**Undocumented in the
U.S. South**

Critical Issues in American Education

Lisa M. Nunn, Series Editor

Taking advantage of sociology's position as a leader in the social scientific study of education, this series is home to new empirical and applied bodies of work that combine social analysis, cultural critique, and historical perspectives across disciplinary lines and the usual methodological boundaries. Books in the series aim for topical and theoretical breadth. Anchored in sociological analysis, Critical Issues in American Education features carefully crafted empirical work that takes up the most pressing educational issues of our time, including federal education policy, gender and racial disparities in student achievement, access to higher education, labor market outcomes, teacher quality, and decision-making within institutions.

Undocumented in the U.S. South

• •

How Youth Navigate Racialization in Policy and School Contexts

SOPHIA RODRIGUEZ

R

Rutgers University Press

New Brunswick, Camden, and Newark, New Jersey
London and Oxford

This book is freely available in an open access edition thanks to TOME (Toward an Open Monograph Ecosystem) — a collaboration of the Association of American Universities, the Association of University Presses, and the Association of Research Libraries — and the generous support of the University of Maryland. Learn more at the TOME website, available at: openmonographs.org.

Rutgers University Press is a department of Rutgers, The State University of New Jersey, one of the leading public research universities in the nation. By publishing worldwide, it furthers the University's mission of dedication to excellence in teaching, scholarship, research, and clinical care.

Cataloging-in-publication data is available from the Library of Congress.

LCCN 2024049492
978-1-9788-2883-4 (cloth)
978-1-9788-2882-7 (paper)
978-1-9788-2884-1(epub)

A British Cataloging-in-Publication record for this book is available from the British Library.

♾ The paper used in this publication meets the requirements of the American National Standard for Information Sciences—Permanence of Paper for Printed Library Materials, ANSI Z39.48-1992.

rutgersuniversitypress.org

This book is dedicated to families and caregivers
for the sacrifices they make to ensure their children
have educational opportunities, like my late
Aunt Jean and mother.

Contents

Undocumented in the
U.S. South

Introduction

●●●●●●●●●●●●●●●●●●●●●

> We came here for a better life. There
> were no jobs and a lot of violence. We
> came here for a better life. But we are
> here now and we don't have rights,
> immigration knocks at the door, and
> it's like being in jail—you can't do
> anything or go anywhere. We are stuck.
> It's hard here. We're free and not free at
> the same time.
> —(Esmeralda, Field Notes, April 27, 2016).

Esmeralda, a recently arrived undocumented youth, articulated her everyday
feelings of isolation, hope, and fear, and how she and those with a similar immigration status were "stuck." I met Esmeralda in the fall of 2015, shortly after I
had begun my ethnographic fieldwork at a local public high school in South
Carolina (Citizen North, pseudonym). Esmeralda, along with all other recently
arrived undocumented youth, was placed in the beginner English as a Second
Language (ESL) classroom with Ava, a bilingual Puerto Rican teacher and
youth advocate. In this conversation, Esmeralda and her peers were discussing the 2016 presidential election and the environment in South Carolina,
and how the undocumented community "needed to know our [their] rights"
because they were "sin *papeles*" [without papers]. Like many of the 11 million
undocumented immigrants in the United States, many of whom are children
and youth, Esmeralda experienced the social, cultural, and psychological fall-
out of the migration process and of being radically transplanted not only into

a new country but into an anti-immigrant Southern state that had uniquely restrictive laws concerning immigrant populations.

While South Carolina had a long history of shunning the Latinx population through anti-immigrant policies (Rodriguez & Monreal, 2017), the aftermath of the election of Donald Trump terrified the undocumented community in this Southern community, due to increased Immigration and Customs Enforcement (ICE) raids in the area and cooperation between local law enforcement and ICE.

Undocumented youth particularly felt ICE's "culture of surveillance" in the school parking lot and near local apartment complexes where they lived. In the face of anti-immigrant policies, Esmeralda and her peers described their everyday lives, local and school-based experiences of discrimination, and the moments of solidarity and belonging they felt in Ava's ESL classroom. They spent the majority of their mornings in that safe space before scattering into hallways of nearly 1,000 other high school students and continuing their day in isolation as newcomers and language learners. The students explained their hopes for a "better life" in the United States (many of them fled poverty and violence in Central America) and how they were met with anti-immigrant national, state, and local policies and practices. Through dialogues in Ava's class, the youth came to understand the illegality of their situation, their limited access to rights and resources, and how to skillfully navigate their community in ways that promoted solidarity and a sense of belonging, Teachers like Ava were uncommon in this school context. Her role as an ESL teacher and "madre," as the students called her, allowed her to form deep relationships with them. She functioned as an important "institutional agent," specifically a cultural guide, which Stanton-Salazar (2011) defines as one who introduces students to new social situations in a new "cultural sphere."

Esmeralda's words, spoken as she and her peers huddled at a round table in Ava's classroom in this small Southern city in a school that feels worlds away from one of the wealthiest cities in South Carolina, provide insight into the lives of undocumented young people across the anti-immigrant South—an understudied geography in academic scholarship—and illustrate the national sentiment toward undocumented immigrants. The complexity of undocumented lives is increasingly highlighted in the media and academic scholarship, specifically the impressive social movement of those eligible for Deferred Action for Childhood Arrivals (DACA) after the 2012 Barack Obama initiative and their continued political presence and activism. While these small victories were critical to their belonging and sense of place in the United States despite their current precarity and limitations, more recently arrived students like Esmeralda continue to face extreme marginalization and barriers to education and social mobility due to their "illegality" (Gonzales, 2016) and newcomer status. In the anti-immigrant South, the lives of students become entwined with national and federal level discourse and politics. Federal (macro) policy has local (meso) and personal (micro) impacts.

Esmeralda's comments in Ava's class highlight one of the central concerns of this book. From a sociological perspective on undocumented youth immigration, race relations, and citizenship, this book reports findings from a four-year ethnographic study that investigated the following: at the macro level, the aggressive immigration policy initiatives, both in Washington and South Carolina, that impacted undocumented immigrants (and those with legal residence and citizenship), especially in relation to the limits of legal citizenship; at the meso level, the school- and community-based experiences of discrimination, isolation, and resistance; and at the micro-interactional level, student and teacher-initiated activities that promoted a sense of belonging, policy thinking, and solidarity (Rodriguez, 2022). Engaging in these macro-, meso-, and micro-level analyses ethnographically provides a major contribution to the scholarship on the sociology of immigration, as it examines the interplay of these levels.

Additionally, the book spotlights an understudied population of high schoolers with liminal legal status, such as being undocumented or unaccompanied; the latter term refers to students who enter the country without a parent or guardian and are then released to a sponsor or guardian. Recently, an increasing number of children are migrating alone or in groups with other children. Between 1970 and 2023, the number of migrants that entered and now reside in the country increased from around 10 million to 45 million (Batalova, 2024). In 2023 alone, over two million people were apprehended by the U.S. Customs and Border Patrol (CBP) along the Southwest border and over 137,000 were "unaccompanied children and single minors" (CBP, 2024). Under U.S. law (Trafficking Victims Protection Reauthorization Act, 2008), children who arrive alone from noncontiguous countries, such as those of the Northern Triangle, are automatically admitted and granted the right to seek asylum. Yet, despite the millions of unaccompanied minors who have been apprehended at the U.S. border over the last two decades, since 2003 only about 700,000 unaccompanied children and single minors have been processed by the Office of Refugee Resettlement (ORR)—the program within the U.S. Department of Health and Human Services (HHS) tasked with their well-being and education (ACF, Press Office, 2024). The volume of recent arrivals since 2014 poses challenges for educational systems (Rodriguez et al, 2024).

This population of unaccompanied and undocumented youth has been less researched in the South in particular, with some exceptions (see, Lopez & Giraldo-Santiago, 2023). Using a multisite ethnographic approach in South Carolina in two Title I public schools, which I call Citizen North and Denizen West, allows for insight into school and community experiences, where youth encounter school-based personnel and local law enforcement and navigate policy and school contexts that maintain barriers to their social inclusion. This is an urgent concern, as law enforcement and immigration personnel increase surveillance in the alleged safe spaces of schools (Verma et al., 2017), and as educational systems are managing the influx of newcomer immigrant students across the United States (Rodriguez, 2021b).

I have three central aims in this book that make significant contributions to the academic scholarship on education and immigration. First, the book focuses on recently arrived high school students who are unaccompanied and undocumented as a population. This is crucial to the sociology of immigration and the education literature because the recent arrival designation distinguishes this population, not only in terms of length of residency, but also in that there has been an increasing number of arrivals to the United States. Many of these unaccompanied and undocumented youth are also ineligible for the DACA program. They are primarily Central American minors who are not fully integrated into U.S. society, and thus are emblematic of the unaccompanied minors who have garnered so much news attention in recent years. This group is analytically unique because, as newcomers from Central America (Honduras, Guatemala, and El Salvador), they are often erased from research that gives extensive attention to DACA-mented students who receive some relief and access to social and educational benefits (Gonzales et al., 2014). Further, even if undocumented youth qualified for DACA, South Carolina is a restrictive policy state where public institutions do not acknowledge DACA (Rodriguez & Monreal, 2017; Roth, 2017), which creates and sustains structural barriers to educational equity. While not all the youth in the project are newly arrived (referred to as newcomers by many schools), one school (Citizen North) primarily was receiving newcomers, many of whom were also unaccompanied, while the other site (Denizen West) had many undocumented youth who had lived in the community since elementary school or earlier. While the legal statuses are important to note, they did not necessarily differentiate the youths' experience of racialization and social barriers. The term *undocumented* is what the community and youth mostly used. *Unaccompanied* was a term less often used, but it came up more regularly during my interactions and observations at one of the schools.

The United States defines an unaccompanied minor as an immigrant who is under the age of 18 and not in the care of a parent or legal guardian at the time of entry, who is left unaccompanied after entry, and who does not have a family member or legal guardian willing or able to care for them in the arrival country (Rodriguez, 2021b). Unaccompanied minors are settling in the United States in increasing numbers due to high rates of violent crime, gang violence and recruitment, and severe economic insecurity in their home countries (Zak, 2020). In 2014, the number of unaccompanied youths arriving in the United States was approximately 50,000. Upon arrival, these youth face strict policies, mistreatment, deplorable conditions, and procedures designed to keep as many of them in custody as possible (López, 2021; Miroff, 2021). They often have limited support to navigate education and immigration systems and have no legal right to counsel. For the schools and districts that serve these students, a lack of federal financial assistance and a reliance on ad hoc local support systems only deepen existing obstacles. In South Carolina, for example, there were approximately 560 unaccompanied migrant youth in 2016 at the start of this research; this number increased to over 1,000 in 2019 and over 2,000 in 2022 (Migration Policy Institute, 2023b).

Secondly, I contextualize these students' lived experiences, ethnographically and longitudinally, in the U.S. South, where anti-immigrant discourse augments a lack of social capital and labor opportunity. In the South, social structures are maintained through state policies that restrict resources and through historically segregated and racialized labor opportunities (Winders & Smith, 2012), making this region a unique variable for studying immigrant incorporation amid racial hierarchies and anti-immigrant sentiment (Brown et al., 2018; Gonzales & Ruiz, 2014). Moreover, while past research has examined undocumented youth experiences longitudinally (Gonzales, 2016), less research investigates the intersection of policies and the everyday lives of recently arrived high-school-aged undocumented youth.

A third aim of this research is to examine undocumented youths' perceptions of citizenship in relation to their racialization in an anti-immigrant state policy context (Abu El-Haj, 2010; Gonzales, 2016; Jaffe-Walter & Lee, 2018; Shirazi, 2018). Youth come to understand their racialized positioning as Latino immigrants and discuss how the intersection of immigration status and racialization impacts them in everyday interactions in the community and school. The study challenges rigid conceptions of citizenship as they present themselves in anti-immigrant policies toward undocumented youth, and it reveals how these youths perceive boundaries of citizenship (Rodriguez & Macias, 2022). By engaging in civic and political practices that are not restricted to U.S. borders or juridical notions of citizenship, youth positioned outside the legal category of "real" citizens nevertheless engage with and resist the stratified opportunity structures in the U.S. South. Critical to this discussion is the concept of racialization and how it contributes to the challenges of *undocumentedness*—a status marker that I reconceptualize as fluid and contested by youth perspectives rather than a fixed component of their identity.

Contexts of Reception: (Un)documented Immigrant Youth Experiences across Education and Social Systems

To understand this book's contribution, it is important to situate it within the scholarship that has chronicled undocumented youth experiences and how they are mediated by the contexts of reception (i.e., countries, states, communities, and schools). The contexts of reception students encounter can present difficulties to students' process of adapting and adjusting to school in the United States. Legal protections exist for students, but so do loopholes; policy contexts, immigration enforcement actions, and both educator support and uncertainty in discussing immigration-related issues all color students' educational experiences (Rodriguez et al., 2018). Specifically, the literature on contexts of reception is critical to understanding how the Southern context sheds light on deeply rooted racism across and within communities and schools. While the South—specifically South Carolina—is the focus here, the relationships between policy and institutions, practices, and interactions are relevant for other U.S. locales that have seen an increase in Latinx populations and migrant groups.

At the national or federal level, undocumented immigrants face contradictory social, political, and economic conditions. They arrive in the United States with some rights and are eligible for some resources, but they maintain a fixed status of "illegality" that governs their everyday lives (Abrego, 2006; Gonzales, 2016). These ambiguities have led many scholars of immigration and sociology of immigration, and education to discuss the important role of contexts of reception. Researchers contend that immigrants to the United States face contexts of reception that are unwelcoming (Portes & Rumbaut, 2001), and they can be affected by discrimination and racism (Suárez-Orozco & Suárez-Orozco, 2001). For newcomer immigrants, adapting to new social and cultural contexts, learning the U.S. educational system, attaining English proficiency, adjusting to school, and acquiring new academic skills may be especially challenging (Hernandez et al., 2009; Ruiz-de-Velasco et al., 2000; Suárez-Orozco & Suárez-Orozco, 2001). Immigrant experiences also vary depending on reasons for migration, economic means, and educational attainment upon arrival. Contexts of reception are multileveled (i.e., they exist at the federal, state, regional, school, and community levels), and thus immigrants encounter potential barriers or supports in many ways. Schools in particular shape the kind of supports immigrants ought to be able to access. Yet research has shown variation in immigrant integration in American schools, and ultimately in their academic success and sense of belonging (Portes & Rumbaut, 2006; Rodriguez & Wy, 2024; Suárez-Orozco & Suárez-Orozco, 2009; Suárez-Orozco et al., 2011).

Legal protections are supposed to ensure equal educational access for undocumented, immigrant-background,[1] and English Learner (EL) students. Of the nearly 11 million undocumented immigrants in the country, approximately 809,000 of them are children (Gelatt & Zong, 2018; Krogstad et al., 2019). Another 5.1 million youth under 18 have an undocumented parent (Gelatt & Zong, 2018). Equal educational access to a free, public K–12 education is one right undocumented students have. *Plyler v. Doe* (1982), a Supreme Court case decided by a 5–4 vote in the early 1980s, determined that the Equal Protection Clause of the Fourteenth Amendment to the U.S. Constitution covers undocumented children. Among other legal findings, the Supreme Court stated that any state resources saved by excluding undocumented students were outweighed by the damage imposed on society at large from denying them an education (*Plyler v. Doe*, 1982; Rodriguez & Crawford, 2022). Thus, states cannot deny students a free public education on account of their immigration status and schools should not engage in actions that result in students avoiding school (*Plyler v. Doe*, 1982; U.S. Departments of Justice and Education, 2014). The decision stands despite attempts to evade *Plyler* over the nearly four decades (American Immigration Council, 2016).

But the legacy of *Plyler* is not without contradiction. Galindo (2012) explains the paradoxical and "unfinished business" of the *Plyler* case (p. 591). Though important to protecting undocumented youth under the Fourteenth Amendment and conferring rights in K–12 education, *Plyler* did not confer a right to a postsecondary education or a pathway to citizenship. Scholars have described the complicated positioning of undocumented children and youth, who have a right to K–12 education but are also "illegal" in the eyes of the broader society and subsequently criminalized (Galindo, 2012; Gonzales et al., 2015).

Federal policies also safeguard students' personal information, provide legal protections for language learners and immigrant-background students, and ensure that schools create opportunities to engage with families (Sugarman, 2017). Because information on legal status cannot be collected by schools, English Learner (EL) is often used as a proxy when referring to immigrant youth. EL students cannot be discriminated against (*Lau v. Nichols*, 1974) and should have meaningful access to education, including access to the same content as their non-EL peers.[2] If issues of legal status are raised in schools, the Federal Educational Rights and Privacy Act (FERPA) prohibits access to student records without a parent or guardian's express permission and places restrictions on third-party access to educational records. Though educational records cannot be shared without permission or legitimate educational purpose, districts can share some information (e.g., name, place of birth, and address) that families in their directories may not want to be made public. One fear is that immigration officials may piece together information to learn a family's whereabouts (Sugarman, 2017). This information is important for contextualizing the ways in which undocumented immigrant populations in South Carolina face significant hardships and a lack of equal educational access as outlined above, to which they are entitled.

While there exist some federal protections for undocumented immigrant youth, the Trump administration, during this study, threatened their livelihood and belonging with the return to large-scale raids (Dwyer, 2018), and enforcement efforts now include more focus on the country's interior as well as the border (Hamilton et al., 2019). Enforcement disproportionately affects Latinx immigrants and Mexican immigrants (Dreby, 2012), and fear and uncertainty have spread through communities (Carlton et al., 2019; Hennessey-Fiske et al., 2019). In August 2019, the largest immigration raid in U.S. history swept up nearly 700 people across seven worksites. More than 200 students in several districts went absent from school, with youth scared to come to school and frightened by a rumor that ICE would come for the children whose parents were arrested (Aleaziz, 2019). While the Biden administration promised to undo many of the Trump administration's restrictive policies, the arrest of noncitizens without a criminal history increased from 39 percent in FY 2021 to 67 percent in FY 2022 (Chishti & Bush-Joseph, 2023). Additionally, Title 42, the emergency Covid-19 order that allowed agents to cite the pandemic to quickly expel migrants without hearing their asylum claims, wasn't lifted until May 2023 and was replaced by an equally restrictive measure barring migrants from seeking asylum if they don't request refugee status in another country before entering the United States (Robles, 2023). Uncertainty over immigration enforcement actions makes it more difficult for schools and educators to establish and maintain trusting ties with their immigrant community members, as well as to know how to meet their needs. Thus, federal political maneuvers loom over the lives of undocumented immigrant youth and their families.

The state context also matters in the educational trajectories of undocumented immigrant students. While *Plyler* supports education for undocumented students through secondary school, no federal policies provide access to higher education. Access is contingent upon state policies, such as permitting students in-state resident tuition rates, scholarships, or state financial aid—without which attending postsecondary schooling is challenging (Bjorklund Jr., 2018; Darolia & Potochnick, 2015). Filindra and colleagues (2011) found that state policies impact the high school graduation rates and educational outcomes of immigrant youth, emphasizing the point that inclusive policies positively impact their educational outcomes. Gildersleeve and Hernandez (2012) analyzed in-state resident tuition for students in twelve states between 2001 and 2011. They found that, even when a policy was intended to be pro-immigration and supportive of increased access to higher education, the policy's language was often contradictory and subversive, resulting in the construction of new forms of immigrant identities reflecting Othered subjects (Abrego, 2008). Gildersleeve and Hernandez (2012) argue that policy defines "who a person is or what makes somebody considered a student" (p. 11). Further, Rodriguez and Monreal (2017) argue that "this subject formation in such a specific manner informs the material conditions in which these students must act. These conditions are different than the normative identity one has of a 'student.' These policies generate unintended consequences and create categories that include and exclude" (p. 768). Other scholars have noted one such consequence is that some immigrants are perceived to be more "deserving" of access to educational opportunities and post-secondary education (Patel, 2015).

In states like South Carolina, access to educational resources is particularly challenging. As will be discussed in chapter 1, Rodriguez (2018a) conducted a policy analysis that revealed the many ways that immigrants are criminalized and excluded broadly, and how undocumented students are excluded from educational opportunities. The policy language in Rodriguez's study refers to immigrants (generally not just undocumented immigrants) as "terrorists" and "aliens" that threaten the social fabric of the state (Rodriguez & Monreal, 2017). Similarly, in a study of 36 undocumented youth between the ages of 18 and 24 in South Carolina, Roth (2017) analyzed how restricted access to higher education affects undocumented youths' "willingness—and ability—to access social capital embedded in ties to high school teachers and staff," if such ties are even available (p. 541). A key finding in Roth's study related to the fact that, regardless of undocumented youths' aspirations or even their documented hard work in school, legal status remained a significant barrier to their mobility. This corroborates research that shows a relationship between educational access and attainment and economic mobility. With federal and state policies that make their status precarious and impact their mobility, undocumented immigrants are entangled in the reproduction of inequality, which is "the very outcome that the Supreme Court sought to avoid through its decision on *Plyler v. Doe*" (Roth, 2017, p. 541; see also Abrego & Gonzales, 2010;).

Thinking back to Esmeralda's comment—"we're stuck"—and positioning undocumented youth experiences in the federal and state landscape of immigration and education policy and practice, we see that restrictive contexts like South Carolina pose additional barriers, especially in schools and K–12 afterschool spaces. Related to the second major aim of this book, I contextualize the lives of undocumented high school students like Esmeralda who feel "stuck" in the New Latino South, in the State of South Carolina, and at the community-level, where surveillance looms over undocumented youth and their families and conditions their schooling. As will be discussed in chapter 4, at the community level, undocumented youth encounter local law enforcement and ICE. They learn how their immigration status and Latinx racial identity impacts how community-level incidents of discrimination and racism occur. The connections between the community-level and school-level incidents where undocumented immigrant youth are subjected to surveillance have provided more evidence of the negative impact on their social-emotional well-being and belonging. Verma and colleagues (2017) have emphasized that the cooperation of law enforcement with immigration enforcement regimes and their encroachment on schools disproportionately affects Latinx immigrants, contributing to increased fear, isolation, and absenteeism in schools. With "immigration knock[ing] at the door," as Esmeralda and youth like her stated, students are living through contradictory social conditions. These youth do not leave their experiences and memories at the door of schoolhouses. They carry with them the trauma of being targeted or having family members deported, as will be shown throughout the book. Further still, they enter schools—supposedly protected spaces—and encounter the larger contexts of racialization, assumptions about them, and stereotyping against Latinx immigrants and non-immigrants alike. These school-based incidents of racialization and discrimination will be highlighted in chapter 3, and how immigrant youth empower themselves in the face of these challenges is the subject of chapter 4.

At the school level, factors such as teacher-student relations further impact access and mobility, which, as Roth notes, limits access to "social capital" for these students, which they otherwise might leverage to benefit educationally or economically. Recent scholarship has shown that the educational system underserves newly arrived immigrant students. In addition to their immigration status, additional factors contribute to students' lack of belonging and access to equitable schooling. Barriers such as low socioeconomic status, economic insecurity, and placement in low-performing, under-resourced, segregated schools (Gándara, 2015, 2017 R. G. Gonzales et al., 2015; Hernandez et al., 2009; Orfield et al., 2014), as well as insecure housing (Ee & Gándara, 2019) and food insecurity (Potochnick, Chen, & Perreira, 2017) limit a quality K–12 education.

Additionally, teacher-student relations are increasingly precarious for undocumented students. This is because educator awareness about policies impacting undocumented students is limited. And yet, their attitudes shape their interactions with immigrant students and the type of advocacy they provide. For instance, recent scholarship investigates teachers' awareness of policies impacting undocumented students and how awareness shapes attitudes toward these students, but there remains a research gap that directly addresses the relationship between awareness and attitudes in relation to teachers' work with undocumented students (Rodriguez et al., 2018). In the first study, Rodriguez and colleagues (2018) qualitatively investigate how teachers become socially and politically literate and empathetic about the specific needs of newcomer youth. Drawing on data from three longitudinal qualitative studies, the authors highlight the challenges of multicultural education and its implementation in the New Latino South, where anti-immigrant policies persist. The authors argue that teachers must develop empathetic relations and policy knowledge to support undocumented students. The teachers in this study refer to their advocacy for undocumented students as ad hoc at best, noting the limited information they received in pre- and in-service teacher training. Yet, the teachers discussed how "hearing [undocumented students'] stories" and "needing to know their rights" was essential for developing "strategic empathy," which included knowledge of the sociopolitical context (p. 5).

Furthermore, Rodriguez and McCorkle (2019, 2020) engaged in a mixed-methods study with a survey sample of 101 teachers in one focal Southern state, and two critical findings emerged. First, we found that teachers were unaware of anti-immigrant policies restricting access to educational and social resources. Second, teachers held false beliefs about undocumented immigrants' access to educational opportunities. All of this research corroborates previous scholarship that points to the importance of teacher-student relations and the teacher's role. In regard to undocumented students in this study, the restrictive anti-immigrant context of South Carolina contributed to the school-based racialization that occurred, specifically moments when teachers interacted with undocumented students in punitive ways or ways that promoted assumptions about their Latinx immigration status.

Instead of looking at these various contexts of reception separately, this book contributes a multilevel analysis that advances regional, state, community, and school-level contexts of reception through an interactive macro, meso, and micro framework to understand the cultural realities of high-school-aged undocumented youth in public schools in the New Latino South and South Carolina. Next, I describe in greater detail the context of the New Latino South and South Carolina, including the conditions of undocumented Latinx immigrants' lives in the state, and provide additional information that will be elaborated upon in chapter 2 before sharing the specific details of the ethnographic project in this book.

The New Latino South

This study focuses on Latinx[3] undocumented immigrant youth in South Carolina, a state in the New Latino South (i.e., Alabama, Arkansas, Georgia, North Carolina, South Carolina, and Tennessee; Kochhar et al., 2005), an important contribution given that previous literature tends to focus on large urban centers that are considered traditional receiving contexts (Winders & Smith, 2012). Kochhar and colleagues (2005) define the New Latino South as a collection of six Southern states that have seen rapid growth in Latinx populations since the 1990s. A budding array of research on undocumented students has largely focused on their activism and educational experiences in larger urban centers, such as New York, California, and Texas. In these contexts, undocumented young people with and without DACA, mostly college-goers, are navigating anti-immigrant policies and a lack of access to higher education. Meanwhile, there is less research about undocumented youth that are high-school-aged, or in rural and Southern spaces where anti-immigrant policies are more severe (Brown et al., 2018; Gonzales & Ruiz, 2014). Specific to the New Latino South context, Lacy & Odem (2009) argue that more exclusionary state and local immigration policies are the result of shifting popular attitudes in the region. They write that "most official rhetoric and policy in the Southeast in recent years . . . seeks to limit especially unauthorized immigrants' access to employment, transportation, housing, health care, higher education, and public benefits" (p. 150). They argue that many local ordinances in Southern localities aim to discourage immigration, make life harder for immigrants, or drive out those already there. One such example is housing regulations proposed in parts of Georgia and the Carolinas that require landlords to verify immigration status and impose fines for renting to undocumented immigrants (Lacy & Odem, 2009). Policies and practices tend to be highly racialized in Southern states due to the legacy of Jim Crow segregation and its impact on contemporary race relations in the South, often rendering a racial binary that ignores the Latinx population (Guerrero, 2017; Marrow, 2011). This unique legacy of segregation and the paradoxical relations with Latinx migrants inform the social fabric of the South in ways that reflect local ideologies toward immigrants and the racialization and lack of belonging that the undocumented youth in this study experience.

In the 2019 book *The Browning of the New South*, author Jennifer Jones examines the impact of doubling down on exclusionary policies and attitudes in a single city—Winston-Salem, North Carolina. A decade ago, North Carolina's Republican leadership was engaged in an attack on Latinx immigrants that looked much like the proposed and enacted exclusionary policies in South Carolina (Rodriguez & Monreal, 2017). To turn out Republican voters and tamp down on growing interest in Barack Obama's popular appeal, would-be state legislators competed to express the most explicitly hateful and racist views, proposing exclusionary policies aimed primarily at harming immigrants that would also in many cases have detrimental effects on North Carolina's native-born minority communities (Jones, 2019).

Jones (2019) also discusses the immigration history of Latinxs, who have been framed as having an unsettled sense of racial identity. In large part, this stems from U.S. relations with Mexico, Puerto Rico, and Cuba in the nineteenth century, at which time colonial endeavors and a domestic understanding of whiteness as tied to property rights, modernity, and global democracy underscored the importance of whiteness (Jones, 2019). A settled Mexican community existed in the Southwest before U.S. jurisdiction was established in 1848 and these people became "involuntary" U.S. citizens when the boundaries of the United States expanded westward (Martin & Midgley, 1994, p. 21). Although the resident population was small (less than 200,000 in 1850), it grew rather rapidly, reaching more than 500,000 by 1900 (Gratton & Gutmann, 2000, pp. 142–143). Over time, this Hispanic homeland (Nostrand, 1980) developed a distinct culture different from both the Mexican and Anglo, and by the early twentieth century the population had deep generational roots. So, in a sense, the term that scholars are using to describe the region—New Latino South—is a misnomer. Immigrants of Latinx descent have long standing roots in the South, but more recent attention to their presence and contributions to local communities is entangled in anti-immigrant rhetoric and racism.

Additionally, Stuesse and colleagues (2017) studied structural racism and race relations in the South. Spurred by demographic changes signaling the increase of Latinx populations across the United States, including in "nontraditional gateway cities" such as rural and suburban areas in the South, Stuesse et al. (2017) examined coalition-building efforts between African American organizations and immigrants' rights groups, and the challenges of whiteness and Blackness as these have been historically and socially constituted in the United States. To expand scholarly understanding of race relations and structuralism toward minoritized groups, while underscoring activism efforts, Stuesse et al. (2017) employ a "racial justice lens" (p. 247) to call people to think about immigration through the lens of Blackness, which still occupies the bottom of the racial hierarchy. The conceptual framework is also informed by critical race scholarship and by those whose voices shed light on the lived experiences of Black people in America. This effort to draw attention to the racialized experiences of minoritized groups in the United States, though not focused on K–12 settings, connects with this book's focus on important concepts such as race, racism, and what will be described below as the racialization of the (un)documented Latinx immigrant youth in this study.

There exists a lack of understanding between U.S.-born and immigrant groups, which is exacerbated by xenophobic and anti-immigrant rhetoric rooted in the contention that immigrants take jobs away from hardworking Americans. The undocumented Latinx youth in the current study address and unravel this idea in their narratives. This claim, though erroneous, gains ground in times of economic downturn and in a neoliberal era in which African Americans and Latinx immigrants compete for access to scant economic resources and jobs. It's made worse by the fact that many African Americans and Latinx people usually compete for the same types of jobs in manufacturing and in the service sector. Such antagonism leads to racial animus intensified by a "zero-sum situation in which working communities of color . . . fight over crumbs" (Stuesse et al., 2017, p. 251). According to Stuesse and colleagues, employers demonstrate a preference for immigrant workers, which fuels further hostility and misperceptions among Latinx and African American workers who are overrepresented in low-wage occupational endeavors. Consequently, "real competition works in tandem with perceived cultural and other forms of difference" (p. 252) to create divisions among African Americans and Latinx immigrants. Stuesse's work, along with that of Jones (2019) and others, draws attention to the false narratives about minoritized groups in the U.S. South and broader racial hierarchies and race relations.

Finally, immigrants who enter the country try to position themselves within its white-Black racial hierarchy. Whiteness and Blackness shape social relations, impacting even those who do not identify with either category. Additionally, because whiteness grants privileges, many immigrants attempt to reposition themselves as white in order to obtain access to those privileges by "distinguishing themselves from Blacks and adopting the cultural diacritica of Whiteness" (Stuesse et al., 2017, p. 253). Immigrants can then become complicit in the workings of white supremacy in hopes of gaining capital at the expense of Black Americans. These intragroup relations often foster division in communities of color in the South and more broadly. The undocumented Latinx youth in the current study are keenly aware of these racial and social relations, and they critique the larger structural barriers minoritized groups face in the U.S. South.

South Carolina and Immigration/Immigrants

As described below in the section on the ethnographic method of study for this book, I call the town where these two public schools are located Denizen. Next, I describe the overall demographic shifts, perceptions, and attitudes toward immigrants in South Carolina, which align with the experiences of undocumented youth in Denizen. Denizen is one of the South Carolina communities that witnessed significant growth in the immigrant population in 2000–2013, with an increase of approximately 74 percent. Roth and Grace (2015) report that the majority of immigrants in South Carolina (91 percent) live in just twenty counties, while ten of these counties account for 76 percent of the total immigrant population.

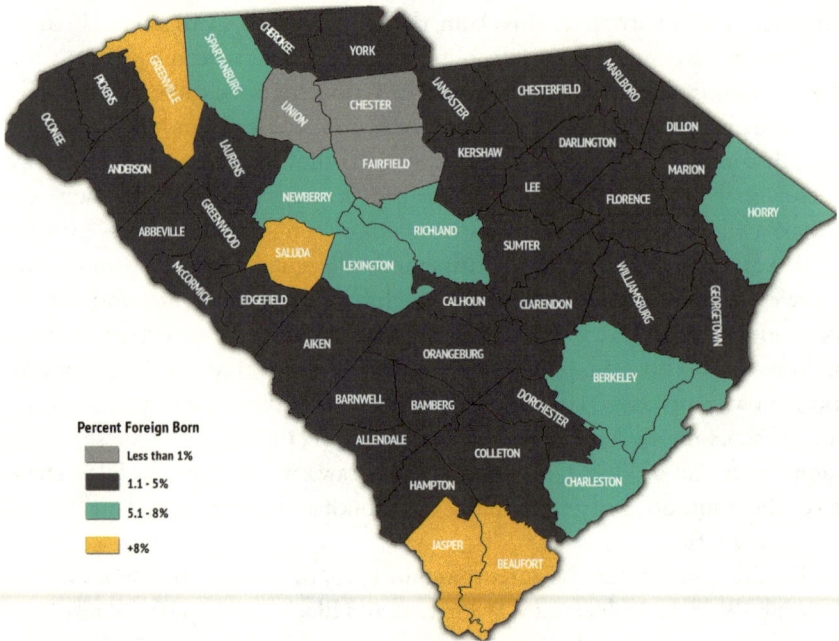

FIGURE I.1 Immigrant Population in South Carolina

Although the state's immigrant population is concentrated in several counties and metropolitan areas, it is also increasingly geographically dispersed and growing rapidly in nonurban counties (Figure I.2). This is reflected in the communities near the two schools in this study, both of which are located in a county that has witnessed an increase in immigration populations in the last decade. While immigrants are generally dispersed across the state, economic opportunity remains a challenge, with 83 percent of immigrants who are noncitizens living at the federal poverty line (Roth & Grace, 2015). In South Carolina, most immigrants are Spanish speaking with some level of English language use, and most live in poverty. Additionally, the bulk of the immigrant population is made up of noncitizens from Latin America. For example, in 2021, there were 271,280 foreign-born individuals in residing in South Carolina (5.2 percent of the total population). This was an increase from 115,978 in 2020 and 49,964 in 2019. In 2021, 121,859 (44 percent) of the foreign-born population was of Latino origin; and 6.6 percent of these were children aged 5–17. More specifically, 95,309 were from Central America, with 3,142 from El Salvador, and 63,603 were from Mexico. In addition, 26,772 were from South America (MPI, 2023). These numbers reflect the growing Latino immigrant population relevant to the study.

Because immigrants are viewed as problems through political rhetoric and media frames, specific policies like those criminalizing immigrants are proposed to control immigrants in the New Latino South (discussed in chapter 2). Rodriguez and Monreal (2017) explore how policy discourse generates categories of knowledge about immigrants, which creates the necessity and rationale for restrictive legislative actions. Critically examining South Carolina policies, they found state-level policy construed immigrants as dangerous, as well as an economic and security threat to the residents of the state. Immigrants thus become the subject of specific types of knowledge and stereotypes (e.g., bad hombres, criminals, job-stealers, terrorists) and the object of targeted policies like increased law enforcement surveillance and continual verification of one's (legal) status (Rodriguez & Monreal, 2017). This research is especially pertinent because construction of a threatening immigrant subject in the New Latino South sets forth the perception that immigrants are undeserving of state resources like education.

Such restrictive immigration policies and contexts not only negatively impact Latinx students, they also place teachers in a conflicting role as they try to navigate competing interests in schools and with the families and children they serve while also remaining apolitical in public schools. Patel (2013) uses the case of Alabama House Bill 56 to illustrate how teachers' desire to serve immigrant students can run counter to the aim of public policy. In the case of Alabama HB 56, public K–12 teachers became de facto immigration agents tasked with reporting undocumented youth to the state education board. Even though this particular provision was disallowed in court, it demonstrates how immigration policy is not enacted in isolation from educational policy. In the case above, schools were no longer considered safe spaces and some Latinx students stopped coming to school (Patel, 2013). Similarly, Marrow's (2009) analysis of 129 semi-structured interviews and additional ethnographic research on Latinx communities in rural eastern North Carolina indicates that some service-oriented bureaucracies—such as schools—are more responsive to immigrants' interests than local and state politicians are. However, whereas public school officials expressed favorable views of Latinx students and worked to provide resources like bilingual ESL teachers, they operated within predetermined "rules of the game" set by restrictive local policies toward immigrants. These examples illustrate that immigration and education policies are highly influential and act jointly in the context of the U.S. South. I turn now to specific barriers for Latinx students in the New Latino South.

Across the New Latino South, educational inequities persist in policy and K–12 school settings. For instance, in writing about education policy and immigrant students, several scholars list uncompromising standardized testing policies (McDaniel et al., 2017), inequitable ESL programs (Tarasawa, 2013), subtractive second language policies (Portes & Salas, 2010), an "English Only" movement (Beck & Allexasaht-Snider, 2002), systemic miseducation (Bohon et al., 2005; Rodriguez, 2022), and "subtractive" schooling (Carrillo & Rodriguez, 2016; Urrieta Jr. et al., 2015). For example, Rodriguez (2018) observes in her critical analysis of sixty-five South Carolina state policies that many educational inequities are enshrined in state policies and then trickle down into institutions such as schools. Consequently, through policy discourse the state becomes an "arbiter of racialized rights" (Rodriguez, 2018, p. 10) and asserts this self-ascribed authority by conferring and denying legitimacy to various groups. This practice carries enormous weight in policy discourse and beyond; the very act of enrolling in school is predicated on proof of legality, in violation of *Plyler v. Doe* (1982). Consequently, access to schooling and educational resources is contingent upon proving one's lawful status. Access to higher education is also compromised for undocumented youth who "face limited options" (Rodriguez & Monreal, 2017, p. 783; Roth, 2017) when applying to higher education institutions in the state due to their status.

While there exist studies about immigrant youth belonging broadly (Katz, 2014), this book unravels the experiences of undocumented high-school-aged youth in a unique focal state in the New Latino South: South Carolina. Both unique in the history of race relations and anti-immigrant sentiment, South Carolina provides a geographic location to study race relations, citizenship, and immigrant youth experiences, focusing on undocumented Latinx youth who are marginalized in their schools and the local society. And while the book makes the argument for the important Southern "context of reception," the issues faced by the youth in this study connect with additional locales that have rising numbers of Latinx immigrants (Hamann et al., 2015). I describe the local community (Denizen), school district, and schools in this study in the description of the ethnographic project.

A Call for a New Theoretical Framework for Understanding Immigrant Youth Experiences of Racialization

I began this study in 2015 with an assumption that immigrant youth in South Carolina would be uniquely positioned given the South's racial history and Black-white binary (Guerrero, 2017). My initial fieldwork revealed the limited services and opportunities for minoritized and immigrant-origin youth in schools; however, my initial conversations with undocumented youth also taught me about the deeply racialized experiences in their communities (i.e., the effects of being a Latino immigrant in a Southern state). Undocumented youth explained the impact and intersection of racialized laws and policies on their everyday lives. Policies have effects, and the larger criminalization and racial profiling that manifests from anti-immigrant federal, state, and local policies have effects on youths' access to resources and their psyche.

I attempt to show the evolving theoretical framework for immigrant youth racialization across multiple levels (at the policy, organizational, and interactional/individual, or macro, meso, and micro, levels) in two major ways (Rodriguez, 2022). First, I expand upon the concept of racialization as the core component of the theoretical framework for this project.

This framework (see Figure I.2) is the guide for reading the historical examination of immigration policy and the local policy analysis in South Carolina, as well as the later empirical chapters. After explaining the theoretical orientation of the project, I then use this lens of "racializing immigration studies" (Sáenz & Manges Douglas, 2015) to provide a historical overview of immigration law and policy, the context of the New Latino South, and how it impacts undocumented youths' everyday lives through processes of racialization in law and policy. My framework has utility and I return to it in subsequent chapters. In chapter 2 I use the framework in my analysis of the macro-historical/policy levels and the meso-organizational level of schools (including racial attitudes of and in schools as expressed by teachers and school personnel), and in chapter 3 I explore the micro-interactional/individual level of racialized experiences in communities. My framework is an interpretive device and I use it and ethnographic data to show how race—as a construct and larger social structure—acts upon immigrant youth. Racialization is not just one thing, or one moment; rather, instances of immigrant racialization occur in/through policy, power relationships, organizational racial attitudes and structures, and interactions.

Immigrant access and mobility

Racialization of immigrant studies

Macro-policy level

Historicizing the immigrant in law and policy

Immigration policy and enforcement

Federal and state policies impacting immigrants

Media and political discourses of immigration (cultural representations in society)

Meso-organizational

Schools as sites that limit opportunity or reproduce inequality

Social networks and actors within organizations

Institutional agents that perpetuate or challenge deficit-based discourses and false narratives about immigrants

Community ideologies and enforcement practices and mechanisms

Micro-interactional/individual

How racialized interactions shape:

perceptions of self and racial/ethnic identity

educator-student relations

peer relations

identity negotiations and values

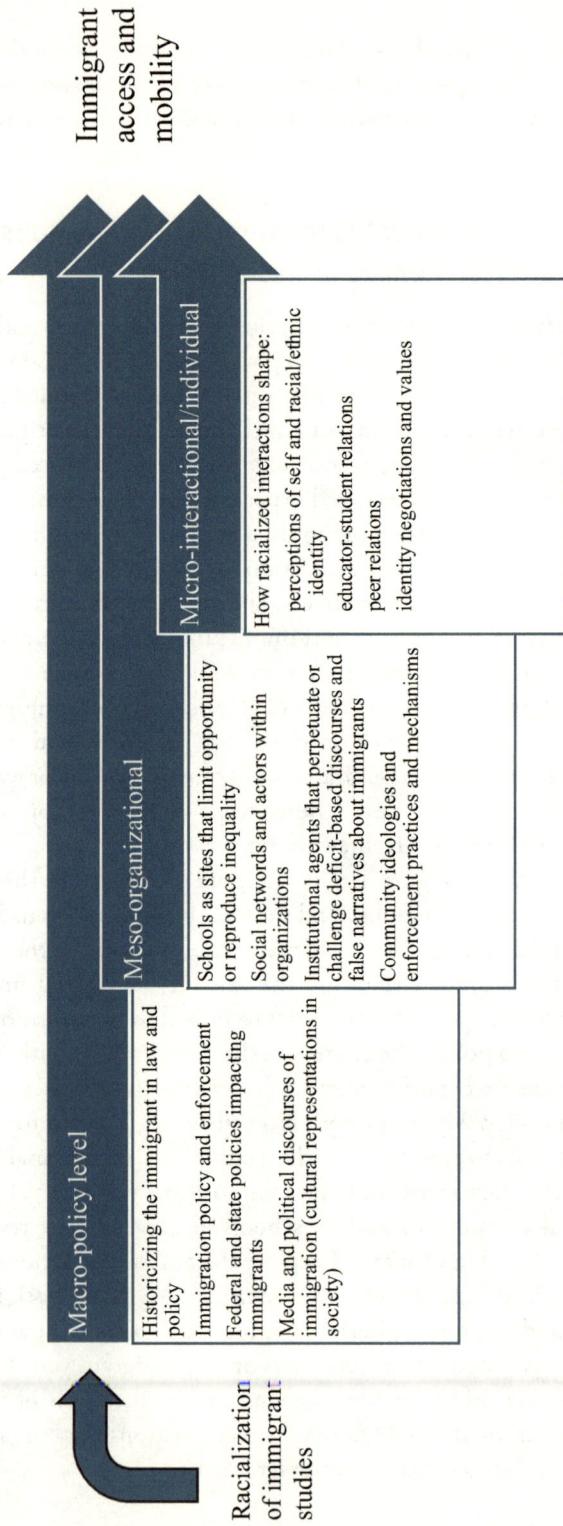

FIGURE 1.2 Multilevel Racialization Framework

Chapter 2 explains the theoretical concepts that underpin the policy and empirical analysis in subsequent chapters. I chart general discussions of immigration policy to provide context for educational policymaking and to underscore that immigration policy shapes and conditions educational policymaking and practice in the context of this study. Specifically, it links histories of immigration law and policy with racialization and citizenship. While this is certainly not an exhaustive immigration history, I connect interdisciplinary scholarship and consider how racialization and citizenship apply to immigrant groups in the United States (Molina, 2015; Ngai, 2006). It is this historical backdrop, examined through the lens of racialization, that is critical for examining policy and the contemporary moment in the South. Additionally, chapter 2 offers a critical analysis of 120 proposed and enacted policies in the focal state of South Carolina. The policy analysis illustrates how state policies set up explicit and implicit forms of exclusion toward Latinx (un)documented immigrants in the state, and how those policies impact the everyday lives of the undocumented youth in this study.

I show that historical and contemporary policies in South Carolina stigmatize Latinx immigrants broadly and undocumented immigrants in particular, which enables policymakers to justify punitive policy "solutions" to these "problems," such as increasing the presence of ICE in local communities, raiding housing complexes, and monitoring local schools (Rodriguez & Monreal, 2017; Rodriguez, 2018). In this discussion, I foreground the notion of "policy problematization" as a rigorous and nuanced theoretical framework that guides the policy analysis and sheds light on how undocumented youth are racialized and targeted through state policy (Rodriguez & Monreal, 2017). The relationship between racialization and problematization, which refers to making people into problems, is reciprocal and mutually informing. For instance, Gulson and Webb (2013) give an example of how a racialized object—the Afrocentric school— became a "problem" *because* it was racialized but also was introduced into a policy context and geography (the city of Toronto) that was already racialized. While it is too rigid to say that racialization occurred *prior to* problematization in this case (particularly given the historical roots of race in North America), the already racialized opening of the Afrocentric school posed new problems related to economics, culture, equity, and justice. Alternatively, Lindblad et al. (2018) explain how the U.S. census was used to address the "problem" of new immigrants following World War II, when "the category of Latino emerged . . . to classify people from, for example, Brazil, Haiti, Argentina and Mexico, among others, as a single population" (p. 206). In these examples, racialization is linked to producing categories of difference in order to make the administration of policies and institutional practices more convenient and efficient (Foucault, 1994). In other words, polices, laws, and practices create categories, groups of people, and problems and ultimately use these categories to differentiate people and often exclude them based on racial/ethnic classifications (Lewis, 2005).

Race and racialized bodies have been inscribed in politics as "problems." In other words, the language in policies makes people into objects of knowledge through practices of racial categorization. The point is not that specific individuals are targets of techniques of power but that power is exercised through the "government of individualization" (Foucault, 1982), which employs strategies of normalization, problematization, and racialization. In other words, these techniques are used to mark individuals as racialized "others," as a strategy for reproducing whiteness as the unnamed, naturalized "normal" and enabling the production of policies and practices that further entrench dominant racial discourses.

In this chapter I introduce the evolving ways in which state policies construct immigrants as deviant problems, on the one hand, or good, deserving immigrants on the other. The binary of deviance or deservingness weighs on the lives of undocumented youth, posing significant challenges for educational attainment and social mobility, as they are forced to navigate hostile and restrictive policies while being fed the false notion that the American dream is theirs to attain if they would only assimilate (this binary is explored throughout the book). Finally, in many cases, the New Latino South and South Carolina maintain the attitude of the immigrant often being more deviant than deserving, and thus subject to anti-immigrant policies of exclusion.

Theoretical Approach: Racialization across Macro, Meso, and Micro Levels

In this introduction, I have engaged with influential concepts I used in my research, specifically racialization and how it cuts across multiple levels and informs categories of citizenship. I expand the literature, moving away from deficit-based assimilationist frameworks for studying immigrant integration and mobility. While assimilation and its variations, including segmented assimilation, have dominated sociological studies of immigration, I move away from them to account for the racialization processes that contribute to immigrant exclusion. Additionally, frameworks such as the contexts of reception and nested contexts of reception have attempted to provide nuance to the study of immigrant experiences of education and social mobility. Next, I provide an overview of these frameworks, and how and why I depart from them. Then, I explain the development of the racialization theoretical framework and how it is used in this study.

Contexts of Reception

Sociologists and migration scholars have long held that the place where immigrants settle is important for the process of incorporation, specifically through the framework of contexts of reception and segmented assimilation. Research about immigrant communities has examined the neighborhood context and the role of ethnic enclaves, but it has assumed that immigrant adaptation, or straight-line assimilation, is inevitable (Brown & Bean, 2006). Segmented assimilation, a hypothesis introduced in the early 1990s, suggests that a variety of factors—including federal policy—shape processes of immigrant integration and, importantly, helps explain why some immigrant groups tend to follow different mobility trajectories into various layers of the social strata. The emergence of the immigrant new destinations literature in the early 2000s has shown that states, counties, and cities have local laws and infrastructural features that impact immigrants' access to resources, and that the contours of the local receiving context vary from one place to the next (Hamann et al., 2015).

More recently, scholars have begun to develop frameworks that capture these different levels of reception to include the neighborhood, city, state, and federal contexts. This provides a multiscalar understanding of how place matters for processes of immigrant incorporation. For example, an unauthorized immigrant (a disadvantaged status determined by laws at the federal level) may live in a state with welcoming laws (such as those that provide all immigrants with access to driver's licenses) but in a neighborhood where they experience some degree of discrimination from neighbors (Menjívar, 2014). Each of these levels of reception may vary along a continuum from hostile to welcoming, and while one level may be more hostile the next level may be more welcoming. In addition to the macro contexts of reception (e.g., host country and state contexts, as well as policies and laws), societal (e.g., reception of cultural groups and their relationship to the dominant group) and institutional contexts (e.g., K–12 education) continue to shape unauthorized immigrant mobility and access to resources, societal discrimination, racism, and racial attitudes toward immigrants.

Considering the governmental, societal, and institutional contexts, Golash-Boza & Valdez's (2018) framework of the "nested contexts of reception" (NCOR) conceptualizes these different levels as a series of concentric circles. Each sphere exercises some influence on the process of incorporation, and the framework offers a much more nuanced understanding of how various factors at the micro, meso, and macro levels impact the mobility trajectories of immigrants. Aligned with this NCOR framework, Perez (2020) shows how nested contexts of reception shape variation in Latinx identity development through processes of racialized immigrant incorporation in an immigrant's new destination. The NCOR framework invites us to consider societal perspectives on race, racial attitudes, and racial discrimination and the roles they play in the lives of immigrants, and how, for purposes in this book, such attitudes might manifest in institutions such as schools. Portes and Rumbaut (2014) describe the racialization of immigrant children in the schools as evidence of the "decisive role" of the context of reception in shaping outcomes (p. 295). Even after controlling for parental variables, demographic characteristics, and early school experiences, youth of Haitian, West Indian, and Mexican origin had a much higher probability of experiencing downward assimilation due to racial identity markers.

These frameworks for assimilation and segmented assimilation account for potential host society views, and NCOR introduces an interactional framework that might also account for discrimination and relationships between dominant cultural groups and immigrants. Yet, these frameworks have explicitly and implicitly "reproduced the privileging of whiteness as the standard of assimilation for immigrants" (Verma et al., 2017). Importantly, then, assimilation, incorporation, or integration of immigrant groups cannot be studied without focusing on how these groups are excluded from access to resources, often (with) held by dominant white groups and institutions. To account for this exclusion, and centering whiteness as a key credential within racial hierarchies in the United States (Omi & Winant, 2014; Ray, 2019; Rodriguez, 2020a; 2021), I move away from these frameworks and call for a framework that includes naming racial exclusion and inequity and locates processes of racialization across multiple levels. I will explain this next.

Racialization and the Construction of Illegality

I expand our understanding of undocumented youth experiences by building a conceptual framework for analysis, shifting the focus from the impact of their immigration status—the notion of illegality—to the interplay between policies and youths' lived experiences and everyday realities. Across the book, I examine three distinct but related levels where racialization occurs (at the macro-policy, meso-organizational, and micro-interactional/individual levels; see Ray, 2019; Rodriguez, 2022) and their interplay with undocumented immigrants' racialized experiences. Providing additional conceptual ground, Hamann & Vandeyar (2018) contend that policy cannot be divorced from the impact it has on immigrant youths' lives (p. 2). In other words, policies and practices are experienced and lived by those they impact. Thus, to study educational and social policies related to immigration necessitates an understanding of undocumented youths' perspectives about the lived effects of racialization in policies, practices, and conceptions of citizenship, in organizations such as the schools they attend, and the interactions within those schools that promote or inhibit belonging and economic and social mobility.

Across the book I center youth responses to policies and discourses at the macro level, their racialized experiences in school and community contexts at the meso level, and how they discuss their everyday resistance at the micro level. I advance this multilevel analysis (see Figure I.2), and then chart the macro-historical and policy levels and processes of racialization of immigrant groups (Brint & Teele, 2006). The macro-policy level perspective provided me with insights of the federal landscape, while attention to state policy in South Carolina revealed the mounting impossibility for undocumented students to go to college, and the ways in which the state criminalized and targeted Latinx youth. K–12 education was low-quality across the state for all minoritized groups and specifically for undocumented youth in this study. In chapter 2, I share youth perspectives on the impact of these macro-level policies and how they structure and hinder opportunity. In chapter 4, I investigate the meso-organizational (school) level, and how schools supported or failed to support undocumented youth. Lastly, in chapter 5, the micro-level analysis examines youth experiences of discrimination, racism, and lack of quality educational opportunity in schools, their relations among teachers and other like youth, and how they enacted forms of resistance through everyday encounters in school. The empirical data that supports this includes ethnographic participant observation and semi-structured interviews with youth, educators, and school-district personnel. Chapter 5 also analyzes youth perceptions of racialized citizenship and how it disrupts normative or traditional understandings of the category of citizenship, in order to show its racialized and relational dimensions.

The three levels in my theoretical analysis ought to be viewed as interrelated, especially since othering and racialization occurred at all levels (in policy, in school systems through a lack of supports, and within/across interactions with educators and community actors such as law enforcement and ICE). To conceptualize this three-tiered analysis of undocumented youth experiences, I focus on how *undocumentedness* shapes access to resources and mobility in light of racialization of immigrants. In addition, I draw from scholars such as Brint and Teele (2006) and Lamont and colleagues (2012), and more recently Victor Ray's (2019) analytic framework for incorporating racialization processes into the study of organizations, where organizations include the racial state (macro), institutions (meso), and interactions (micro). Brint and Teele (2006) explain that school advantages can be illuminated through macro (historical and policy), meso (institutional, i.e., school), and micro (interactional and relational) levels, and this illustrates perspectives of minoritized group disadvantage. I leverage this multilevel analysis to understand the intersectional frame of policies and schools and how both bear on and constrain everyday lives, as well as how youth utilize cultural tools to respond and navigate their community. I utilize ethnographic evidence to show this "problem framing [in federal and state policies] and institutional settings [two Title I public high schools]" (Lamont et al., 2012 p. 45). Lamont et al. (2012) utilizes this macro-, meso-, micro-level approach to conceptual how minoritized groups respond to and negotiate constraints on their everyday lives and personalize "accounts of exclusion" (p. 45). Similarly, Deaux (2006) calls for attention to the macro (immigration policy and practices), meso (social networks and links between individuals and social structure), and micro (individual values and attitudes) to explain immigrant experiences of exclusion. Adapting and building on these models, I provide a conceptual base for studying the undocumented youth perspectives that give texture to the evolving realities and effects of policies and immigration enforcement on youths' lives. Critical to this conceptual base, and currently not in the literature, is a framework that leverages the concept of racialization to analyze these levels (see Figure I.2).

This interactional framework shows the intersections of policies, school and community phenomena and practices (e.g., school systems and supports, networks, and ideologies within schools; Deaux, 2006; Ray, 2019; Rodriguez, 2022), and interactions between undocumented youth, educators and school-based personnel, and peers. Important to this work is the notion of racialization. In the next section I define the concept and further explain how I apply it in this study.

Racialization

Broadly, racialization is a process of othering (Gans, 2017). Scholars have defined racialization in myriad ways, such as a racist ideology where all intergroup differences are highlighted, a dialectical process between dominant and subordinate groups (Miles, 1982), a process by which physical differences are reflected in social hierarchy and shape lived experiences (Banton, 1977), and a peripheral process born out of Eurocentrism (Fanon, 1968). Racialization, as a component of the conceptual orientation, also offers a way to understand the material effects of race and racism on racialized immigrant bodies. As Fassin (2011) argues, "Racialization processes may be brutal or subtle. They may result in genocides or everyday racism, but also in consciousness and empowerment" (p. 421). Racialization is depicted as a process combining racial ideology and culture with an embodied form of discrimination linked to psychological processes of interiorization and symbolic violence. In other words, it means that individuals assign meaning to phenotypic characteristics through social practices and processes in order to understand race (Hochman, 2019), or racialization is seen as a process of racial classification (Omi & Winant, 2014).

Racialization is a process of othering that reproduces inequality within and across social institutions and social life (Ray, 2019), and it has relevance to discussions of undocumented youth experiences. Racialization is important because it cuts across all the levels of analysis that impact undocumented youths' lives and educational experiences. In addition, youth are positioned as "illegal" and thus excluded from society, institutions, and resources. The data illustrate how this category is maintained through racialization, criminalization, and discrimination in policy and practices at organizational and interactional levels. Specifically, this framework (Figure I.2) shows how the binary of illegal/legal, when applied to undocumented youth, is lived in punitive ways that impact their belonging because they constantly interface with policies, practices, systems, and ideologies that desire their marginalization. Further, showing how youth are racialized in/through policy and school practices sheds light on how the youth are actively categorized and targeted (De Genova, 2002). At the macro-historical and policy level, processes of racialization occur by targeting different groups and excluding them from citizenship. At the meso (institutional) level of the school, youths' narratives underscore the problematic constructions of illegality, and how educators assume all Latinx immigrants are "illegal" due to the "spillover effects" of racialized categorization (De Genova, 2002, p. 11). At the school level, notions of illegality are reproduced through assumptions and stereotyping about Latinx populations, as well as educators' lack of awareness about policies impacting immigrants (Crawford, 2017, 2018; Dabach, 2015). At the macro and meso levels, legal limits and social contradictions arise, and thus examining the layers in relation to the relational and interactional (micro) level is necessary to intervene in the reproduction of illegality and inequality for undocumented youth (De Genova, 2002; Negron-Gonzales, 2014).

In sum, it is important to understand how undocumented youth experience social and legal contradictions, disrupt the binary of legal and illegal (Ybarra, 2018), and exploit racist ideologies and processes of racialization to encourage their empowerment. Important for educators and policymakers is linking policies and practices with the impact they have on the everyday lives of undocumented youth. As such, this framework underscores youth voices and perspectives as a form of resistance to the damaging racialization processes that intersect with their everyday lives. The study was framed this way to examine the discursive policy level and how policy affects the material realities of undocumented youth, underscoring how their micro-level interactions and voices give rise to a resistance narrative about their experience.

Key Concepts in the Book

Given the understudied geography of the New Latino South, and the emerging conversation about race relations and immigration issues (Jones, 2018), this book raises such issues as racism and racial othering and how these processes intersect with what it means to be a citizen in the United States and the South through the eyes of undocumented Latinx immigrant youth. The unexamined geographies of the New Latino South can help us to understand concepts such as race and racial othering—what sociologists of race Omi and Winant (2014) call *racialization*—and citizenship.

Racialization

To build on broader issues of race and education, and the experiences of Latinx undocumented youth, I draw from the racialization literature in sociology, which is part of a larger racial formation theory (RFT) of society (Omi & Winant, 2014; Sáenz & Manges Douglas, 2015). From RFT, I focus on the concept of racialization—an iterative process where immigrant youth are "placed into the U.S. racial paradigm based upon perceptions and experiences of exclusion, surveillance, and profiling"—to critically explore Latinx undocumented youth experiences and promote equity for immigrant youth (Verma et al., 2017, p. 210). A racialization framework helps to make sense of the ethnographic data in my study that revealed how undocumented youth talk about and experience race, racism, and the ascription of identity, and how they negotiate the racialization process to give voice to their own experience of identity and belonging. Silverstein (2005) explains that race is a "cultural category of difference that is contextually constructed as essential and natural—as residing within the very body of the individual" (p. 364). The ascription of racial categories to people with perceived common traits is not a politically neutral act. Rather than a fixed aspect of identity, race is a "system of categorization" (Delgado & Stefancic, 2017) designed for the purposes of power and hierarchy (Omi & Winant, 2014; Weitz 2015). This system of categorization is a historical and ongoing process that Omi and Winant (2014) call *racial formation*: a "process by which social, economic, and political forces determine the content and importance of racial categories, and by which they are in turn shaped by racial meanings" (p. 111). Important to the ongoing process of racial identification is acknowledging race as a "master category" that shapes life courses, and considering racialization, which is the process of categorization into a racial hierarchy. In the context of this study, the youth come to understand their racialized identity as Latinx and its intersection with undocumented immigration status as part of a larger racialized system of the South. Seeing racialized systems helps contextualize the importance of their self-articulated identity expressions, because youths' perceptions of themselves are impacted by institutional and structural factors. The youths' dialogue reflects a counternarrative to racialized policies and practices in their schools and local communities. In the context of this study, youths come to recognize how their identities are racialized, which generates dialogue and critical awareness that they leverage to educate themselves politically and to organize locally in their schools and communities.

Latinx Racialization

The category of "Latino"[4] is an example of how racialization processes relate to power. There is frequent debate over whether the term *Latino* is an ethnic or racial category, as can be seen in discussions over how the term is used in the U.S. Census (Telles, 2018). "Latino" (or Hispanic), however, functions as a racial category in that race is, in large part, a category that is ascribed to people regardless of how they self-identify (Cobas et al., 2015; Vargas et al., 2017). So, Latino is a racial category because people ascribe to it a certain set of essentialized common traits. Latino as a racial category is also ascribed to individuals who are assumed to be nonwhite or not clearly African American, and this racial ascription has consequences. Accordingly, Vargas and colleagues (2016) explain, "The notion that others may define one's race regardless of one's own identity is known as 'socially assigned race' or 'ascribed race,' and it has proved to be a very important measure in predicting the level of discrimination an individual will encounter as well as his or her health outcomes" (p. 500). These racial ascriptions enable Latinx groups to think of themselves in racial terms. While recent immigrants from Latin American countries may identify more with their nationality (as was the case in this study), later generations (i.e., second- and third-generation Americans) identify as Hispanic or Latino (Perez & Hirshman, 2009). The example of Latino racialization shows not only how racial formation is never absent from power negotiations but also how people are part of the meaning-making of that process.

Racialization and Everyday Experiences

As mentioned above, racialization processes are negotiated via day-to-day interactions over time. This racial negotiation process can either re-inscribe current racial classifications or challenge them. The data below reflects this negotiation process for undocumented youth. While newcomer immigrants arriving from Central and South America and Mexico may identify, for example, with their nationality, they still navigate a society that racializes these identities.[5] It is against this background of history, politics, and geography that the racialization of Latinx undocumented immigrant youth is informed. Additionally, racialization occurs within their schools and in the South Carolina policy context, and it affects how they view themselves and respond to racialization processes. Just as Verma and colleagues (2017) call for examining racialization and immigrant youth, and the factors that inform racialization, this study expands our understanding from the grassroots level of the salient factors that inform and perpetuate racialization (e.g., instances of surveillance in the community; youths' interactions with teachers and school-based personnel; formal and informal school structures that classify youth, such as placing all the newly arrived students in ESL classrooms without formal assessments and providing limited services at the school and district levels). This study also illustrates how youth make sense of their complicated racialized identities, in which race, ethnicity, and countries of origin are entangled and conflated with their immigration status in South Carolina. Both Latinx immigrants and U.S. born Latinxs experience forms of racialization and the othering processes due to perceived race/ethnicity and immigration status. It is important to note how Latinx undocumented youth across two divergent school contexts experience racialization and racism, and how they are criminalized in their everyday lives through identity formation and limited educational and community-based supports/opportunities.

Citizenship

FitzGerald (2017) posits that citizenship acquisition, historically and in its current form, is a highly racialized process. Importantly, prior to 1870, whites were the only racial group to enjoy full citizenship rights in the United States (FitzGerald, 2017). Correspondingly, while Blacks were denied citizenship rights until after the Civil War and during World War II Japanese Americans were stripped of their citizenship and placed in internment camps following the Japanese attack on Pearl Harbor, German Americans and Italian Americans did not face retribution in the aftermath of the involvement of Germany and Italy in that war (FitzGerald, 2017). As the United States engages in processes of racial othering in relation to citizenship, the plight of Latinx immigrants continues. One example relates to the racialization of Mexican immigrants. Molina (2014) argues that Mexicans' links to Indigenous people marked them as "culturally nonwhite" (p. 4); this relationship to indigeneity became the basis for subjecting Mexicans and other Latin American populations to racialized immigration practices. (These historical issues are taken up in chapter 2.) Further, I discuss the racialization experiences of Latinx immigrant youth with varying legal statuses, as well as U.S. born Latinx students with foreign-born parents, and how they navigate assumptions, racial stereotyping, and racialization.

Theorizing Racialized Citizenship

Central to this book is the link I make between the concept of racialization as an ongoing process of othering and citizenship and its meaning in the United States. To date, scholarship has not fully linked these important processes, which also have deeply impacted Latinx immigrants, especially those in this study who are undocumented. In what follows, I link citizenship and racialization through a poststructural approach. While previous sociocultural studies connect citizenship and belonging, they generally employ the concept of citizenship through juridical and legal definitions without attention to how this perspective is racialized. These definitions of citizenship are useful to some extent in thinking about the nation-state, but they have been problematic because of their nativist tendencies. Additionally, this normative view of citizenship limits what or who can count as a citizen (i.e., born in the nation or not). Considering a transnational and racialized lens of undocumented youth starts to extend the conversation beyond the normative view of citizenship. To begin this effort, I leverage a poststructuralist lens of citizenship that frames it as a process of racialized subject-making. Youth in this study disrupt normative views and account for the social-relational and racialized dimensions of citizenship. Abrego (2019) argues that undocumented youth develop consciousness about citizenship that "empowers them to enact practices of citizenship as they attempt to claim rights, resist unjust policies of exclusion, or effect political subjectivities that resist the power of the nation-state" (p. 644). Important to this study is what I call *racialized citizenship*, and how youth respond to it as part of their subject-positioning as noncitizens. I found that Latinx groups are criminalized broadly in this Southern context, which reflects the national projection of immigrants as outsiders and threats to a fabricated sense of unity in America within a racist nativist frame (Huber, 2009). Despite national rhetoric and policy initiatives that threaten undocumented lives, K–12 schools are supposed to be safe spaces under *Plyler v. Doe*. And yet, these spaces are compromised by the threat of ICE enhancing the "culture of surveillance" in many communities such as the one in this study (Rodriguez & Monreal, 2017).

Citizenship as a Process of Subject-Making

These discursive shifts signal an opportunity for a poststructural approach, which I advance to open several important points that expand on legal considerations of citizenship: 1) Possessing citizenship is not synonymous with inclusion or belonging, especially when viewed through racialized perspectives (Abu El-Haj, 2007; Shirazi, 2018); 2) citizen-subjects are embodied and formed through everyday practices of civic-minded engagement (i.e., learning about rights and resisting racialization processes as the undocumented youth in this study do); and 3) transnational migration may include a country of origin, a country of residence, third countries, and countries or cultures that inform identity and (in)visibility (Abu El-Haj, 2007; Jaffe-Walter & Lee, 2018; Shirazi, 2018). Regardless of contentious geopolitical recognition, transnational migrants' perceptions of citizenship and belonging are informed by overlapping and sometimes contradictory spheres of identity, inclusion and exclusion, and a collective social imaginary (Vaquera & Aranda, 2015).

I theorize citizenship as a process of subject-making in relation to how Latinx undocumented youth enter racialized hierarchies in the U.S. South, enact activist/resistive identities, and articulate perceptions of citizenship (Foucault & Lotringer, 1989; Ong, 1996). Drawing on Foucault's notion of subjectivity, this study understands citizenship as a process of subject-making, which means that normative categories of citizenship are sustained through legal and risk-threat discourses (Rodriguez, 2018b), and it defines citizenship as a set of cultural practices and beliefs produced through power relations (Ong, 1996). The Foucauldian notion of citizenship connects to the power/knowledge nexus.[6] Different discourses construct different subject positions, such as being "illegal" or being deemed "at risk" in schools.

Alongside how subjects are made through power and policies that potentially subjugate them, the study considers how undocumented youths' perceptions of citizenship and belonging comprise their "self-knowledge." Examples of such self-knowledge include learning the limits of legal citizenship and how they cannot access drivers' licenses, and that they "break the law every day" to get to work, as one youth said. The youth narratives "disrupt" and resist the institutional and legal processes that make them into subjects (i.e., noncitizens or "criminals") (Foucault & Lotringer, 1989, p. 212). The socially constructed categories generated in legal and political discourse in the state have effects, one of which is to determine who is entitled to state resources and who is not. Relevant to this current study, the discourse and enactment of citizenship varies for undocumented Latinx youth in the South and is intimately tied to U.S. immigration patterns and histories of Jim Crow segregation in the South (Brown et al., 2018; Guerrero, 2017). This theoretical framework raises important questions about how the category of citizenship is constructed but also contested through the perceptions and actions of undocumented youth.

Moreover, Ong (1996) explains that citizenship refers to the practices and meanings forged by the individual in relation to and in conjunction with the state. Ong (1996) theorizes citizenship as a process through which the subject is made simultaneously within the state through the power of governmental and social institutions and through the subject reflexivity that occurs in response to this being-made. Cultural citizenship is *not* (and cannot be) an autonomous construction of either entity but is produced by both. Further, Ong (1996) notes that racially informed conceptions of citizenship are fluid and influenced by grassroots-level experiences as a counternarrative to neoliberal colorblind ideologies in the United States that shape American values, such as the practice of "good citizenship" being regarded as one in which the good subject attains success on the basis of self-sufficiency—a current strategic narrative used by the Trump administration in its attempt to implement the "public charge" initiative and limit the type of immigrants that come to the United States. Ong (1996) explains that this is a "process of self-development that in Western democracies becomes inseparable from the process of 'whitening'" (p. 739). The white-dominant narrative sustains racial hierarchies and narratives of economic worth in the country and makes subjects out of immigrant labor, which in turn determines immigrant deservingness of rights and resources. For immigrants, Ong (1996) highlights the importance of the subject-making process and how it associates citizenship with whiteness. Ong (1996) reminds us that, despite the state's role in constructing racial categories of exclusion/inclusion, these categories are continually replicated in everyday life, the "product of people's maintenance of their 'comfort level' of permissible liberal norms against the socially [culturally] deviant newcomers who disturb that sense of comfort" (p. 740).

However, a global world requires a change in the normative, white-dominant, and legal views of citizenship. To this end some scholars began using the word *cultural* when discussing conceptions of citizenship. Citizenship, according to FitzGerald (2017), can be subject to ethnicization or racialization in what he describes as four distinct instances. Racialization can take two forms: 1) a positive preference that privileges a particular group over others, or 2) negative discrimination against a particular group or groups. These concerns about who counts as a citizen intersect with the racial hierarchy in the United States. In each of the subsequent chapters, I show how undocumented youths' citizenship status intersects with racialization processes. This is accomplished through multiple levels of analysis—the historical-policy (macro) level, the school-community (meso) level, and the everyday interactions with teachers and peers (micro) level. To investigate the ways in which these youth endure processes of racialization, identity formation, and belonging, I undertook an ethnographic study that involved policy analysis, participant observations, and interviews with youth and school-based personnel such as teachers, principals, social workers, and counselors; these interviews helped me gain understanding of the youths' everyday lives and experiences with social and educational systems in the South.

The Ethnographic Project

The longitudinal multisite critical ethnographic project explored three interrelated research questions: 1) How do undocumented youth talk about the policies that impact their daily lives? What levels of policy awareness do they exhibit, and what are the policy effects they experience? 2) What institutional structures exist to support recently arrived undocumented youth in their school and community contexts? 3) To what extent do undocumented youth articulate a sense of belonging to their schools and community in relation to their perception of their citizenship/immigration status?

The study included multiple data sources, including extensive fieldwork and participant observations at two Title I high schools, interviews with undocumented youth ($N = 63$), and focus groups. In addition, I engaged in policy analysis of South Carolina education, social, and immigration policies that impacted the everyday lives of undocumented youth and their families (Rodriguez & Monreal, 2017; Rodriguez, 2018a). At stake in each of these questions are the ways in which access and opportunity are excluded from the lives of undocumented youth. Answers to these questions will show the ways state policies constrain the everyday lives and school experiences of undocumented youth (Rodriguez & Monreal, 2017; Rodriguez, 2018a), as well as how youth talk about such constraints, the variation in school support they receive, and how this affects their sense of belonging at school. The answers to the research questions are imperative for educators, school districts, and policymakers to better understand the conditions that undocumented youth navigate and how they advocate for their educational rights and social supports.

Two School Sites, Same Racialization Processes

I conducted ethnographic research in the Denizen community for three and a half years (2015–2018). I noticed population growth on my morning drives across the river onto the island where new housing emerged along the marsh. Meanwhile, the youth lived in trailers tucked away from the major thoroughfare. All of this is on the outskirts of a small, wealthy Southern city. Despite the gentrification near Denizen West, the district maintains a flexible choice policy so that many of the students of the newer white population on the island were attending charter and magnet schools in the area.

Denizen County School District (DCSD) serves almost 50,000 students. This group includes 23,547 white students (47.1% of the total), 19,536 Black students (39.1%), 4,692 Hispanic students (9.4%), and 785 Asian students (1.6%). Additionally, 3,851 students were identified as English language learners, and 4,778 are identified as special education students. Having studied how minoritized youth and communities struggle for equitable policies and practices by protesting in front of the school board (Rodriguez, 2021; Rodriguez et al., 2019), I learned about the deeply rooted segregation and lack of equity in Title I schools in the DCSD, and I witnessed how community members fought for equity in their schools to no avail.

The two sites were selected for their rising population of undocumented Latinx students. To give a brief example, Citizen North witnessed the number of designated English language learners (ELs) significantly increase from approximately 100 students in 2015 to over 300 in 2018, suggesting an unprecedented volume of immigrant youth entering the under-resourced school. While Denizen West did not see as much of an increase in ELs, the late arrival language learners (Allard, 2015) struggled to acquire English, and there were no services for them at the school or translators/bilingual staff.

Citizen North is a large comprehensive Title I school with nearly 100 percent minoritized youth, including an influx of recently arrived undocumented immigrants. It serves the largest area of students in the district, covering a zone of 15 miles that extends into many rural areas. Denizen West is a uniquely small rural school that youth refer to as "the island school" because it is situated on an island about 15 miles west of the urban city center. This island school also has mostly minoritized youth (1 percent of students are white). Despite claims about their threat to economic and national security in state law and policy efforts (Marrow, 2011), the Latinx community has a long-standing presence in the area surrounding the school. This is primarily due to the federally funded migrant farms and the nearby poultry industry. Families rarely leave the island because they are ineligible for a driver's license due to their immigration status and there is no public transportation to this school.

Data Sources

The data sources included field notes from participant-observations, semi-structured interviews ($N = 63$ across both sites) with high school undocumented youth ages 14–17, and quasi-focus groups ($N = 12$), including multiple focus groups with 3 to 4 students in each. Protocols were used to elicit standard answers across domains of inquiry (e.g., definitions and perceptions of citizenship, policy awareness, immigrants' rights, race relations, and border-crossing stories). Given the longitudinal nature of the study, a subset of youth in this were interviewed 4–6 times over the course of the study. The quasi-focus groups emerged in more organic ways, as youth gathered in school social worker's office. The core group in this study convened daily and was there when I arrived on campus. After the 2016 election, the youth desired more knowledge about their rights and local politics, so that became the bulk of our discussions. The youth participants all self-reported as undocumented to me or to the school social worker, who helped me connect with youth in her office during school hours.

Organization of the Book

Chapter 1, "I don't feel welcome here," is Ethnographic Interlude I. This chapter shares the role ethnographic evidence can play in understanding the impact of policy. I introduce my evolving ethnographic self as it pertains to my learning from undocumented youth. During our conversations, I became advocate, friend, listener, and researcher. I was challenged in this project due to the extreme marginalization youth faced and sharing the stories we held in common took the research in different directions at times.

Chapter 2 is titled "'This state is racist with its policies toward Hispanics. We work, but don't have rights.': Racialization of immigrants at macro-historical and policy levels." This chapter uses a historical and policy-analysis perspective to consider the legacies of segregation in the South and how they shape the contemporary social and political structures and processes that negatively impact undocumented immigrants' lives. The chapter begins with a brief discussion of policies impacting foreign-born immigrant groups to show how the normative categories of citizenship are problematic and details how citizenship has been racialized in the United States, excluding different groups at different times based on U.S. political interests. Then, I discuss the policy context of South Carolina, where this study occurred. Based on a review of 120 state policies in South Carolina, a critical policy discourse analysis revealed the ways state policies set up explicit and implicit forms of exclusion toward undocumented Latinx immigrants. This chapter argues that policies seek to problematize Latinx immigrants broadly—and undocumented immigrants in particular—which enables policymakers to justify punitive policy solutions (Rodriguez, 2018a; Rodriguez & Monreal, 2017). This chapter reveals the evolving ways in which state policies construct immigrants as "deviant" and "problems" on the one hand, or good, deserving immigrants on the other. The binary of deviance or deservingness weighs on the lives of undocumented youth, posing significant challenges for educational attainment and social mobility as they are forced to navigate hostile and restrictive policies while being fed the false notion that the American dream is theirs to attain if they would only assimilate.

Chapter 3, "We call them coolers—immigration rooms are cold," is Ethnographic Interlude II. This chapter shares ethnographic narratives from undocumented youth to show how migration shapes and is shaped by their educational aspirations. The students' migration journeys and the fact that they come to the United States without papers significantly impacts their everyday lives. The story of Juan reveals the deep trauma and hardships that youth endure and the residual effects upon entering U.S. schools. Juan points to the "ignorance" of many adults and peers in the school about what it means to be an immigrant. Youth reveal the conditions and consequences of living in South Carolina without documentation.

Chapter 4, "'I was born at the border, like the wrong side of it': Racialization and discrimination at Denizen West High and Citizen North High," introduces the research sites in the study and key concepts of racialization as they relate to Latinx immigrant youths' feelings of isolation. It traces how Latinx immigrants and undocumented immigrant youth are constructed as deviant problems in two Title I high schools, how they endure racialized encounters in their schools through teacher-student interactions, and how they critique and resist racialization through their dialogues. It examines the ways in which state policy delimits many legal, political, and institutional barriers for youth as they attempt to socially integrate. This chapter emphasizes youth voice and experience in relation to institutional barriers to educational opportunity and attainment. As such, this chapter provides insight at the level of school as the major socializing institution. The chapter explains the two sites in the ethnographic study and includes analysis of interviews from teachers, district leaders, and district personnel to share their perceptions of these youth, while utilizing youth narratives to counteract the racism and discrimination espoused by the school and its agents. This chapter argues that not only are these young people forced to "navigate their everyday illegality" (DeGenova, 2002, 2004; Rodriguez, 2017b), they also encounter little reprieve and support in these schools due to the ways in which policy impacts district-level and school-based personnel's and teacher's perspectives and propensity to believe in false narratives about undocumented youth. Drawing on the shared experiences of youth across sites, along with interviews from teachers in the schools and district personnel to shed light on the racialized institutional and school-based perspectives, I highlight how youth articulate a sense of belonging within the affinity groups they form, which empowers them to become activists in their schools and communities as an act of resistance to the larger narrative about them in policy and school.

Chapter 5, "'Even being a citizen isn't a privilege if you're Hispanic here': Undocumented youth perceptions of racialized citizenship," takes a more intimate look at undocumented youth perspectives of citizenship and responses to how they are racialized and cast as outsiders in their school and community—specifically how youth come to define and interpret citizenship in theory and practice in the restrictive state. Drawing on field notes and group interviews with youth, this chapter shares how critical these weekly (sometimes daily) impromptu sessions in the school social worker's office became as youth desired policy knowledge about issues that were impacting them in the state. In this space, youth made sense of their citizenship status and built networks of support. This chapter rigorously theorizes citizenship and uses youth voices to contest the boundaries of juridical and political citizenship (Abrego, 2019) to focus on its relational dimensions. To chart a nuanced theoretical position on citizenship, this chapter also attends to scholarly debates about migration and citizenship, which focus on citizenship as membership and rights in the nation-state. The previous scholarship examines how immigrants are excluded from formal citizenship within the boundaries of liberal democratic states, emphasizing the tensions between citizens' rights in democracies and the "engendered inequalities in capitalistic societies" (Ong, 1996, p. 737). This chapter will ultimately argue for a brand of racialized citizenship, rooted in the experiences of youth as they build policy knowledge to expand their activist identities in the community and school. To understand the meaning-making processes of this type of membership, I share undocumented youth perceptions of citizenship, identity, sense of belonging, and policy thinking in a particularly restrictive state policy context.

The book's Conclusion contains a discussion of key policy and practice implications for school-based personnel and educators.

Part 1

Macro-Level History and Policy Perspectives

● ●

1

Ethnographic Interlude I

• • • • • • • • • • • • • • • • • • • •

"I don't feel welcome here.":
Ethnographic Encounters,
Methodological Notes, and
Policy Effects

"Are you in the same situation as us?" Daisy wondered aloud. We were huddled in Cookie's office at Denizen West, which used to be a storage closet. It snugly fit a desk and a round table with two chairs, where Daisy and I sat while Cookie, the school social worker, rummaged through papers while standing behind the desk, occasionally looking at us and listening. Daisy explained that in her school many students were undocumented. She shared that despite the small community, there were moments of uncertainty about disclosing immigration status with peers or adults in the school. Cookie, however, was a safe person for many of the students. Aracely, another youth in the office, nodded along quietly. She was grappling with being Latinx in the South, her citizenship status, and what it felt like to live in the United States. She said: "I'll never lose my Mexican side. I don't feel welcome here. They say we're taking stuff. And in history class, white students stand up for the flag. Why should I pledge to a country that can't solve its problem?" This encounter with Aracely and Daisy is an example of the substance of our dialogues in Cookie's office. Often running between classes, Cookie let me sit in the office as youth would come in from class or if they needed a safe space. I often helped with homework or just talked about their experiences in the school, the interactions they had with teachers, and the effects of their immigration status on their perceptions of their future or how their status impacted their family members.

As I listened to the youth, I noted that their experiences of navigating their status and identity dynamics and enduring daily microaggressions in their school and the local community were persistent patterns. Their perceptions of what it meant to be American and a citizen while being a Latino in the South, and of immigration policy and law, emerged in our conversations along with the racist encounters they had in the local Southern community of Denizen. For instance, Luisa told me, "People are still not going to like us even if we are citizens or not," referring to the discrimination she and other Latinx students and their families experienced in the community.

In individual and group interviews, observations, and school-wide surveys, youth commonly reported family and economic reasons for coming to the United States and noted the assumptions that "whites" had about immigrants "stealing stuff," such as jobs. Quickly, their descriptions shifted from everyday encounters with local "white supremacists with a Confederate flag in a big truck at McDonald's" in the community, to the many examples of discrimination at school (discussed in later chapters), to broader commentary about the Trump administration, U.S. policies and perceptions toward Latinos, and their families' economic contributions and reasons for migration.

In an effort to make sense of the swirling conversations, and to think theoretically about how racialization operates within and across multiple levels—that is, policy (macro), organization (meso), and interactional (micro) levels—I took notes during my fieldwork about youths' stories. My ethnographic encounters offered insight into the grassroots-level experiences of undocumented youth as these larger social and societal structures and ideologies were at play. Anthropologists Faier and Rofel (2014) refer to ethnographies of encounter as "part of a movement to understand how the cultural (i.e., cultural meanings, practices, objects, identities, and subjectivities) is made and remade in everyday life" (p. 364). *Encounter* refers to the "engagements across difference: a chance meeting, a sensory exchange, an extended confrontation, a passionate tryst. Encounters prompt unexpected responses and improvised actions, as well as long-term negotiations with unforeseen outcomes, including both violence and love.... These highlight relational dynamics, identities, and unequal relationship" (p. 364) to shed light on new cultural meanings. My encounters with the youth in this study comprise the cultural meanings, specifically the political and material effects of the racialization of immigrant youth. Learning about and observing their everyday realities in the local context of schools and the community enabled me to understand their unequal positioning in society because of social structures that maintain their inferiority and lack of power. The encounters in Cookie's office, the lunchroom, courtyard, or walking down a barren road on the island reflect ground-level experiences in the context of school and policy. From here, I shed light on the racialization processes undocumented immigrant youth face and how these shape their aspirations, mobility, and ultimately educational outcomes.

Initially, I entered the field with commitments to the immigrant community and hoped to improve their schooling experiences and belonging. Moving to South Carolina in 2014, I was new to this political context but quickly understood the legacies of Jim Crow segregation. My office was near the elementary school that was the site of the first attempt in the city of Denizen at desegregation in 1974, and it represented the many efforts in South Carolina to thwart or blatantly deny integration efforts post-*Brown*. Even though I had taught on the history of American education and landmark Supreme Court cases impacting educational equity for minoritized young people, it was not until I moved to South Carolina that I learned about the "corridor of shame" and the *Briggs v. Elliott* (1952) case that was part of the *Brown* set of cases. I also learned about *Abbeville v. South Carolina* (2014), where the state supreme court found that schools were failing to provide students with a "minimally adequate education." All these cases documented the abysmal educational inequality for Black students in South Carolina over decades. This history was sewn into the fabric of the state and local community.

Furthermore, it was clear to me how racial tensions and ideologies lived through local monuments, such as graveyards for enslaved people under the campus buildings that I walked by every day on the way to work. Despite the glaring racial inequity for the Black community, it was less clear initially how Latinx immigrants were treated and where they lived. Thus, to think about immigrant youths' lived experiences, I had to locate the hidden, sometimes invisible population, or what scholars refer to as a "shadow population" (Reynolds, 2014). After investigating and connecting with a local community-based organization working on dropout prevention, I was able to identify two high schools with Latinx students and support staff (counselors and school social workers) funded through various grants secured by the community-based organization. Drawing on my previous experience as an ethnographer of community-school partnerships and Title I high schools, I was able to navigate the dynamics of locating sites for fieldwork. However, the policy and political landscape and the nature of race relations in the community were new to me. They were not novel or surprising, but nonetheless I knew I needed to gain a deeper understanding of how race and racialization operated in the Denizen community. To do that, I began building relationships on the ground while also thinking about and analyzing policy documents at the state level.

Previous scholarship often focuses on the abstract policy or the discourses and effects of policies on immigrants' access to resources (Abrego, 2008; Rodriguez, 2018a), the multilayered ways that policy compounds immigrants' everyday lives through the actions of ICE and its cooperation with local law enforcement (Arriaga, 2017; Menjívar, 2014b), or more broadly, how initial and return migration impacts families and the life course of youth (Heidbrink, 2020). As discussed later in this chapter, U.S. immigration policy is uneven at best, but in 2016 it felt like every day youth had to navigate it or stay alert to the newest Trump administration policy or practice. Of course, South Carolina had a long history of racist or exclusionary policies toward immigrants (Rodriguez, 2018a; Rodriguez & Monreal, 2017), but I was interested in how youth "interpreted" these policies to shape their lives (Hamann & Rosen, 2011, p. 4). In South Carolina, I observed a system of racist policies and practices that were understood and lived by youth, so pointing out systemic racism and acknowledging that racism in this Southern context was endemic was neither new nor useful to them.

Instead, I considered how to make sense of policies and processes of racialization that occurred at multiple levels. My analysis of these intersections and interactions of the racialization process—the "ethnography of policy"—is the major contribution of this study. Recalling Daisy's comments, I explored through youths' eyes what it meant to live through/in policies, how the youth wondered if other students were in the "same situation," and how they would grapple with feeling "unwelcome" in South Carolina and the United States broadly. Youth commonly noted in the early years of the study how U.S. border policy influenced their sense of belonging. Aracely said of her migration journey, "I remember the thorns in my feet. I get flashes." Her view of immigration policy and citizenship status as part of federal policy is also complicated by her perceptions of living in South Carolina, such as feeling the state "benefits from our [Hispanic im/migrant] labor."

And yet, policy discourse and effects didn't just happen in a vacuum. Ana noted that "citizenship wasn't necessarily a privilege here," explaining that Latinx immigrants were targets of racism and surveillance. Similarly, Odie shared, "Citizenship doesn't matter to me; it's just a paper; papers can be burned; we have to deal with other stuff every day," referring to how racism in the community was connected to immigrant youths' lived experiences of policies and practices. In each of these conversations, youth explained how they and other Latinx immigrants navigated policy barriers. The lived experience of policy was intertwined with familial and educational dimensions. As such, I was not just documenting a particular homogenous culture. There was significant diversity in the experiences and identities of the 63 youths interviewed or observed in this study. And given the ad hoc policies, programs, and practices across macro, meso, and micro levels, capturing a singular experience was unproductive and not useful. Similarly, I did not trace a particular policy, its implementation, and its impact on their lives. Instead, I viewed policy broadly as shaping ideologies and discourses toward Latinx immigrants in South Carolina and I examined the effects of policy and ideologies (Ball, 1993; Hamann & Rosen, 2011).

In addition to broadening the definition of policy, ethnographic studies that engage with policies and policy analysis necessarily engage with different methods and units of analysis. While the bulk of this project was fieldwork, including participant observation at multiple schools and semi-structured individual and group interviews, analyzing U.S. and South Carolina policies, including exclusionary educational policies in the state, was critical for understanding these youths' everyday lives. I viewed policies in some sense as actors and policymaking as a "sociocultural practice" (Hamann & Rosen, 2011, p. 8) that was brought to bear upon undocumented youths' lives. Methodologically, I studied policy to better understand my research questions, and to align with my commitment to understanding the broader phenomena—how racialization processes at macro, meso, and micro levels impacted undocumented youths' lives and their access to mobility and resources—in relation to the social context of South Carolina, a particularly restrictive state. Across the levels of analysis, and utilizing theoretical framing of racialization, I examined federal and state policies in relation to the systems of social relations youth encountered; ideas and beliefs of and about immigrants in the state; narratives, values, and perspectives about national, state, and school-level policy; receptivity toward immigrants; and interactions with students, teachers, staff, and community members. This holistic view is central in ethnographic research. And while each undocumented youth story differed in some way, the "stories they held in common" (Bettie, 2003, p. 8) related to their lived experience of anti-immigrant policy and the racialization processes, including at the macro policy level, which is the subject of chapter 2.

Moreover, the social organization of the school and community was largely influenced by policy discourses and effects at the federal, state, and local levels. Considering policies helped make sense of the ethnographic data, and even though youth did not always name specific house bills or pieces of legislation, it was their lived experiences that helped map the contoured effects of policies. Thus, I would research the language of policies impacting immigrants to learn about and share specifics of their educational rights and together we also were able to inform some school staff and teachers interested in advocating for them.

In addition to having to learn the policy context, I also needed to consider my own role and commitments as an educational sociologist and ethnographer. As I reviewed policy documents such as South Carolina's "Show Me Papers" law, youth commented that the state was "racist toward Hispanics." This was in reference to the minimum-wage jobs available to them while being under immigration surveillance (Rodriguez & Monreal, 2017). The deeper into my engagement with policy, the more my own irritation and anger about the blatantly racist and exclusionary policies showed with youth. I had to share my own experiences with them to build trust in the beginning, and I did this, in part, by sharing my personal and professional journeys and beliefs. As we explored the policies in South Carolina, I did not shy away from sharing my deeper commitments and opinions about racial injustice and educational inequities experienced by immigrants. The policies were not new to them, but they wanted to learn about "their rights," because they understood that, though they were limited, they did have rights.

I often reflected on the differences and similarities among us. While introducing my interest in policies as actors and critical data sources in this ethnography, I was also an actor: as Erickson (1984) notes, "it is 'I' who was doing the fieldwork, not somebody else. Thus, assumptions and prejudices are central to the study and analysis" (p. 60). Being in school spaces with youth means experiencing strong relationships with whomever else is there. For me this meant my relationships with the kids. Some of these "relationships may feel good, and others may hurt" (Erickson, 1984, pp. 60–61). As noted, the 2016 election brought intense emotion to the research, and sometimes I felt that I could not and should not proceed with asking youth to share their fears and uncertainties about the future, policies, and living in an anti-immigrant state during such a volatile political administration. There were rumors in the community about ICE raids at local apartment complexes where the youth lived. At times, it was difficult to know what to say to the youth because they would ask what could happen to them or their families. Deportation was a real threat in this community. Many of the youth witnessed friends and family members deported during the study.

I spoke with two of the teachers at Citizen North who were very involved in assisting youth when they brought immigration-related documents to school, Ms. Ava and Ms. Constance. I was able to draw on my experience as a former English as a second language (ESL) and literacy teacher in New York City and Chicago public schools to work closely with these two ESL teachers. Ava was new to South Carolina but had been a teacher elsewhere for over a decade. After the election, I was able to co-plan lessons with her to help share resources and information about educational and political rights for undocumented youth since all her students were newcomers. Many were undocumented and some were unaccompanied and lived in the apartment complexes that were being raided. My commitment to ensuring they knew about their rights in case they encountered ICE was prioritized and shaped the data collection process in Ava's class. In other words, the subject of the lessons and group interviews became integral to the conversations in Ms. Ava's class. Undocumented youth shared their families' reasons for migration and their perspectives about the economic contributions of immigrants in South Carolina, such as when one youth commented, "We [Hispanics] do the work they [white people] don't want to do."

The newcomer undocumented youth at Citizen North were much shyer and more afraid in their demeanor and had more questions regarding local policies and their rights, while the undocumented youth at Denizen West had lived in the community longer, in some cases since they were young children. Despite having to navigate ICE near the school, cooperation between ICE and local law enforcement, and family deportation, the Denizen youth expressed less fear and more frustration. This is not to say they were unafraid, but in comparison to the more recently arrived students, I found this to be true. In terms of my reflexivity and my political commitments, and the design of critical ethnography, I entered the study and the evolving methods for collecting data with the intention of analyzing sensitive issues related to the racialization of undocumented immigrant youth. While this ethnography included policy analysis and knowledge-sharing, my primary aim was to theorize the relationship between larger structures in society and structural inequalities and agency for youth empowerment (Atkinson et al., 2007). These critical perspectives were always discussed, but in terms of talking with the youth, I would ask open-ended questions about what they perceived their rights to be and what they thought policymakers should do to support immigration reform. Next, I share specifics about my social location as a researcher and how that influenced my relationship-building with the undocumented youth.

Shared Stories We Held in Common: Context, Class, and Identity

When I present this research, I am often asked how I was able to build relationships with the undocumented youth. There is no easy answer. All ethnographers enter the field uncertain and flexible. While the Latinx youth in this study were undocumented, they arrived between birth and 14 years of age and many of them spent most of their childhood in the United States (Gonzales, 2016). Others arrived the school year I began the study in 2015. I perceived my role as similar to my role as a middle and high school teacher, to build initial relationships with them. They viewed me as an advocate from the beginning. My relationships with them, I would later learn, were reciprocal in the sense that they felt I was an advocate for them, or a friend who listened when they talked about the struggles they faced. One youth referred to participating in my research as having a "platform" where she could share her story (Rodriguez & Kuntz, 2021).

Another way I was able to connect with the youth was having grown up impoverished. While I am a U.S. citizen, I am the child of a foreign-born Cuban immigrant. Sharing my experiences of growing up low-income and with a single mother helped me connect with youth; specifically, we discussed our identities, our friendships in high school, and feelings of isolation and embarrassment growing up poor. My ethnographic encounters of difference (Faier & Rofel, 2014) allowed us to connect despite immigration status and social class differences, and now the unequal power dynamic given I was a university professor and researcher. These differences did not outweigh our shared experiences (Bettie, 2003; Rodriguez, 2019).

The youth and I connected on social class and on our identity struggles. I spoke of being racialized in my higher education experience, and being one of only a few Hispanic students in my high school. I shared that at times, I felt "white" having grown up with a white mother, but that I felt torn because of my Cuban heritage. I often would let people decide for me what my identity was. In one encounter, I was sitting at a conference table at Citizen North High School with three female youth discussing identity. One youth, Eggy, shared, "I'm considered a BLACK-xican—guata and Mexican." We all laughed, but Eggy described how she has darker skin and is Indigenous, Guatemalan, and Mexican, so her friends call her "Black-xican." These conversations led us to make sense of their identity in this Southern context; specifically, because they lived in the context of a Black-white binary, most community members and school personnel did not understand the diversity of *Latinidad* (Gamez & Monreal, 2021). Most of the youth regularly commented that "American" was not part of their identity and they did not "fit in."

In sum, my ongoing reflexivity pushed me to consider our similarities and differences. My own history and identity intersected with the research, and at times I felt a sense of healing in talking about class and identity struggles with the youth in the study. While I was an outsider to their community in many ways, we were all outsiders in this unique Southern context. Yet, our encounters, including dialogues, silences, laughs, and walks, were evidence of our relationship as an act of love, healing, and reciprocity in the research (Rodriguez & Kuntz, 2021; Rosaldo, 1997). Despite the deep personal relationships I forged, I considered their stories as part of the nuance of ethnography and the tensions between their experience and larger social structures.

As the youth shared how "this state is racist," I sought to uncover how, in what way, and through which mechanisms the state and local contexts maintained racist, exclusionary systems, policies, and structures. It is difficult to capture the intimate relationships and moments of tension, uncertainty, and sadness, especially when youth cried or told a story about a family member being deported. Irwin (2006) refers to this as the "dark heart of ethnography," where we must face the realities of the relationships we are forming and our shortcomings as ethnographers in shifting violent, harmful policies. I often felt powerless in this regard. Nonetheless, I explored the policy, school, and relational dynamics to shed light on these youths' cultural meanings and sensemaking of their experience as undocumented in the South. Noticing in my conversations with youth how the overlapping layers of government (macro), school (meso), and relational (micro) policies converged to racialize them, I developed a theoretical framework to analyze these policies that would accurately capture their lived experiences. This framework guides the chapters in this book.

2

"This state is racist with its policies toward Hispanics. We work, but don't have rights."

• •

Racialization of Immigrants at the Macro Level

You know immigration came to visit my house a few days ago. They knocked at the door. I didn't know what to do. They asked for ID or any identification. They were looking for someone else, but they told us to be careful because we don't have a license and we drive so we break the law every day to go to school and work. Sometimes I don't know what to do so I don't come to school, or if I do I bring the immigration letters to Ms. Ava.

—Undocumented youth, Field Notes, April 2016

In the above quote, an undocumented youth explains the impact and intersection of racialized laws and policies on their everyday lives. Policies have effects, and the larger criminalization and racial profiling that manifests from anti-immigrant federal, state, and local policies have effects on youths' access to resources, as well as on their psyche. This chapter has two aims. First, I expand upon the concept of racialization as the core component of the theoretical framework for this study. This framework offers a way of understanding the macro, meso, and micro dynamics of immigration policy, school-level dynamics, and interactional relations between immigrant youth. After explaining the theoretical orientation of the project, I then use this lens of "racializing immigration studies" (Sáenz & Manges Douglas, 2015) to provide a historical overview of immigration law and policy, the context of the New Latino South, and how it impacts undocumented youths' everyday lives through processes of racialization in law and policy. The theoretical framework in the Introduction refers to the macro level, where racialization processes occur through historicizing immigration law and policy, federal and state policies impacting immigrants, immigration enforcement, and media and political discourses of immigrant illegality (see Figure I.2 in the Introduction).

The chapter begins with the theoretical concepts that underpin the policy and empirical analysis in subsequent chapters. To underscore how immigration policy has shaped educational policymaking and practice in the context of this study, I chart general discussions of immigration policy, linking histories of immigration law and policy with racialization and citizenship. While this is certainly not an exhaustive immigration history, I connect interdisciplinary scholarship and consider how racialization and citizenship apply to immigrant groups in the United States (Molina, 2014; Ngai, 2005). It is this historical backdrop that is critical to examining policy and the contemporary moment in the South. Additionally, this chapter offers a critical analysis of 120 proposed and enacted policies in the focal state of South Carolina. The policy analysis illustrates how state policies set up explicit and implicit forms of exclusion toward Latino (un)documented immigrants in the state, and how those policies impact the everyday lives of the undocumented youth in this study.

In my policy analysis, I examined how South Carolina state policies racialized and targeted immigrants broadly and undocumented youth specifically, making them into problems in the policy discourse and enabling policymakers to justify punitive policy "solutions" to these "problems," such as increasing the presence of ICE in local communities, raiding housing complexes, and monitoring local schools (Rodriguez, 2018a; Rodriguez & Monreal, 2017). The relationship between racialization and problematization, which refers to making people into problems, is reciprocal and mutually forming. For instance, Gulson and Webb (2013) give an example of how a racialized object—the Afrocentric school—became a "problem" *because* it was racialized but also was introduced into a policy context and geography (the city of Toronto) that was already racialized. While it is too rigid to say that racialization occurred *prior to* problematization in this case (particularly given the historical roots of race in North America), the already racialized opening of the Afrocentric school posed new problems related to economics, culture, equity, and justice. Alternatively, Lindblad et al. (2018) explain how the U.S. Census was used to address the problem of new immigrants following WWII when "the category of Latino emerged . . . to classify people from, for example, Brazil, Haiti, Argentina and Mexico, among others, as a single population" (p. 206). In these examples, racialization is linked to producing categories of difference to make the administration of policies and institutional practices more convenient and efficient (Foucault, 1994). In other words, policies, laws, and practices create categories of people and problems, ultimately using racial categories to differentiate people and often exclude them based on racial/ethnic classifications (Lewis, 2005).

The point is not that specific individuals are targets of techniques of power but that power is exercised through the "government of individualization" (Foucault, 1982), which employs strategies of normalization, problematization, and racialization. In other words, these techniques are used to mark individuals as racialized others, as a strategy for reproducing whiteness as the unnamed, naturalized norm that enables the production of policies and practices that further entrench dominant racial discourses.

This chapter reveals the evolving ways in which state policies construct immigrants as deviant problems on the one hand, or good, deserving immigrants on the other. The binary of deviance or deservingness weighs on the lives of undocumented youth, posing significant challenges for educational attainment and social mobility, as they are forced to navigate hostile and restrictive policies while being fed the false notion that the American dream is theirs to attain if they would only assimilate. The New Latino South and South Carolina maintain the attitude of the immigrant often being more deviant than deserving, and thus subject to anti-immigrant policies of exclusion.

Theoretical Approach: Racialization across Macro Policy and Historical Moments

In the introduction, I engaged with influential concepts in this project, specifically racialization and racialized citizenship. To expand the literature, I move away from deficit-based assimilationist frameworks for studying immigrant integration and mobility. While assimilation and its variations, including segmented assimilation, have dominated sociological studies of immigration, I move away from them to account for the racialization processes that contribute to immigrant exclusion. Additionally, frameworks such as the contexts of reception and nested contexts of reception have attempted to provide nuance to the study of immigrant experiences of education and social mobility. Next, I provide an overview of these frameworks, and how and why I depart from them. Then, I explain the development of the theoretical framework for this project.

Contexts of Reception

Sociologists and migration scholars have long held that the place where immigrants settle is important for the process of incorporation, specifically through the framework of contexts of reception and segmented assimilation. Research about immigrant communities examined the neighborhood context and the role of ethnic enclaves, but assumed that immigrant adaptation, or "straightline assimilation," was inevitable (Brown & Bean, 2006). Segmented assimilation, a hypothesis introduced in the early 1990s, suggested that a variety of factors—including federal policy—shape processes of immigrant integration and, importantly, helped explain why some immigrant groups tended to follow mobility trajectories into various layers of the social strata (Portes et al., 2009). The emergence of the immigrant new destinations literature in the early 2000s showed that states, counties, and cities have local laws and infrastructural features that impact immigrant access to resources, and that the contours of the local receiving context vary from one place to the next (Hamann et al., 2015).

More recently, scholars have begun to develop frameworks that capture these different levels of reception to include the neighborhood, city, state, and federal contexts. This provides a multiscalar understanding of how place matters for processes of immigrant incorporation. For example, an unauthorized immigrant (a disadvantaged status determined by laws at the federal level) may live in a state with welcoming laws (such as those that provide all immigrants with access to driver's licenses) but in a neighborhood where they experience some degree of discrimination from neighbors (Menjívar, 2014a). Each of these levels of reception may vary along a continuum from hostile to welcoming, and while one level may be more hostile the next level may be more welcoming. In addition to the macro contexts of reception (e.g., federal, state, policy, and law contexts), societal (e.g., reception of cultural groups and their relationship to the dominant group), and institutional contexts (e.g., K–12 education) continue to shape unauthorized immigrant mobility and access to resources, societal discrimination, racism, and racial attitudes toward immigrants.

Considering the Governmental, Societal, and Institutional Contexts

Golash-Boza and Valdez's (2018) framework of the "nested contexts of reception" (NCOR) conceptualizes these different levels as a series of concentric circles. Each sphere exercises some influence on the process of incorporation, offering a much more nuanced understanding of how various factors at the micro, meso, and macro levels impact the mobility trajectories of immigrants. Aligned with this NCOR framework, Perez (2021) shows how nested contexts of reception shape variation in Latinx identity development through processes of racialized immigrant incorporation in an immigrant's new destination. The invitation in the NCOR framework to consider societal perspectives is an important step for considering the role race, racial attitudes, and racial discrimination play in the lives of immigrants, and how, for our purposes, such attitudes might manifest in institutions such as schools. Portes and Rumbaut (2014) describe the racialization of immigrant children in schools as evidence of the "decisive role" the context of reception has in shaping outcomes (p. 295). Even after controlling for parental variables, demographic characteristics, and early school experiences, Haitian, West Indian, and Mexican origin youth had a much higher probability of experiencing downward assimilation due to racial identity markers.

These frameworks for assimilation and segmented assimilation account for potential host society views, and NCOR introduces an interactional framework that might also account for discrimination and relationships between dominant cultural groups and immigrants. Yet, these frameworks have explicitly and implicitly "reproduced the privileging of whiteness as the standard of assimilation for immigrants" (Verma et al., 2017). Importantly, then, assimilation, incorporation, or integration of immigrant groups cannot be studied without focusing on how these groups are excluded from access to resources, often (with) held by white-dominant groups in institutions. To account for this exclusion, and centering whiteness as a key credential within racial hierarchies in the United States (Omi & Winant, 2014; Ray, 2019; Rodriguez, 2020a, 2021), I move away from these frameworks and call for a framework that includes naming racial exclusion and inequity and locates processes of racialization across multiple levels. I will explain this next.

Racialization and the Construction of Illegality

I expand our understanding of undocumented youth experiences by building a conceptual framework for analysis, focusing not only on the impact of their immigration status—the notion of illegality, but also the interplay of policies and youths' lived experiences and everyday realities. Across the book, I examine three distinct but related levels where racialization occurs and impacts immigrants (macro-policy, meso-organizational, and micro-interactional) (Ray, 2019) and their interplay with undocumented immigrants' racialized experiences. Providing additional conceptual ground, Hamann and Vandeya (2018) contend that education and social "policy cannot be understood apart from what does" (p. 2). In other words, policies and practices are constituted, and lived, by those they impact. Thus, to study education and social, policies related to immigration necessitates an understanding of undocumented youths' perspectives about the lived effects of racialization in policies, practices, and conceptions of citizenship, in organizations such as the schools they attend, and in their interactions within those schools that promote or inhibit belonging and mobility.

This chapter charts the macro-historical and policy levels and processes of racialization of immigrant groups (Brint & Teele, 2006). I center youth responses to policies and discourses at the macro level, their racialized experiences in school and community contexts at the meso level, and how they discuss their everyday resistance at the micro level. I advance this Multilevel Racialization Framework (see Figure I.2 in the Introduction). This macro-policy level perspective provided me with insights regarding the federal landscape, but attention to South Carolina state policy revealed the mounting impossibility for undocumented students to go to college, and the ways in which the state criminalized and targeted Latinx youth. K–12 education was low-quality across the state for all minoritized groups, specifically for undocumented youth in this study. I share youth perspectives about the impact of these macro-level policies and how they structure and hinder opportunity. In subsequent chapters, I investigate the meso-organizational (school) level and how schools supported or failed to support undocumented youth, as well as the micro level. An analysis of levels reveals youth experiences of discrimination, racism, and lack of quality educational opportunity in schools, their relations among teachers and other like youth, and how they enacted forms of resistance through everyday encounters in school.

The three levels ought to be viewed as interrelated, especially since othering and racialization occur at all levels (i.e., in policy, in school systems through lack of supports, and within/across interactions with educators and community actors such as law enforcement and ICE). To conceptualize this three-tiered analysis of undocumented youth experiences I focus on how *undocumented-ness*—a term I use to illustrate the fluidity of the status rather than fixing identity—shapes access to resources and mobility in light of the racialization of immigrants (Rodriguez, 2020a). In addition, I draw from scholars such as Brint and Teele (2006) and Lamont and colleagues (2012), and more recently Victor Ray's (2019) analytic framework for incorporating racialization processes into the study of organizations, where organizations include the racial state (macro), institutions (meso), and interactions (micro). Brint and Teele (2006) explain that framing experiences of schooling and advantage can be illuminated through the macro (historical and policy), meso (institutional, i.e., school), and micro (interactional and relational), illustrating perspectives of minoritized group disadvantage. I leverage this multilevel analysis to understand the intersection of how policies and schools bear on and constrain everyday lives and how youth utilize cultural tools to respond and navigate their community. I utilize ethnographic evidence to show this "problem framing" in federal and state policies and "institutional settings" (two Title I public high schools) (Lamont et al., 2012, p. 45). Lamont and colleagues (2012) utilize this macro, meso, and micro level approach to conceptualize how minoritized groups respond to and negotiate constraints on their everyday lives and personalize "accounts of exclusion" (p. 45). Similarly, Deaux (2006) calls for attention to the macro (immigration policy and practices), meso (social networks and links between individual and social structures), and micro (individual values and attitudes) levels to explain immigrant experiences of exclusion. Adapting and building from these models, I provide a conceptual base for studying the undocumented youth perspectives that give texture to the evolving realities and effects of policies and immigration enforcement on youths' lives. Critical to this conceptual base, and currently not in the literature, is a leveraging of the concept of racialization as a framing device to analyze these levels.

This interactional framework shows the intersections of policies, school and community phenomena and practices (e.g., school systems and supports, networks, and ideologies within schools) (Deaux, 2006; Ray, 2019), and interactions between undocumented youth, educators and school-based personnel, and peers. Important to this work is the notion of racialization, which I define and further explain in the next section. I examine the macro-level policies in the United States and in South Carolina through this lens of racialization, and explain how I will apply it in this study.

Racialization

Broadly, racialization is a process of othering (Gans, 2017). Scholars have defined racialization in myriad ways, such as a racist ideology where all intergroup differences are highlighted, a dialectical process between dominant and subordinate groups (Miles, 1982), a process by which physical differences are reflected in social hierarchy and shape lived experiences (Banton, 1977), and a peripheral process, born out of Eurocentrism (Fanon, 1968). Racialization, as a component of the conceptual orientation, also offers a way to understand the material effects of race and racism on racialized immigrant bodies. As Fassin (2011b) argues, "Racialization processes may be brutal or subtle. They may result in genocides or everyday racism, but also in consciousness and empowerment" (p. 421). Racialization is depicted as a process combining racial ideology and culture with an embodied form of discrimination linked to psychological processes of inferioritization and symbolic violence. In other words, it means that individuals assign meaning to phenotypic characteristics and enact discrimination through social practices and processes (Hochman, 2019), and use racialization to create racial classification and a racial hierarchy (Omi & Winant, 2014). In addition to using phenotypic characteristics to racialize and classify groups, people use various identifiers or signals of race, such as accents (W. Roth, 2016).

Racialization is a process of othering that reproduces inequality within and across social institutions and social life (Ray, 2019) and has relevance when discussing undocumented youths' experiences. Racialization is important because it cuts across all the levels of analysis that impact undocumented youths' lives and educational experiences. In addition, youth are positioned as illegal, and thus excluded from society, institutions, and resources. The data illustrate how this category is maintained through racialization, criminalization, and discrimination in policy and practices at organizational and interactional levels. Specifically, this framework shows how the binary of illegal/legal, when applied to undocumented youth, is lived in punitive ways that impact their belonging, because youth constantly interface with policies, practices, systems, and ideologies that desire their marginalization. Further, showing how youth are racialized in/through policy and school practices sheds light on how youth are actively categorized and targeted (De Genova, 2002). At the macro (historical and policy) level, processes of racialization occur by targeting different groups and excluding them from citizenship, which is the topic of this chapter. At the macro level, legal limits and social contradictions arise, and thus examining this level in relation to the micro (relational and interactional) level is necessary to intervene in the reproduction of illegality and inequality for undocumented youth (De Genova, 2002; Negrón-Gonzales, 2014).

In sum, understanding how undocumented youth experience social and legal contradictions, disrupt the binary of legal and illegal (Ybarra, 2018), and exploit racist ideologies and processes of racialization is an important step toward their empowerment. Important for educators and policymakers is linking policies and practices with the impact they have on the everyday lives of undocumented youth. As such, this framework underscores youth voices and perspectives as a form of resistance to the damaging racialization processes that intersect with their everyday lives. This chapter shows the discursive policy level and how policy affects the material realities of undocumented youth.

Looking Back to Understand the Contemporary Moment: Racialization of U.S. Immigration Policy and Normative Categories of Citizenship

U.S. Immigration policy is confusing and complex. At various points in the country's history, the government established laws that rendered some immigrants illegal; often this decision was tied to political interests (Golash-Boza & Valdez, 2018). For example, the first U.S. citizenship law, known as the Naturalization Act of 1790, conferred citizenship rights via naturalization to immigrants who were "free white person[s] . . . of good character," thus excluding slaves, free Blacks, and Native Americans (Library of Congress, n.d., p. 103).

This act also extended citizenship rights to the children of U.S. citizens who were born overseas.

In 1798, President John Adams enforced the Alien and Sedition Acts in response to what was perceived to be a military threat from France. To alleviate concerns about a weakening presidency, the Adams administration scapegoated foreign nationals who were thought to threaten society. The three alien laws, which mostly targeted Irish and French immigrants, prolonged the waiting period for naturalization from five to fourteen years, made possible the detention of foreign nationals whom the government considered suspicious, and gave the president the authority to expel any foreign national he regarded as dangerous. The Naturalization Act of 1802 repealed what were the most gregarious provisions of the 1798 Alien and Sedition Acts, doing away with punitive measures and reducing the waiting period for naturalization to five years; however, naturalization was still limited to whites (Library of Congress, n.d.).

Historically, the United States is one of the only countries that conceived citizenship as a status distinct from nationality (FitzGerald, 2017). For instance, Blacks who resided in the United States were considered U.S. nationals (FitzGerald, 2017), but they were excluded from citizenship in accordance with the *Scott v. Sanford* Supreme Court ruling of 1857. While citizenship itself was not clearly defined at that time—other than to indicate which groups would be excluded from it—in 1866 Congress passed the first Civil Rights Act, the first federal law to define citizenship (White, 2012). The act was designed to protect the civil rights of persons of African descent and support the Thirteenth Amendment; the law was opposed by President Andrew Johnson but was later enacted when it became ratified in 1870. This ratification followed the passage of the Fourteenth Amendment, which stated that "all persons born or naturalized in the United States, and subject to the jurisdiction thereof, are citizens of the United States and the State wherein they reside" (para. 5). Also in 1870, the Naturalization Act finally granted Blacks full citizenship status; access to naturalization was still blocked for Native Americans and other people of color who were not classified as being of African descent (Taparata, 2016). Native Americans had to wait another fifty-four years before they were able to attain U.S. citizenship under the Indian Citizenship Act of 1924 (Law Library of Congress, n.d.).

As more immigrants of color began to pour into the United States, immigration policies became particularly restrictive for nonwhite immigrants who were deemed unassimilable (Rodriguez, 2018a) and threatening to the nascent republic whose image and white, Christian, and European bonafides would be tarnished by their presence (FitzGerald, 2017). For instance, while the Naturalization Act of 1870 was beneficial to African Americans, it revoked the citizenship rights of naturalized Chinese Americans. Exclusionary immigration policies such as the Page Act of 1875, which barred the entry of Chinese women who were considered "immoral" (Peffer, 1986, p. 28) and the Chinese Exclusion Act of 1882, which prohibited the migration of Chinese laborers to the United States, worked in concert to ensure that no Chinese people would be allowed to enter the United States. The Scott Act (1888), the Immigration Act of 1891, and the Geary Act (1892) added new restrictive measures vis-à-vis immigration from China (Lee, 2002). Restrictions on Chinese immigration remained in effect until they were finally repealed through the Magnuson Act of 1943, which also granted citizenship rights to Chinese Americans and made possible the naturalization of Chinese immigrants (Chang, 2003).

Historicizing the Present Problem of the Immigrant

The image of the immigrant in America is one of hope and promise, difference and otherness, inclusion and exclusion. The paradoxical positioning of the immigrant who comes for a better life and is received but also expected to contribute economically is long established in United States policy and popular discourses and was enshrined in the purpose of schooling and curriculum in the late nineteenth and early twentieth centuries (Olneck, 1989; Reese, 2005). These paradoxes (Lindblad et al., 2018) position the immigrant as both included and excluded, wanted and unwanted, part of the American community while also positioned outside it (Abbott, 1917).

To link the "problem of the immigrant," and American society, education and social policy, and public schooling, Grace Abbott, an American social worker, immigrant rights advocate, and reformer (1917) wrote:

> Our educational policy also has some-times completely ignored the problems of the immigrant. Some years ago, at a meeting, the subject under discussion was what could be done in both day and evening schools to prepare more successfully the immigrant children and their parents for American life. An "educator" who was present rose and, with a display of a very popular kind of Americanism, said that we had an "American system of education" in this country and that if it did not suit the immigrant, he ought not to come, or, having come, if he is dissatisfied, he should go back. It was, of course, quite evident to those who listened that this educator would resent any interference with his "system" on behalf of the American boy or girl just as he did on behalf of the Italian or Lithuanian man or woman. The problem of adapting successfully our school system to meet the needs of the community has not been created by the presence of the immigrant; but each national group is a new element to be considered if the adaptation is to be scientifically made. A real service is, therefore, rendered the Native American, as well as the immigrant, in every demand that the schools be made flexible and is constantly adapted to changing conditions.

Abbott's argument remains relevant over a hundred years later as America struggles to provide equitable educational opportunity and value what immigrant children bring to the school system. However, immigrants continue to be labeled through deficit-based or at-risk discourses, and they are encouraged to learn English and contribute to society (Rodriguez, 2015).

Historicizing the figure of the immigrant (problem) yields a litany of U.S. policies that illustrate a range from anti-immigrant to inclusion (see Golash-Boza & Valdez, 2018; Goodman, 2015; Ngai, 2005). One salient feature of uneven (open borders approach vs. restrictive policies) immigration policy in the United States is that it has long been racialized. For instance, Golash-Boza and Valdez (2018) and others (e.g., Goodman, 2015) explain how immigration issues related especially to restriction or anti-immigrant sentiments date back to the Page Act (1875) and the Chinese Exclusion Act (1882). These policy restrictions were specifically targeted at Chinese immigrants. At the time, these anti-Chinese laws were challenged in the Supreme Court Case *Fong Yue Ting v. United States* (1893) when three Chinese nationals argued they had a constitutional right to avoid deportation. The court ruled that "deport[ing] noncitizens was inherent to the nature of sovereignty and that constitutional protections did not apply" (p. 2). This case was important because it gave the U.S. government the right to deport as part of an "administrative" procedure (p. 2). The effect of anti-immigrant policies on Chinese immigrants illustrates how immigration policies were racialized and reinforced exclusion, even when immigrants were citizens (Chung, 2018; Ngai, 2017). Thousands of Chinese workers were banned and excluded due to their perceived racial inferiority (Chung, 2018).

Historicizing immigration policy and law shows how immigrants were impacted and othered based on their racial/ethnic classification in similar ways to the targeting of immigrants in our contemporary moment. Other than to indicate which groups were excluded, citizenship was not clearly defined until 1866 when Congress passed the first Civil Rights Act, which provided a federal juridical definition of citizenship. To ensure that the definition of citizenship would survive in the event that the 1866 Civil Rights Act was repealed, similar language was included in the first clause of the Fourteenth Amendment, which stated that "all persons born or naturalized in the United States, and subject to the jurisdiction thereof, are citizens of the United States and the State wherein they reside" (para. 5).

The entire process of naturalization presumes that immigrants are outsiders and thus need to become "natural" somehow. And that process is determined by policymakers and the U.S. government, the groups that hold power in such institutional structures. Similarly, immigration policy and enforcement created additional guidelines to determine which groups could or could not be made "natural." Groups that were excluded in the early 1900s were prostitutes, criminals, and the poor, because they were thought to commit acts of moral turpitude; this linked otherness with race, ethnicity, and morality. In these examples, policies target particular groups to manage them. Michel Foucault (2008) developed the concept of biopolitics to refer to how governing structures include and exclude for the management of the population. While biopolitics is useful for theorizing such management, alone it "misconstrues how profoundly race and racism shape the modern idea of the human and dismisses theorizations of race and subjection" (Smith & Vasudevan, 2017), without attention to the racialization or racialized othering that is embedded in social life. Related to migrant bodies, especially nonwhite ones, it is important to consider the intersection of (bio)politics, policy, and race (Silva, 2016). Thus, Smith and Vasudevan and others (e.g., da Silva, 2011) argue that scholarship should consider how race manifests in policy problems across modernity, evidenced in our historicizing of immigrant integration discourse and practice.

Moreover, the process of making people "natural" entailed policies and programs in schools in particular. Since school is the major public socializing institution that immigrants interface with, curriculum, educational policy, and practice become a relevant technology of power for surveillance and discipline in the management of marginalized populations. The policy problem of immigrants, and their criminalization through law and policy, creates additional policy windows (Kingdon & Stano, 1984) for schools and other institutions to generate interventions and possible ways to manage the populations. In many ways, the problem of the immigrant could be managed through the discourse of belonging and integration, which ultimately centers whiteness and assimilationist ideologies in policy and practice (Verma et al., 2017).

Managing Immigrant Populations through Policy

The 1900s heralded an era in which the federal government assumed more control over immigration policy. Through the Naturalization Act of 1907, the federal government mandated that newly arrived immigrants learn English and pledge an oath of allegiance to the United States as part of the naturalization process (USCIS, n.d.). This law also conferred upon U.S. district attorneys the authority to initiate denaturalization proceedings. Further restrictive legislative measures include the Immigration Act of 1907, which introduced the notion of the "public charge" (Canaday, 2009, p. 22); the Immigration Act of 1917, which imposed literacy tests on immigrants and barred admission of migrants from the Asia-Pacific zone (Powell, 2009); the Emergency Quota Act (1921), which established quotas on immigrants from Southern and Eastern Europe (National Park Service, 2017); and the Johnson-Reed Act of 1924, which predominantly targeted Asian and Eastern and Southern European immigrants and put in place a large immigration apparatus with the creation of the border patrol (Canaday, 2009; Molina, 2014).

In 1942, the United States and Mexico signed the Mexican Farm Labor Agreement, marking the beginning of the Bracero Program (Goodman, 2015). Under this program, migrant laborers from Mexico would be provided with shelter, food, sanitation, and a wage of 30 cents per hour in exchange for farm labor. The Bracero Program brought 4.6 million temporary Mexican laborers to the United States over the course of twenty-two years; at the same time, a large number of women and children who were relatives of farmworkers entered the United States illegally, which led to six million deportations (Goodman, 2018). According to Goodman (2018), the Bracero Program—which amounted to labor exploitation of Mexican workers—resulted in long-term family separations that took a toll on children.

The McCarran-Walter Act of 1952 continued in the tradition of restrictive immigration policy by retaining pre-established quotas while also putting a preference system in place. That system was used to further stratify immigrants and distinguish the desirables from the undesirables (Bennett, 1966). It was also the first immigration law to link naturalization to good character and establish the basis for the exclusion of those deemed to be afflicted with "moral turpitude" or moral deficiency, an assumption made on the basis of race, socioeconomic status, and sexual orientation (Canaday, 2009, p. 24).

The 1960s saw a turn to a slightly more inclusive immigration policy through the 1965 Naturalization and Immigration Act, which loosened restrictions based on race, abolished previously established quotas that disproportionately favored white immigrants, and eliminated nationality and national origin as a basis for entry (Ludden, 2006). It did, however, retain and further develop a preference system by establishing what became known as chain migration, giving preference to immigrants related to U.S. citizens and permanent residents, as well as immigrants with "special" skills (Ludden, 2006). The 1980s also witnessed less restrictive immigration policies that were premised on creating more inclusive categories: the Refugee Act of 1980 was established to create a systematic procedure and apparatus to facilitate refugee admission and resettlement in the United States (Office of Refugee Resettlement, 2021). Simultaneously, in 1986, Congress passed the Immigration Reform and Control Act, which provided amnesty and a pathway to citizenship for most illegal immigrants who arrived in the country before 1982 (Coutin, 2005). While gaining legal status was significant for Mexican laborers at the time, because they could work in the United States and return home to Mexico to visit family, the act also made it a crime for employers to knowingly hire illegal immigrants.

The last major comprehensive federal immigration policy reform was passed in 1990 by President George H. W. Bush. It is generally considered to be a more inclusive legislative act, having created more visa categories and, thus, more opportunities for migration, while also raising the cap on the number of immigrants admitted (Leiden & Neal, 1990). It also lifted the testing requirement imposed on the naturalization process through earlier legislation. However, in 1996, immigration legislation reverted to its restrictive nature through the Illegal Immigration Reform and Responsibility Act, which focused on "cracking down on illegal immigration" (Kerwin, 2018, p. 192). Kerwin (2018) posits that this piece of legislation formed the basis of the cruel and inhumane immigration practices enacted today by instituting detention as common practice, removing due process for illegal immigrants apprehended by Border Patrol, and placing significant obstacles to the attainment of asylum. Similarly, in 2006, President George W. Bush signed into law the Secure Fence Act, which provided funding for and authorized the creation of a fence spanning 700 miles along the U.S.-Mexico border.

Citizenship as a Contested and Racialized Category

To understand the myriad definitions surrounding citizenship, it is imperative to examine the United States' current political and social climate. As Abu El-Haj (2015) states, "citizenship, with its attendant rights, is a key site that regulates inclusion and exclusion from the state. The question of who warrants consideration for citizenship has been, and continues to be, hotly contested across modern nation-states" (p. 77). This contestation of citizenship has deeply embedded roots and is connected to scholarly discussions of immigration—and American immigration history in particular—given that the United States is often described as a "nation of immigrants." Despite this, the presence and integration of immigrants in U.S. society has been fraught with tension (Rodriguez, 2018b). In this section, I provide evidence that undocumented youths' counternarrative speak to the "privileges of citizenship" in its normative and legal definition (Rodriguez, 2020a).

De Genova (2002) links immigration, citizenship, and the notion of being illegal with racialization—a process of racial profiling and othering. Golash-Boza and Valdez (2018) explains that being undocumented is associated with being illegal, especially for Mexican immigrants. The notion of illegality influences what it means to be an immigrant in the United States. Bickham Mendez and Nelson (2016), drawing on De Genova's work, explain that the notion of illegality is racialized and formed by an "assemblage of institutional practices, discourse, and day-to-day interactions. The association of the category 'illegal' with particular phenotypes and cultural identifiers has resulted in its extension to all Latinos and those who resemble them" (p. 134). In other words, if a person is perceived to be Latinx, then that person will experience racialization—othering and presumption of criminality/illegality—throughout their everyday life, regardless of documentation status (Flores-González, 2017;

Molina, 2014; Rodriguez & Macias, 2022). De Genova (2004) further contends that if illegality produces deportability, then immigrants become a risk that is disposable, regardless of whether they are in the country illegally. This is critical because, even if immigrants are not actually deported, the threat of deportation governs their everyday lives.

Illegality, or what I refer to as *undocumentedness*, is a socially constructed identity marker—a fabrication—that individuals move in and out of. Moreover, immigration laws are espoused as "race-neutral," and yet it is Latinx immigrants who are often subject to legal threats, along with other racialized minorities. I use the term *undocumentedness* as a conceptual, analytical, and political move because I view it as a socially constructed term that has material effects on the racialized bodies of the youth in this study. The term *citizen* carries a variety of connotations, depending on who you are and the racial classification you have upon entering the United States.

Today the United States' legal definition of citizenship encompasses two distinct forms of citizenship: birthright citizenship and naturalization (Bloemraad, 2004). Birthright citizenship is premised on two dimensions (FitzGerald, 2017; Shachar, 2009). The first is *jus sanguinis*, understood as the principle of descent; this means that citizenship can be passed on from parents to children on the basis of blood ties. For example, citizens of the United States can pass their citizenship status to their children, even if the children are not born on U.S. soil (Alvarez et al., 2019). The second component of birthright citizenship is *jus soli*, or the principle of the soil, whereby citizenship is determined by one's place of birth. This means that a child born in the United States is, according to the law, invariably entitled to U.S. citizenship, except in the case of the children of diplomats.

The United States Citizenship and Immigration Services (USCIS) defines naturalization as the process through which U.S. citizenship is granted to a foreign citizen or national once they meet one of the following eligibility criteria: a) completing five years of permanent resident status obtained through work authorization/company sponsorship; b) completing three years of permanent resident status attained through marriage to a U.S. citizen; c) being a member of the U.S. military who has served the United States in times of peace and war; or d) being a foreign-born child of a U.S. citizen who wishes to sponsor their child for U.S. citizenship (USCIS, n.d.). Additional requirements include passing the U.S. Naturalization Test (also known as the American Civics Test), proficiency in English, proof of U.S. residence, and, remarkably, having good moral standing, which is defined as being "a person of good moral character" (para. 2). Naturalization can also occur through family adjustment status, meaning that a U.S. citizen can sponsor their spouse, child under 21, or parent (if the citizen is at least 21 years old) for permanent residency, which would then grant them a pathway to citizenship (USCIS, n.d.). Moreover, refugees can legally work in the United States upon their arrival to the country and are eligible to apply for permanent residency status a year from the day they arrived; concurrently, persons who have been granted asylum can also apply for permanent residence a year after they entered the country, provided that they meet the definition of a refugee, or are the spouse or child of a person designated as a refugee (USCIS, n.d.).

Adam Goodman (2015) discusses the evolution of migration in his article "Nation of Migrants, Historians of Migration." He asserts that "by normalizing migration, rather than borders, U.S. historians have the opportunity to depoliticize, to an extent, the highly controversial nature of public and academic debates about immigration. Focusing on migration rather than immigration leads historians away from an 'us vs. them' mentality and shifts the emphasis from the supposed history of American exceptionalism to U.S. history as a part of world history, and the United States as one of many nations of migrants" (pp. 9–10). He also complicates the U.S. view of immigration by postulating that "despite the prevailing political and popular idea that immigration is a domestic issue, scholars have shown that it is unquestionably an issue of foreign relations, shaped by large structural economic transformations, geopolitical relations, and shifting international migration control policies, among other factors" (p. 12). Acknowledging the United States' role would take the onus off the im/migrants, and to this end the United States would be an active and responsible agent in the im/migration paradigm. Instead, in the United States narratives of risk and threat are the pervasive ideology (Rodriguez, 2018b; Rodriguez & Monreal, 2017).

In the U.S. context, undocumented migrants are perceived to pose imminent racialized criminalized threats (Chavez, 2020; De Genova, 2002), even though the United States relies upon their labor in new receiving contexts, such as in the Southeastern portion of the United States (Guerrero, 2017; Marrow, 2011; Odem & Lacy, 2009). The risk is part of a made-up crisis and a series of policy problematizations (Rodriguez & Monreal, 2017) rendering migrants as risky problems and thus undeserving of social mobility and educational achievement (Rodriguez, 2018a). The contradiction, of course, is that while immigrants have long been considered threats to a fabricated American national identity, attempts to assimilate and Americanize them have persisted, especially through policies and K–12 public schools. The point in this scholarship is that immigrants have simultaneously been problems and risks to American national identities and unity while also being targets of assimilation, integration, and Americanization efforts.

Gary Gerstle (1997) aimed to examine immigrants' experiences in the period 1880–1920. He argues that Americanization was not linear (i.e., a specific set of steps taken once someone entered the United States that led to becoming an American). He found the process of Americanization to be an act of alienation rather than being emancipatory, grounded specifically in terms of class. Just as Gerstle emphasized the nonlinearity of Americanization and the role of class in relation to Americanization, segmented assimilation as explained by Alejandro Portes and Min Zhou (1993) assert that "instead of a relatively uniform mainstream whose mores and prejudices dictate a common path of integration, we observe today several distinct forms of adaptation" (p. 82). They further explain the consequences of assimilation where one version (straight line) is predicated upon "parallel integration into white middle-class," while another (downward assimilation) leads to a life of poverty in the underclass.

Lastly, Portes and Zhou (1993) are mainly concerned with what causes immigrants to assimilate in different ways. They identify three features that significantly affect the success of second-generation immigrants: racial identity and skin color, location, and absence of mobility ladders. The difference in generations of immigrants is also discussed by Gerstle (1997) when he posits that "Americanization movements, and generational succession within ethnic communities, all contributed to the collapse of cultural inventions. Historical circumstances and social structures undermined experiments in the fashioning of identity" (p. 546). Both Portes and Zhou and Gerstle identify systemic factors that either bolster or inhibit the success of second-generation immigrants, and in some cases they underestimate the role of racial discrimination in the United States.[1] In part, this is because the process of racialization as it relates to immigration policy and law has not been explored in depth. That experience of racialization is a key vector that shapes the lives of the Latinx undocumented immigrant youth in this book.

Immigrants and Immigration in the New Latino South

Research on Latinx undocumented immigrant youth in South Carolina, a state in the New Latino South, is an important contribution given that previous literature tends to focus on large urban centers that are considered traditional receiving contexts (Winders & Smith, 2012). Kochhar and colleagues (2005) define the New Latino South as a collection of six Southern states that have seen rapid growth in Latinx populations since the 1990s. Meanwhile, less research about undocumented youth that are high-school-aged exists in rural and Southern spaces where the effects of anti-immigrant policies are severe and varied when compared to national trends that suggest activism and positive mobility, though this is not to take away from the significant barriers that all Latinx undocumented immigrants face (Brown et al., 2018; Gonzales & Ruiz, 2014). Policies and practices tend to be highly stymied and racialized in Southern states due to the legacy of Jim Crow segregation and its impact on contemporary race relations in the South, often rendering a racial binary that ignores the Latinx population.

In a recent history of the Nuevo South, Guerrero (2017) argues that scholars must understand the "legacies of Southern history in terms of dealing with racial difference and economic development" (p. 9). This relates to how Southern plantation owners' success was contingent upon the exploitation of labor by migrants in the region. One aspect that is important to understanding the labor structure of the South is the passage of the North American Free Trade Agreement (NAFTA), which brought an aggressive private sector recruitment campaign for Latinx agricultural laborers to the South and led to a significant increase in Latinx immigration to the region (p. 99; see also Ribas, 2016). This unique legacy of segregation and the paradoxical relations with Latinx migrants inform the social fabric of the South in ways that reflect local ideologies toward immigrants. In the eyes of youth in this study, this legacy influenced their parents' perspectives on education and the opportunities they would have in South Carolina. While South Carolina has yet to be studied in depth, sociologists and anthropologists have examined similar issues related to race, immigration, criminalization, and stratification. This research showcases the importance of context and racial relations, and how those factors impact the everyday lives of immigrants broadly and Latinx undocumented immigrants specifically.

In a study of Mississippi, Steusse (2016) shows how racial tensions between African Americans and immigrants emerged. She highlights two key factors in the South that contribute to racial tensions and a lack of collaboration among marginalized groups: economic competition between African Americans and immigrants, and the effects of structural racism in the social positioning of Latinx immigrants. There exists limited understanding between U.S.-born and immigrant groups, which is exacerbated by xenophobic anti-immigrant rhetoric rooted in the contention that immigrants take jobs away from hard-working Americans. This claim, though erroneous, gains ground in times of economic downturn and in a neoliberal era in which African Americans and Latinx immigrants compete for access to scant economic resources and jobs. (These ideologies are held by some of the educators in this study, as will be discussed in chapter 2.) It's made worse by the fact that many African Americans and Latinx people compete for the same types of jobs in manufacturing and in the service sector. Such antagonism leads to racial animus, intensified by a "zero-sum situation in which working communities of color . . . fight over crumbs" (Stuesse et al., 2017, p. 251). According to the authors, employers demonstrate a preference for immigrant workers, fueling further hostility and misperceptions among Latinx and African American workers who are overrepresented in low-wage occupational endeavors. Consequently, "real competition works in tandem with perceived cultural and other forms of difference" (p. 252) to create divisions among African Americans and Latinx immigrants.

Immigrants enter into a racial hierarchy premised on a white-black binary. Steusse (2016), for example, contends that "Whiteness and Blackness shape social relations," impacting even those who do not identify with either category. Additionally, because whiteness grants privileges, many immigrants attempt to reposition themselves as whites in order to obtain access to those privileges by "distinguishing themselves from Blacks and adopting the cultural diacritica of Whiteness" (p. 253). Immigrants can then be viewed as competitors to African American labor-seekers, but both groups are competing for undesirable jobs. There has been additional historical scholarship that offers a colorblind, whitewashed view of immigrants in which they are accused of "acting white" in order to gain economic and social mobility (Weise, 2015). Additionally, there is a tradition in sociology and education that posits the involuntary minority rejects a positive perspective about the benefits of the educational system, which creates explanations for why minoritized groups underachieve in in education (Ogbu, 1978, 1987). These scholarly perspectives fail to account for structural racism in society that creates the condition for the lack of educational achievement of minoritized groups. These cultural-deficit models and straight-line assimilationist models do little to address racism and discrimination in society (Alba et al., 2011; Warikoo & Carter, 2009). Part of the racial hierarchy is set up by federal, state, and local policies, or what scholars call contexts of reception (Filindra et al., 2011; Golash-Boza & Valdez, 2018).

As noted in the Introduction, research shows that immigrants to the United States face contexts of reception that are unwelcoming (Portes & Rumbaut, 2001), and they can be affected by discrimination and racism (Suárez-Orozco & Suárez-Orozco, 2009). Contexts of reception are multileveled (i.e., federal, state, regional, school, and community), and thus immigrants encounter many potential barriers to accessing resources. Schools in particular shape the kind of welcoming support immigrants ought to access. Yet, research has shown variation in immigrant integration in American schools, and ultimately in their academic success and belonging. Additionally, schools have largely shaped immigrant educational success and mobility through their practices and policies. Scholars use the cultural difference model to explain immigrant student achievement. This model problematically positions educational outcomes as a product of the cultural practices of immigrants. In other words, deficit-based and racialized perceptions of immigrant ability shift burdens of learning and belonging, or achievement, employability, and integrability onto individuals rather than acknowledging structural racism and racial hierarchies in the United States.

Racialized Immigration Policy: From Federal to Local Enforcement

Stereotypes of immigrants or discourses, including in South Carolina's policy discourse, condition how people think about and interact with immigrant groups. Embrick and Henricks (2013) argue: "It is through everyday discourse, as critical race scholars have shown, that racist structures are reinforced and legitimated. Discourse conditions how people think about and interact with others. It fosters a medium through which the racial order crystallizes in everyday interaction, also known as the racialized social system" (p. 199; see also Rodriguez, 2015).

Jones (2019) references the changing sociopolitical context on the federal and, particularly, on the state and local levels in Southern states such as North Carolina to explain a change in immigration policy and enforcement apparatuses, as well as a shift toward a much more punitive approach that has resulted in the stigmatization of undocumented migrants and a lack of opportunities for upward mobility. She notes that in the 1990s and early 2000s, North Carolina was more welcoming of Latinx immigrants, including the undocumented, largely providing access to resources and supports to assist immigrants as they settled into life there and allowing for upward mobility and opportunity. However, in 2011 all of this came to a grinding halt. Jones (2019) attributes this change to two key factors: (1) the delegation of immigration policy enforcement from the federal to the state and local levels; and (2) post-9/11 border securitization and militarization.

Jones (2019) posits that immigration policy has always and continues to be "considered in light of racialized ideology" (p. 70). Racialized forms of immigration policy date back to the Immigration Act of 1917, which created categories of exclusion on the basis of race and ethnicity, the Johnson-Reed Act of 1924, which created quotas and preference systems based on race, and 1954's Operation Wetback, a vicious process of deportation of Mexicans residing in the United States. While 1965's Immigration and Nationality Act abolished race-based quotas, legal immigration for Mexicans was restricted, followed by an increase in border militarization efforts in the 1970s and 1980s. However, during that same time period (1970s–1980s), amnesty was granted to undocumented immigrants. Illegal immigration and the maligning discourse of illegality surfaced after 1986 when restricting federal immigration policy became a priority. The 1996 Illegal Immigration Reform and Immigrant Responsibility Act placed an emphasis on more punitive anti-immigrant policies, linking immigration to domestic policies such as welfare reform and social services. Today, we see several anti-immigrant states maintaining restrictive policies in the New Latino South (e.g., Alabama, Mississippi, South Carolina) and elsewhere, such as in Arizona.

However, the real shift in immigration policy purpose and scope occurred after 9/11, culminating in the passage of the Real ID Act in 2005 and the shift in enforcement from federal to local actors and agencies. Jones (2019) references the Delegation of Immigration Authority Section 287(g) (authorized by the Illegal Immigration Reform and Responsibility Act of 1996), which is an example of local and federal partnerships that significantly impact the immigration landscape, with individuals taking it upon themselves to "protect" the border and immigrants becoming defined as "unwanted and deportable subjects" (p. 70). As a result of 9/11, immigration is now linked to terrorism, and the former has been deemed a national security issue so that "fighting a war against terrorism came to mean fighting immigrants" (p. 72). Likewise, the racialized nature of immigration policy rendered Latinx immigrants not only "racialized minorities, but also potential threats to the state" (p. 72), giving rise to *crimmigration*, the criminalization of immigration.

Another example of how 287(g) impacts the everyday lives of Latinx immigrant communities exists in North Carolina (Arriaga, 2017; Browne & Odem, 2012). Arriaga (2017) investigates the relationship between the public and crimmigration entities in North Carolina to gain an understanding of everyday life for North Carolinian Latinx immigrant communities in a racial state that relies on Section 287(g) to keep managed immigrant populations in check. ICE's 287(g) Program is designed to "curb the increase and survival of the Latino immigration community at the local level" (Arriaga, 2017, p. 417). Arriaga explains how local crimmigration entities (i.e., police, courts, and commissioners) work together to respond to the Latinx immigrant "threat" through intergovernmental programs (p. 429). Arriaga recognizes how the racial threat theory builds on the foundation of Blumer's (1958) group threat hypothesis. The hypothesis is focused on the relationship between dominant and subordinate racial groups, and suggests that dominant racial groups (i.e, whites) have prejudice toward minoritized groups due to a perceived or real threat. Local-level partnerships with ICE have led to the creation of immigration law problems for people who lack U.S. citizenship (p. 419). Through interviews with several judges, Light and colleagues (2014) found differential treatment on the basis of noncitizenship as well as a cultural divide between Hispanics and non-Hispanics. The 287(g) Program allows local law enforcement to detect, detain, and deport unauthorized immigrants through an agreement with ICE. Arriaga (2017) argues that county governments, in conjunction with the criminal justice system, respond to the new Latinx threat by working with ICE programs to foster a form of racialized social control meant to constrain the bulk of the Latinx population regardless of age, gender, or immigration status (p. 420).

Of the one hundred North Carolina counties, only five sheriff offices operate with 287(g) programs. Those counties are Henderson County, Gaston County, Cabarrus County, Wake County, and Mecklenburg County. Arriaga (2017) used data from these five counties to categorize her findings into three key areas of interest: (1) program adoption rationale and implementation; (2) program ownership; and (3) nonexistent community relationships. Arriaga's analysis shows how the sheriff's offices in these five counties partnered with ICE to verify undocumented residents during any public safety infraction. Residents who are identified as undocumented are detained for deportation. Some scholars claim that in detaining individuals for being undocumented, local law enforcement is overreaching its jurisdiction (Arriaga, 2017, p. 423). The programs were implemented in visible and overt ways, such as immigration officials sitting outside migrant health clinics and waiting to stop individuals, and they were designed to focus on the Latino Threat (Chavez, 2020). Success stories were strategically chosen to reiterate a sense of moral panic and justify strengthening the programs (Longazel, 2013).

Arriaga's (2017) analysis also includes program ownership, which was shown to be unclear, as it is uncertain whether ICE officers operate within cities' or sheriffs' law enforcement jurisdictions. ICE is concentrated on efforts from the sheriff's departments rather than city departments. ICE officers are allowed to come into local sheriff's departments and provide training to deal with the Latinx threat. In the 2015–2016 legislative session, House Bill 318 (Protect Workers Act) was passed; it states in section 15(a) that "No County [or city] may have in effect any policy, ordinance, or procedure that limits or restricts the enforcement of federal immigration laws to less than the full extent permitted by federal law."

Finally, the third area of analysis discussed the nonexistent relationships that existed between ICE program officers and the communities in which they operated. Community members were still unclear as to the role of ICE in their communities. With the passing of HB 318, many community members were eager to see the relationship between ICE and local law enforcement end. This deeper analysis of local policy is critical for understanding the contexts of reception and the power of local contexts to criminalize immigrants. Similar to North Carolina, South Carolina maintains partnerships between local law enforcement and ICE. These partnerships maintain racialized exclusion, rooted in the Latino threat discourse, and have consequences for immigrants' access to resources, mobility, and belonging. Later in this chapter, I show how similar state policies in South Carolina do this.

Criminalizing and Racializing Immigrants

The presence of ICE, coupled with racial profiling as part of the apprehension and detention process, gave rise to civil rights violations (Jones, 2019, p. 73) and led to the erosion of trust between law enforcement and immigrant communities in the New South. Although policy rhetoric dictated that only migrants who had committed violent and serious crimes would be apprehended, immigrants began to be targeted and detained for minor offenses such as traffic violations. In response, many in the undocumented community isolated themselves from nonimmigrants as a protective measure. Additionally, the lack of access to a driver's license, higher education, social services, and other supports led to the entrenchment of the isolation and marginalization of the undocumented community in the South. This was achieved chiefly through macro-level "institutional closure" (Jones, 2019, p. 77), which included increased police and ICE presence and restricted access to higher education and social services. Not only were migrants' opportunities for upward mobility severely limited, but their very survival was put at stake by inhibiting their ability to find jobs and move freely within their communities. In particular, the loss of the ability to procure a driver's license proved detrimental in localities such as Winston-Salem and other areas of the South where public transportation is limited. Racial profiling played a large part in crimmigration, with measures such as 287(g) being used to target Latinx immigrants almost exclusively.

Browne and Odem (2012) describe the racialized experiences of Dominicans and Guatemalans in Atlanta, Georgia. They argue that "Legal status thus becomes a second axis in the racialized category of 'Latino'" (p. 330), which means that Latinx groups are never just racialized as Latino or Hispanic—their immigration status also factors into how they are identified and excluded. Using the concepts of racial formation and the racial state, Omi and Winant (1994) contend that race is continually "socially constructed" at multiple levels—from individual interactions to state policies (p. 322). Browne and Odem (2012) importantly demonstrate how immigration laws (SB 529, HB 87, and Section 287[g]) are used by the state "to racialize Latinos in a way that casts them in a homogenized frame as 'illegal,' 'Mexican,' and unwanted" (p. 324). Comparing these laws to Jim Crow laws in the American South, they name this phenomenon "Juan Crow," arguing that discriminatory laws and policies result in "Denied access to health care, education, and other social services," additionally Latinos face "increased levels of police surveillance, arrest, detention, and deportation" in addition to fear and harassment for others (p. 329). These acts of exclusion impact individuals as "Latino" becomes a race rather than an ethnicity within the domain of these laws and ordinances, and as police and the public identify Latinos' through particular types of bodies—those that appear "Mexican" and "speak with an accent" (p. 329). The contexts in North Carolina and Georgia are similar to the anti-immigrant South Carolina context and have significance and implications for how the Latinx undocumented youth in this project navigated their everyday lives.

Race Relations, Racialization, and Advancing Racialized Citizenship

Thinking about the relationship between race, history, immigration, and the politics of citizenship has been a task of scholars. The racial dynamics, including the black-white binary, and the whitewashing of immigration stories in the South set up dynamics for what citizenship means and how it is constituted (Guerrero, 2017). While this chapter shows how Latinx immigrants, and even citizens, are criminalized broadly as they are considered "problems," it is critical to understand how citizenship has historically been racialized in the United States.

FitzGerald (2017) explains that historically and currently citizenship acquisition is a highly racialized process. As previously addressed, prior to 1870 whites were the only racial group to enjoy full citizenship rights in the United States (FitzGerald, 2017). Correspondingly, while Blacks were denied citizenship rights until after the Civil War and Japanese Americans were stripped of their citizenship and placed in internment camps following the Japanese attack on Pearl Harbor, German Americans and Italian Americans faced only minimal retribution in the aftermath of Germany and Italy's involvement in World War II (FitzGerald, 2017). As the United States engages in processes of racial othering in relation to citizenship, the plight of Latinx immigrants continues. One example relates to the racialization of Mexican immigrants. Molina (2014) argues that Mexicans' links to Indigenous peoples mark them as "culturally nonwhite" (p. 4); this relationship to indigeneity became the basis for subjecting Mexicans and other Latin American populations to racialized immigration practices.

The racialization of Mexican immigrants, coupled with the increase in Mexican immigration, set in motion a particularly vicious persecution by the U.S. immigration apparatus and a rhetoric matching that practice, which portrayed Mexicans as disposable and deportable "aliens" (Golash-Boza & Valdez, 2018). While there are no racial quotas in the most recent immigration legislation, 97 percent of deportees in the United States hail from Central and Latin America; this staggering percentage speaks to laws that generate disparities even in the absence of explicitly racially discriminatory language, laws that therefore form part of the larger institutional structure that legitimates racial discrimination (Golash-Boza & Valdez, 2018).

Racialized language plays a significant part in the state's efforts to delegitimize, disparage, and dehumanize undocumented migrants; migrants' very humanity is questioned through the discourse of illegality (De Genova, 2002), which reproduces them as "aliens" unrecognizable by the state. The discourse of illegality renders migrants deportable, and thereby disposable, subjects, which in turn exposes them to exploitation through menial, low-paying jobs that provide employers with cheap human labor (Golash-Boza & Valdez, 2018; Rodriguez, 2018a).

Citizenship as a construct and status is weaponized to occlude and exclude racial minorities who are portrayed not only as undeserving, but also as threatening to the social status quo and racial hierarchy that sustains the dominant status of whites and the power of white supremacy. Citizenship is a racial project operated by a "state of exception" (Agamben, 2005, p. 1) that uses its power to diminish opportunities for people of color and inhibits their chances for social mobility. Whether the discussion is about birthright citizenship or citizenship by naturalization, traditional and normative conceptions of citizenship are part of a larger state apparatus poised to disenfranchise communities of color and uphold an inherently unjust and unequal racial order.

Racialization of naturalization includes limiting eligibility for citizenship to only certain racially defined groups (positive preference) while excluding racialized others who are part of undesired groups. FitzGerald (2017) argues that in order to spot racial discrimination one should not focus on naturalization rules alone but on conceptualizing and analyzing naturalization as a "whole system of policy regulating admission and membership" (p. 131). Discrimination through the use of race as a criterion in immigration policy has been sharply reduced since the 1930s; however, racial discrimination continues to be practiced in covert ways through positive preferences for certain ethnic groups rather than negative discrimination against identified groups, which would constitute a more overt form of discrimination.

Next, I connect the concept of racialization with historical, sociological, and policy-analysis work as it relates to South Carolina.

Immigration and Education Policy in South Carolina

The research in this book builds upon previous scholarship that seeks to understand ways in which racialized immigrants in the South are excluded from public spaces broadly and schools specifically. The previous literature speaks to how state policy contexts shape the lives of immigrants, and it underscores how these policies emerge out of ignorant fear, racism, and discrimination.

Demographic trends that indicate the sharp nationwide increase in the Latinx population are well-documented; however, scholarship has generally been less attentive to the high influx of Latinx people in the South, particularly Southeastern states like South Carolina, the "site of a rapidly growing Latinx population" that is now termed by many as the "New Latino" or "Nuevo South" (Rodriguez, 2018a, p. 3). Southern states including South Carolina responded to this population growth with restrictive policies that deny educational opportunities to Latinx youth and adversely affect the general well-being of the Latinx population by reducing access to resources and opportunities for social mobility. The history of Latinx presence in the state suggests that this is not a new trend and that the state has, since the nineteenth century, discriminated against its Latinx residents, portraying them as lazy, unassimilable, and a drain on the state's resources, a narrative that has carried through to this day (Weise, 2015). Thus, while Latinx communities around the country have been negatively impacted by Trump-era anti-immigrant policies and discourse, Latinx communities in states like South Carolina have always lived in a climate of fear and trepidation due to the state's restrictive policies and have seen these fears magnify as a result of Trump-era policies.

Education policies directed at Latino immigrants, or policies designed and implemented to directly impact this population, have varied in terms of whether they have helped or hindered academic and social outcomes for Latino immigrant students, especially in spaces like the South, other rural areas, and Midwestern geographies. Hamann (2004), for example, points out how in areas that are nontraditional locations of the Latinx diaspora, including the New Latino South, many organizations and schools contain non-Latinx and non-Spanish-speaking leaders, district-level administrators, and policymakers who make decisions about their educational trajectories. These decisions, and the subsequent ideological perspectives about immigrants in these nontraditional contexts (Winders & Smith, 2012), deeply impact the life chances of immigrant children. And despite the group of scholars studying new immigrant destinations (Wortham et al., 2002), there remains little scholarship about places like the New Latino South, and South Carolina specifically (Rodriguez, 2018a; Rodriguez & Monreal, 2017).

One exception to this is Hamann's (2004) study of the Georgia Project. For this ethnographic study of educational policy implementation, Hamann drew from interviews, observations, surveys, newspaper accounts, and informal "check-ins" with the parties involved. The study focuses on Dalton, Georgia, and the first school district in Georgia to enroll a majority Latinx student population. The majority of students in Dalton are described as Mexican immigrants or the children of immigrants, English language learners, and from low socioeconomic backgrounds with highly mobile families. Schools in Dalton struggled to accommodate the growing numbers of Latinx students who, in turn, performed poorly academically. To combat this, the Dalton School District launched the Georgia Project in the 1990s, which brought together staff from the Universidad de Monterrey in Mexico and several important Dalton citizens; this partnership resulted in bilingual Mexican teachers being assigned temporarily to Dalton schools, Dalton teachers receiving training in Mexico, and the district producing its first ever needs assessment of Dalton's Latinx community. The Georgia Project garnered accolades and spread to other parts of northwestern Georgia; however, by 2001, the partnership diminished into a single nonprofit entity and district involvement became minimal.

The Georgia Project was born out of the efforts of a prominent Dalton attorney who contacted a CEO with Mexican business connections who, in turn, contacted Universidad de Monterrey; this attorney subsequently petitioned the Dalton schools superintendent to draft a letter supporting what became the Georgia Project initiative. Meetings were arranged, and supportive articles were featured in local newspapers. The project's launch was promising, particularly when the City Council allocated $250,000 per year for each of the next three years to help fund the project. The initiative also secured $500,000 in Title VII funding. However, these arrangements were met with protests and anti-immigrant sentiment among the locals—a sentiment which began to be reflected in local media coverage as well. While the project drew positive recognition for the steps it took—such as the partnership with Mexican teachers, the teacher training in Mexico, and the needs assessment conducted vis-à-vis the local Latinx community—in 1998 the district began withdrawing from the project. This was signaled by its decision to scrap the visiting instructor component of the project, and the visitor program was finally terminated when a new superintendent assumed the position in 2000. At that point, only the summer training initiative survived.

The failure of the Georgia Project demonstrates that educational policies designed with the Latinx population in mind ultimately fail to address the pivotal question of how to best address the needs of newcomer students. Such policies seem to be more preoccupied with bureaucratic issues, such as power-driven conflicts about the role of the superintendent, school district officials, and university scholars. Additionally, while the project's crafters correctly diagnosed the problem (the lack of support and school district resources for the growing Latinx student population), there was a lack of a clear and strong consensus about how to address it. Finally, the fact that Dalton is located in a culturally conservative part of the country and the state further impeded the project's sustainability.

While this study took place nearly two decades ago, the stagnant policies that enable persistent inequality for immigrant students, especially newcomers, remain. In the South, where newcomers have more recently been English language learners and in many cases are undocumented, stagnant policies are compounded by explicit anti-immigrant ideology, especially in Alabama and South Carolina. Even though the Georgia Project appeared to be an inclusive policy, Southern states are overrun by ideologies of racism and fear of foreign-born groups (Guerrero, 2017; Jones, 2019).

As state-level legislation related to immigration rises dramatically (National Conference of State Legislatures, n.d.), it is necessary to understand why state and local legislatures seek and adopt immigration policy. Chavez and Provine (2009) found that common rationales, such as threat rhetoric and negative economic and criminal perceptions, are not associated unilaterally with restrictionist legislation. Instead, citizen ideology, not government ideology, was significantly related to reductionist immigration policy. Building on that research, Ybarra et al. (2016) used cross-section time-series analysis to find that economic recession paired *with* changing demographics was correlative of increased immigration policy at the state level. Interestingly, local growth in the Latinx population yields increased restrictive policies while growth in the Asian population had no measurable impact. This speaks to the racialized hierarchies of immigrant groups, specifically the model minority stereotype that positions Asians as honorary whites and not as significant to the social or economic status quo in many states (Goodman, 2015). Thus, anti-immigrant anxieties, and the ensuing racialization of immigrant groups (Sáenz & Manges Douglas, 2015; Verma et al., 2017), is tied directly to the expansion of Latinx populations in the historically segregated South.

Another reason Southern states have enacted strict immigration laws creating restrictive local policy contexts for newcomers relates to popular white supremacist attitudes in the formerly Jim Crow South. Lacy and Odem (2009) argue that more exclusionary state and local immigration policies are the result of shifting popular attitudes in the region, writing that "most official rhetoric and policy in the Southeast in recent years seeks to limit especially unauthorized immigrants' access to employment, transportation, housing, health care, higher education, and public benefits" (p. 150). These scholars, and others (Arriaga, 2017; Oboler, 2010), argue that many local ordinances in Southern localities aim to discourage flows of immigration, make life harder for immigrants, or drive out those already there. For example, communities in Georgia and the Carolinas maintain housing regulations that require landlords to verify immigration status and incur fines for renting to undocumented immigrants (Lacy & Odem, 2009). This racialized practice is akin to what Bonilla-Silva and Dietrich (2011) call the "new racism," in which aspects of social life are restricted through policies, processes, and mechanisms that undercut or outright deny minoritized groups access to a standard quality of living or living wage jobs. Local unease was compounded by the Trump administration, which seeks tighter enforcement of immigration laws while rolling back protections such as the DACA program. Latinx communities in the South must also worry about increased ICE activities and re-established 287(g) programs (Arriaga, 2017) that seek to further constrain their lives.[2]

Alabama, like South Carolina, has enacted anti-immigrant policies. Patel (2013) illustrates how teachers' desire to serve immigrant students counters public policy objectives to criminalize immigrant students. In the case of Alabama HB 56, public K–12 teachers became de facto immigration agents tasked with reporting undocumented youth to the state education board. In other words, teachers were forced to investigate students' immigration status despite protections under *Plyler v. Doe* (1982). Schools were no longer considered safe spaces and some Latinx students stopped attending (Patel, 2013). Verma et al. (2017) illustrate how the encroachment of immigration policy into schools, as part of a larger immigration surveillance apparatus, paired with racialization processes in schools, leads to a school to prison to deportation pipeline.

The examples above illustrate how state policies in the South impact the everyday lives of both undocumented and documented immigrants and suffocate their protected status in school and right to educational opportunity under *Plyler*. These examples also underscore how the powerful processes of racialization, disciplinary surveillance, and deficit-based discourses frame immigrant students as deviant and threatening to the fabric of the state(s). This position, then, enables the justification and rationale for systemic racialization, leading to systematic practices of exclusion and structural racism in these Southern states in particular. I note these examples to point out the uniquely hostile context of the New Latino South, and how this context bears upon immigrants' lives. These examples illustrate that immigration and education policies are highly influential and act jointly in the context of the U.S. South. I turn now to specific barriers for Latinx students in the New Latino South and offer an analysis of South Carolina state policies.

Racialization in South Carolina Policy

The South is experiencing rapid growth in its Latinx population (Winders & Smith, 2012). However, states like South Carolina continue to enact discriminatory policies toward Latinx youth and Latinx communities that, in conjunction with the Trump administration's anti-immigrant rhetoric and actions, have magnified fears among the local Latinx community and hinder social mobility opportunities for Latino youth.

Rodriguez and Monreal's (2017) critical analysis of South Carolina's immigration policies uncover co-opted notions of deservingness premised on immigrants' perceived ability to assimilate to American society and betray a racialized hierarchy in which Latino groups occupy the bottom tier. Constructions of Latinx immigrants as lazy, unassimilable, and a drain on state resources permeate policy discourse and migrate from policy documents to the everyday realities that Latinx communities and youth encounter in South Carolina. Policy discourse's criminalization and delegitimization of Latinx people leads to material effects such as restricted access to educational services and resources for undocumented youth, lack of access to higher education institutions, and an unwelcoming environment at K–12 educational institutions. For example, in 2018, 6,500 undocumented students and recipients of DACA were present in South Carolina (Kovacs, 2018; Roth, 2017). However, South Carolina restricts DACA students from attending public institutions of higher education and thus a significantly lower number attend college.

Implicit and Explicit Exclusion in Policy, Problematization, and the Trope of "Deservingness"

Analyses of South Carolina policy documents demonstrate a consistent pattern of discrimination against Latinx youth and communities through a racialized discourse predicated on conceptualizing and criminalizing immigrants as "alien" others who pose a security threat to the state and, by extension, the nation itself. Policy problematization is useful in exposing the "hidden truths" (Rodriguez & Monreal, 2017, p. 769) contained within policy discourse. These analyses show how policy discourse is used to generate and then circulate a body of knowledge that serves as the premise for the enactment of exclusionary policies. Rodriguez and Monreal (2017) utilize a critical discourse analysis (CDA) approach to policy because CDA focuses on uncovering the connections between language (policy discourse) and the material effects of such policies on people's lives.

A CDA-based analysis reveals a "language of othering" (p. 781) that dehumanizes immigrants and constructs them as problematic subjects that need to be "fixed" and in some cases even "combatted" (p. 781). Policy discourse also sets up the conditions for a "culture of surveillance" (p. 784) as a response to the conception of immigrants as threats (a conception co-opted by the state through policy discourse), whose actions and bodies therefore need to be placed under constant scrutiny and control by the state apparatus. Immigrants are also presented as an "epidemic" (p. 779) that needs to be contained by the state.

Policy discourse and enactment in South Carolina promote ideologies about immigrants that are transmitted to the public and form the basis of popular opinion about immigrants in states like South Carolina. In Rodriguez's (2018a) analysis of state education policies, she argues there is an "us vs. them" dichotomy predicated not only on a comparison between immigrants and citizens, but also between "deserving" and "undeserving" immigrants (p. 5). This trope of deservingness erects barriers for undocumented youth and marks boundaries that both include and exclude. Tropes of deservingness undergird common sense narratives around ideas of national unity, in which groups are cast as either contributing to such ideals or undermining them, giving rise to the notion of the "good immigrant" and the "bad immigrant." "Good immigrants" are portrayed as assimilable, hard-working, and self-sufficient, reinforcing bootstraps narratives and meritocratic models. On the other hand, "bad immigrants" are unassimilable and lazy, and they form a burden to the state by relying disproportionately on state resources for their well-being. In my extensive analysis, it is clear that South Carolina explicitly and implicitly excludes Latinx immigrants from public and social resources and sets up a binary of "good immigrants" (white and European), who are economically useful, and "bad immigrants" (non-White and Latinx), who "are viewed as less human and less deserving" by comparison (Rodriguez & Monreal, 2017, p. 782).

In addition to racial and ethnic origin, "bad immigrants" are also defined by their "illegality," invariably linked to their identity as Latinx. Consequently, the state, through policy discourse, becomes an "arbiter of racialized rights" (Rodriguez, 2018a, p. 10) and asserts this self-ascribed authority by conferring and denying legitimacy to various groups. This practice carries enormous weight in policy discourse and beyond; the very act of enrolling in school is predicated on proof of legality, in violation of *Plyler v. Doe* (1982). Consequently, access to schooling and educational resources is contingent upon proving one's lawful status. Access to higher education is also compromised for undocumented youth who "face limited options" (Rodriguez & Monreal, 2017, p. 783) when applying to higher education institutions in the state due to their status.

Within the historical and policy contexts, this chapter shows the interrelationship between immigration and racialization. Additionally, the policy analysis illustrates the interplay between language and reality; mechanisms of exclusion do not merely manifest on the symbolic level but are enacted through policy proposals and implementation. The effects of this policy context are visible in this study. For instance, schools function as a site of the unequal racial dynamics inscribed in policy materials by being less welcoming to undocumented youth who "are often ignored or isolated" and experience a "lack of institutional supports" (Rodriguez & Monreal, 2017, pp. 790–791). In addition, access to basic employment rights such as work compensation is contingent upon immigration status, as is access to state-provided services (including educational services).

These studies serve to highlight how the State of South Carolina constructs notions of good immigrants and bad immigrants that are predicated on tropes of deservingness. These notions, inscribed in policy discourse, form the premise for the enactment of mechanisms of exclusion that deny undocumented Latinx youth and their families access to educational resources and services. The limited resources available to undocumented youth make life nearly unbearable for them and their families. Next, I briefly discuss some of the educational barriers that will be explored in subsequent chapters.

Educational Barriers for Undocumented Youth

While barriers for English-language-learning immigrant children and youth are not unique to the South, responses and interventions for improving their schooling experiences are stymied in a hostile policy context. Broadly speaking, schools have mostly responded in an ad hoc and impromptu manner to changing demographics and the increasing Latinx populations in the South (Hamann & Harklau, 2010). (This demographic change was noted in the Introduction.) For example, schools lack certified interpreters and burden Spanish teachers with the additional role of unofficial interpreter (Colomer, 2010; Harklau & Colomer, 2015). Schools and service providers rely on deficit-based notions of Latinx culture (Villenas, 2001, 2002) and construct Latinx communities as problems (Murillo Jr., 2002). Latino immigrants often become the targets of racist discourse at schools, such as the construction of a "Trump Wall" at a North Carolina school (Szathmary, 2016) and a recent incident where a substitute teacher in Charlotte told students to "go back to where you speak Spanish" (Patton, 2017). Unfortunately, these types of instances were common, especially in schools, as will be shown in later chapters.

Language learning services, policies, and programs compound marginalized education policies for Latinos in the New Latino South. English for Speakers of Other Languages (ESOL) programs do not meet the needs of individual schools, lack certified teachers, and employ deficit-based approaches toward second language development (Mellon et al., 2018; Portes & Salas, 2010; Tarasawa, 2013)—if those programs exist at all. One youth in my study explained the failure of the English as a Second Language (ESL) program in her school, sharing that she had to take a mandatory ESL exam yearly, but was given no ESL support throughout the academic year. A school leader at Denizen West corroborated this youth's experience, saying, "This population [language learners] are not seen; they are invisible. The advocates are making things happen." This school leader was a strong supporter of bilingual education but noted how the district neglected "bilingual education as a topic of conversation." Often, this district had no policy for language learning services. While the district's policies were neglectful at best, this school leader and many advocates raised the issue and pushed for strengthening language services, including bilingual education programs and advocates. Leaders like the one above noted the "moral imperative" to support the population of language learners, and yet systemic change and support were limited.

Insufficient second language programs are unsurprising given Southern policy attempts to craft deleterious English-only policies aimed at rapid Americanization (Beck & Allexsaht-Snider, 2002). In my study, the above school leader at Denizen West discussed this "English-only" mentality. The school leader stated that "You can't even get information from the front office [or] a school or a central office unless it's English," and commented on the lack of translation available for families and lack of multilingual support. Beck and Allexsaht-Snider's (2002) case study of language minority education policy in Georgia revealed the Spanish language skills of immigrant and Latinx students were framed as a problem (see also Ruiz, 1984). Further, Georgia policymakers attempted to use education policy as a way to demand assimilation, gauged by English proficiency, while erasing primary language support (Beck & Allexsaht-Snider, 2002). The authors assert that such policies are acts of cultural erasure, symbolic violence, and systemic miseducation (Beck & Allexsaht-Snider, 2002). The policies also perpetuate popular stereotypes regarding Latinx inability/ unwillingness to assimilate and use language as a proxy for race. As chapter 4 shows, language learning services vary from poor to nonexistent in the Denizen community.

If somehow Latinx immigrants can navigate the school system, despite the systemic miseducation of immigrant youth in the New Latino South, they still face significant inequality, racism, and discrimination, specifically engendered in state policy and law. Bohon et al. (2005) conducted qualitative interviews and focus groups to identify six key barriers to Latinx educational attainment in Georgia: a) lack of understanding of the U.S. school system; b) low parental involvement in the schools; c) lack of residential stability among the Latino population; d) little school support for the needs of Latino students; e) few incentives for the continuation of Latinx education; and f) barred immigrant access to higher education. They concluded that "with the massive influx of Latinos to Georgia, new forms of educational inequalities have surfaced ... the immediate future looks dim" (Bohon et al., 2005, p. 56). One youth in my study expressed sorrow that her friend who arrived in the United States in the third grade could not attend college despite enrolling in all AP classes, due to not having a social security number and not qualifying for DACA. She stated, "He is the reason why I passed some of my classes, so why is he stuck behind?"

This research shows how state policies in the New Latino South, such as limited access to higher education, exclude Latinx students from the schooling process and impede social mobility. Even Latinx students who are able to successfully navigate unprepared and unresponsive public schooling systems face questions about their intellectual abilities (Carrillo & Rodriguez, 2016), along with restrictions to higher education due to their legal status or the legal status of their parents (Bohon et al., 2005; Rodriguez & Monreal, 2017).

Next, I connect the implications of U.S. immigration history, racial discrimination, race relations, and politics, and explain how they have manifested in the New Latino South and South Carolina. Through the youth voices in subsequent chapters, I show how they navigate the produced subjectivity of illegality while disrupting their state of undocumentedness through their dialogues and acts of everyday resistance (Scott, 1985).

"This state is racist.": Implications of Historical Policy Analysis

As undocumented students manage their immigration status in anti-immigrant states like South Carolina and within the broader national climate, and are excluded from educational and social resources, their master status of illegality becomes a key factor in shaping the course of their lives (Gonzales, 2016). As Flores et al. (2018) contend, "Illegality studies reminds us that the category of the illegal gets reproduced over time and becomes more and more important over the life course and that 'place' ensures that levels of legality are relative" (p. 29). I build on that research in this project regarding the notion of undocumentedness—a resistive category rather than a prescribed one—which is lived and resisted by undocumented youth.

At the macro level—examined in this chapter—I showed how historical and policy contexts racialize and exclude based upon racialization processes embedded in conceptions of and policies toward immigrants in the United States. These historical and contemporary ideologies toward immigrants frame undocumented Latinx youth experiences in this study, particularly in the anti-immigrant restrictive policy context of South Carolina. At the meso (institutional, chapter 4) level of the school, youths' narratives underscore the problematic constructions of illegality, and how some educators assume all Latinx immigrants are illegal due to the spillover effects of racialized categorization. At the school level, notions of illegality are reproduced through assumptions and stereotyping about Latinx populations, as well as educators' lack of awareness about policies impacting immigrants (Crawford, 2017, 2018; Dabach, 2015; Gallo & Link, 2016; Rodriguez, 2020a). At the macro and meso levels, legal limits and social contradictions arise, and thus examining the layers in relation to the micro (relational and interactional) level is necessary to intervene in the reproduction of illegality and inequality for undocumented youth (De Genova, 2002; Negrón-Gonzales, 2014).[3] Undocumented youth experience social and legal contradictions and disrupt the binary of legal and illegal (Ybarra, 2018). Chapters 4 and 5 also showcase school- and community-based racialization and show the micro-interactional level that contributes to understanding the racialized encounters undocumented youth experience and their perceptions of resistive, racialized citizenship.

Regarding the notion of undocumentedness, I intentionally use this term as a political act of resistance. It is the accumulation of the ways that undocumented youths' status of illegality and broader ideologies perpetuated about them are reproduced and constructed through history, law, and policy. As the youth at the outset noted, "I break the law everyday" as he drives to school and work. While he has a right to attend school, he is restricted from obtaining a driver's license in the state as an undocumented immigrant. Another youth commented that "This state is racist. They want Hispanics to do the work they don't want to do, but they don't want us here," referring to the hypocrisy of exploiting undocumented labor while criminalizing and excluding Latinx immigrants. These youth voices disrupt the everyday discourse about immigrants in this context and destabilize the notion of illegality by demonstrating undocumented immigrants' acts of resistance.

By acknowledging the space they occupy—their undocumentedness—I disrupt and destabilize the power relations that circulate around their being to underscore their dialogues and actions as a form of resistance. I refer to undocumentedness to underscore the grassroots-level experiences of youth that disrupt essentialized, deficit-based views of them—often perpetuated through school- and community-based racialization processes that other and exclude them from opportunities and resources (Rodriguez, 2020a)—in productive ways to build solidarity, exploit discrimination, and access limited resources across multiple levels (i.e., micro-level interactions, meso-level school and community contexts, and macro-level policy constraints.

This chapter has shown that a key factor in Latinx immigrants' and undocumented youths' everyday lives is socially and legally produced through the condition of illegality and racialization processes in policies and laws that have excluded them, particularly defined categories of normative citizenship. This status is deeply racialized, and it is reproduced through policy ideology, discourse, and enactments. This status structures the everyday decision-making that undocumented immigrants engage in, from when to go to the grocery store, to how they learn about and encounter immigration enforcement and courts, and it takes a toll on their families, even if they are separated from family members. Recent scholarship has directed more explicit attention to the context-specific effects of illegality as it intersects with other vulnerabilities (Menjívar & Kanstroom, 2013), such as labor relations (Goldring & Lanholt 2012), and the limits of social reproduction—the set of structured practices that make up "the fleshy, messy and indeterminate stuff of everyday life" (Bickham Mendez & Nelson, 2016). From this perspective, healthcare, education, childcare, housing, and access to community spaces comprise the fabric of social reproduction. Limiting Latinx immigrants' access to space within new settlement sites, as scholars have pointed out, not only constrains their social reproduction but also limits political, economic, and social rights (Odem, 2009). This book advances the context-specific realities of undocumented youth in South Carolina while also attempting to advance the ways they resist the social and legal reproduction of inequality through their undocumentedness.

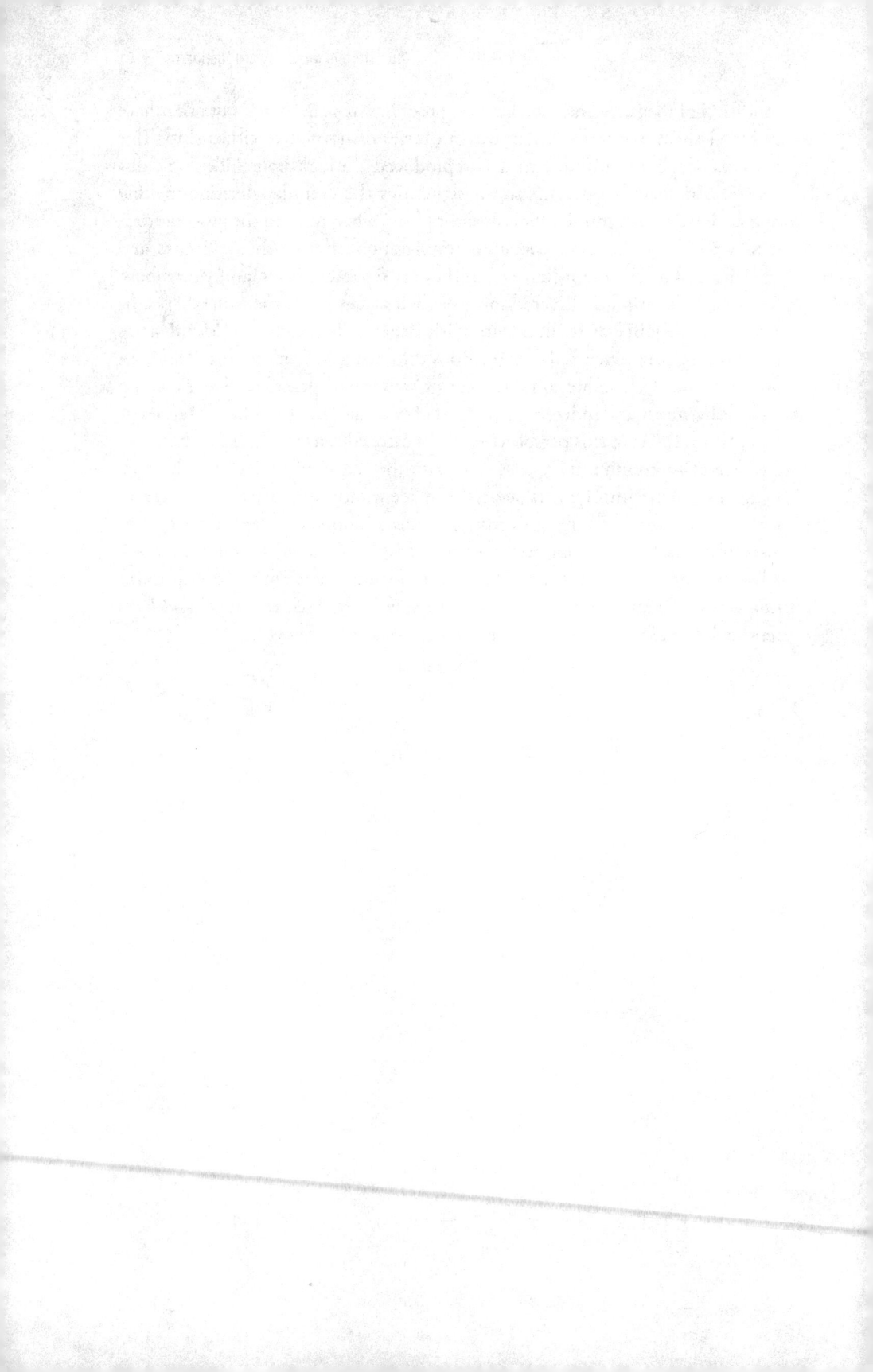

Part 2

Meso-Level Organizational Perspectives

• •

3

Ethnographic Interlude II

• • • • • • • • • • • • • • • • • • • •

"We call them coolers–
immigration rooms are cold.":
Students' Migration Journeys
and the Lived Effects of
Policies upon Their
Entering U.S. Schools

> They don't know that I grew up more on
> the street than I did in my house, and
> well now they are scared of me, or think
> bad of me, and it's not that I am bad but
> I always walk alone. I'm always alone
> because I haven't found a friend to be my
> friend really here.
> —Juan, undocumented youth, interview,
>   March 2016

In 2016, while in Ms. Ava's newcomer ESL class at Citizen North, I remember Juan twirling his soccer ball while sitting in the desk across from me, not making eye contact when I asked him to tell me a little bit about where he grew up. Stopping the ball, he said, "I was born in El Salvador, and had the almost perfect childhood before becoming lonelier when I came here." Initially, we talked about his desire to play soccer and go to college. Having arrived in the United States about a year prior to the interview in 2015, he was still learning about scholarships and postsecondary opportunities, and determining what his aspirations were for after high school. He expressed strong views about the purpose of education, discussed in (outlined further in chapter 4): "There are two types of education; the first type of education happens at home with the parents, and the second education is in school that is academic to prepare and will wake up the mind and know what is the good one can do with one's own goals, and I think that is what education at school helps us with to improve our own personalities and achieve the goals one has." He believes that education at home is more learning about "responsibility, honesty, and respect for others," while "the education at school is more for learning about life and to develop the brain and know what goals are. Things like learning math and science and things you don't learn at home." He felt that at school there is a lot of "ignorance," noting that "some people will say I can't study and succeed in something because I am an immigrant, and I don't know what they want." He went on to describe the many layers of ignorance in his school, including peers' ignorance and teachers' ignorance about immigrants and Latinos, and their reasons for coming to the United States. In the next chapter I return to these moments that Juan and other youth felt misunderstood and alienated. They felt that adults in the school had lower expectations of them due to their immigrant backgrounds and language learning needs, and that some adults in school lacked understanding about the (pre)migration journeys and the racialized interactions they had prior to and in school and the local community. It was evident to me in this moment how thoughtful and sentient Juan was, despite his apprehension about talking with me.

As our interview moved through the topic of ignorance, I asked him if he felt there were differences in how Latinx students were viewed at the school versus in the Latinx community, given that he was an undocumented newcomer. He pointed quickly and somewhat robustly to the racial ignorance of the school, but also complicated racial dynamics among other Latinos in the school. He explained: "The Latinos, you'll see the majority of children of Hispanics that were born here, the majority think they're better than those who came here and they think they can do everything just because they have a paper or something like that, and sometimes I see that it's so ridiculous that a Hispanic like us thinks like that." At the core of Juan's frustration with education and the low expectations in the school and in general was the fact that he felt he had sacrificed a great deal to come to the United States and then had to deal with anti-immigrant sentiment in his community and school, and within Latino groups due to various immigration statuses. On the one hand, people in Denizen assumed all Latinos were immigrants and undocumented, while the youth understood the nuances within the Latino and immigrant community—which ought to prompt educators and policy-makers to learn from these youth. I listened to Juan's journey to understand the pre- and post-migration experience and, in some instances, the trauma.

"It was fast, my dad had already been going back and forth. He called in the night and said he paid for a coyote, and I had to pack my stuff." I had asked Juan if he felt comfortable sharing his migration story. He explained that due to his age he had to go to Guatemala and cross the river. "I said to myself, what am I doing here? What am I doing here? I don't belong on this path and I don't know I asked God for strength to maybe make it to here. Then I got to Guatemala to a house where there were dog fleas and things like that and I wasn't used to that, and after that I wanted to go back, but I said, 'How am I going to go back? I'm in Guatemala.' I spent one night there and then left." He explained how difficult it was traveling alone and through Guatemala due to some of the language differences, but by the end of one day he left for the border to Mexico. He recalled:

We passed into Mexico to a place that was beautiful, there was like a lake with blue water, like light blue, it was perfect. Up until there everything was going well, and then a car that carries cows came and they put us in there and left us there for a night in the woods waiting for someone to come for us. In the morning a car came, just one, for like 45 people, and they put us one on top of the other, it was like a 2 hour trip. I was in a crouched position with 45 people. We were on top of each other. My legs got hurt, that is when I first hurt my knee. After around 2 hours we got to a house but there was no food or anything, we were there 4 days and we only ate once, and after 4 days we left for— I forget the name, but we were there a week and in that house there wasn't a bathroom, nothing, and they gave us food once a day.

I asked how he found these people and if he had networks or connections to them. He said: "I don't know . . . well, there in my country it was dangerous and that's why my dad made the decision to bring me here, so they paid for them to bring me, they paid like 8,000 dollars. So the guy we paid was coming to the north and he had his contacts that would go passing the people along the way. I only knew the coyote, but he pulled people from all over El Salvador and we all came together there and left, we were 45 but I didn't know anyone."

At times it was difficult to follow Juan's narrative and recollection of the journey. The number of hours and days as well as the number of people he encountered shifted. As an ethnographer, I wanted to deeply and sincerely understand these events by seeing them through Juan's eyes, and to share with readers the nonlinearity of the migration experience (Jackson, 2010). I listened as he explained how he felt as a teenager trying to unite with his father in the United States. He explained:

I felt like the world was falling on top of me, and I don't know, sometimes I felt like crying because I had no way of communicating, I couldn't communicate with my mom for the whole 3 months, call her or anything like that. So we were in that house and we left for a trip that was like 9 hours to somewhere in Mexico, it was before getting to Mexico City. We went by car like this [*extending his arms but keeping them close to his body*] all cramped together the whole way. But that time there were 2 cars, so we were more relaxed, but my leg was already bad, you can see it was left a little irritated [*shows scars on knee*] because in those cars sometimes they have a place to tie the car and it rubbed against me like this and it cut me there, so at that point I couldn't even crouch or anything.

And after that we spent like 3 days in that house but it was different, I always slept on the floor, always on the floor, but at this house there was ceramic floors that were cold and my back hurt and afterwards, from the day we left for Mexico City, we went 2 days without eating anything, without drinking anything, to wait for a bus to take us to the border of the United States with Mexico. Then we got there and we got to a house where there were more than 100 people, it had 2 floors but it was very small. I slept 29 days on the stairs. Then finally people started to leave, but I slept the same, sitting [and] things like that because there was nothing and there were a lot of lice and—do you know what those are? I always tied a bag or something over my head to protect myself and I was the only one without lice. Afterwards we arrived at another house and spent 15 days there, but the woman saw that my back was hurting [and] gave me a mattress to sleep and I felt more relaxed.

As Juan continued, he explained that he had to attempt to cross the U.S.-Mexico border more than once. In his second attempt, he said,

We crossed the river in a small boat to the car that was waiting for us on the other side and suddenly there was the airplane, the helicopter and it illuminated us [shined lights on them] and the police came so we had to run back, and since I always played soccer I didn't run faster than the guy in charge of us so I didn't lose him, but I was running right behind him, but then all of a sudden I watched him fall into a hole, and then I came and we all fell into the hole, and we fell into the water from the river, the "bravo" river [*Rio Bravo is the Spanish name for the Rio Grande*], and we ended up in the river and had to walk like 4 hours in the water to where the boat was. They only caught 2 and then we went back to the house, we were all wet and I got sick. So we had a few unsuccessful trips.

During the fourth attempt, he explained that a dog started barking and immigration discovered them. As they ran, several in his group were detained again, and in the end only a few of them made it. He said once he made it he had to hide until a car came. He said, "I felt like I was to die of cold, it was so cold and they had taken away my jacket, because mine was too bright of a color. I was shivering to the point that my teeth were chattering, and I thought 'Now what do I do? Where do I run? I don't have anywhere to go.'" The next morning he was picked up and taken to another house on the U.S. side of the border.

Once in the United States, somewhere in southern Texas, he stayed a week in a house with 60 people.

We all slept cramped and the bathroom was disgusting and we got food once a day, but a man would cook it and the food was so bad that it hurt me, and I was really skinny from not eating. You could see these bones and these bones [*points to collarbone and cheek bones*] so I was like that. I could only take a week of that; I couldn't take it anymore I didn't sleep well or anything for two months or more. We had to walk for so many hours, sometimes full days of walking to avoid checkpoints. The saddest thing I saw was one of the guys that was with us sat down when they let us rest and he just stayed like that and I went to wake him up and he was cold, he couldn't even move, even the air was coming out of him because he was already dead and he was just sitting there. And we looked around and a snake had bitten him, it was next to him, and I just stood there because I was already empty [also translates to *spent*] and we left him there. I wanted to go back and see if he was just sleeping but they didn't let me go back.

Then we arrived at the house, I was really sick and I couldn't take it anymore, I was really skinny, my body was really thin. A car arrived and they put us in groups, I was in a group of 32 and they put us in a really small car, a truck with 4 doors. I said, "I'm going in the front in the cabin," they had taken the seat out of the back seat, but I said "I'm going here because last time it was bad in the back," but I didn't know it was going to be even worse. They put 2 people on top of me and below me—it was hot [and] I was on the side, like really close to the tire and it was burning me, and that's how I got a scar here [*points to back of leg*]. It was so hot, I last 5 hours driving in that car and arriving to Texas on the truck so that it didn't look really low so he stopped to take it off and you could see Texas, Houston, really close we were in a little town before it on a road and there was an immigration car, we were like 15 minutes from Houston when we stopped and there was immigration. So he [the driver] went crazy and we went towards a ravine and the truck hit a tree and we all felt it.

When I got out, I wanted to run but I couldn't, I fell because my legs were asleep. I stood up and looked at the houses. The ones that were in the back couldn't breathe and were taken to the hospital. So since I couldn't take it I saw a little house with a porch and I sat down and I couldn't stand it anymore. I just sat there like this and I watched how they were grabbing them. Since I was so white a lot of people were confused and spoke to me in English. So I was sitting and all of a sudden a woman came out and put her shotgun up to my head. And she talked to immigration. I stayed there looking at the woman and she spoke to me in English but I didn't understand anything. I didn't move, it didn't matter, I just stayed there sitting until immigration came and threw me on the ground and put the ties around my legs and hands and then I arrived at, we call them the "coolers" where immigration is, they have the rooms cold. I spent 6 days there. I only had a thin shirt like this one and I wore it like this [*puts arms inside of shirt*] and I covered my legs and I didn't get up because I had muscle cramps. Six days, and then they started moving me around until I was close to the border with Mexico. And I said, 'If they leave me here at the border, I'm going to call the guy that brought me to pick me up and cross again.'

After this long journey, Juan was sent to California and then Chicago, where he had food but was recovering from malnourishment and the trauma of crossing the border and being detained. He was ultimately released to his family and landed in South Carolina.

Sharing this portion of Juan's story is important because it illuminates the lived effects of racialized migration-border policies. While it may feel long to read, my intention is to illustrate the story, from Juan's perspective, of a young adult who experienced the months it took to leave his family in El Salvador and arrive in the United States.

Migrant Youth Movement and Trauma

Youth experience trauma, starvation, and long journeys, and yet they still hold positive views toward education and aspirations once here. Yet upon arriving in the schools, from racialized illegality that is reified through macro policies (Menjívar, 2014b, 2021), they encounter a new version of racialized social systems in schools and communities. Juan's narrative is that he began this abrupt journey with strangers. However after some unsuccessful attempts, we gain a clearer understanding of the physical and mental toll that this process takes, as sooner or later almost everyone is captured. He provides very descriptive details of his surroundings and experiences, such as "passing into Mexico to a place that was beautiful, with a lake with blue water, like light blue it was perfect," or the way he describes the extremely cold weather he endured. The amount of time in which he was traveling felt longer and his limited knowledge of the language or his environment seemed to impact the ways in which he processed his experiences. He was also forced to confront the realities of migration, which include death, specifically the death of one member of the group as they were making their way up a mountain. Furthermore, he has several scars from his trip as well as potential trauma from having a shotgun pointed at his head. These real and symbolic scars remain as young people like Juan enter U.S. schools.

Many youths at Citizen North had similar experiences of migration and having come to the United States without papers. While the macro-level policies deeply impact youth, the lived effects of these policies reverberated across school and community spaces. In addition, youth enter the racialized social system of school and community contexts. Stories like Juan's were common among many youth.

Below, I share field notes from when I sat with a group of youth at Denizen West to learn about their migration journeys and discussed their experience of not having *papeles*. Carolina arrived when she was younger and did not have much recollection of the journey; rather, she recalled the struggles throughout her childhood since her arrival. Rafaela, on the other hand, had arrived more recently, and she shares her migration story below. My ethnographic field notes here are intended to walk alongside the youth as they share their experiences so that we might learn from these grassroots-level perspectives.

Field Notes Excerpt

RAFAELA (R) My story is very long, but if you want I can tell it.

SOPHIA Go ahead . . . take your time.

R I was left at 1 year old with my grandparents until I grew and was 14 years old and met my parents, and they told me that I should come here so I made the decision and at 13 years old I came, without papers.

CAROLINA (C) How did you get here without papers? [*Asks another student*] Did you come with papers or without papers?

R Without papers.

C And you came in a car? They didn't detain you? That's pretty amazing.

R At 13 years old I also came in *carro*, but they did get me. They grabbed me and asked me so many questions in English that I didn't know and then they returned me, they put me in a car like a van and from there they sent me to a place for underage people and there they gave us food, there was one bathroom.

C Almost like being in jail.

SOPHIA Were you alone in the place they took you [a detention center]?

C Who were you with?

R I came alone. From there, they asked for my papers because they sent me to Mexico and held me there and asked for my papers. Then when I turned 14, my parents told me to come again and I said okay, so I tried again. On that try, they almost grabbed me again because we were crossing and immigration came and there were some [unknown word] there that I had to cross and I couldn't run anymore. I said to my uncle—because this time I came with my 2 uncles—so I couldn't run and said "You go because I know how you'll suffer and I don't want you to suffer," and he said "No, you can go on." And the car stopped where the [unknown word—possibly referring to a land obstacle, like a hole] was and we jumped from there and it was all broken, and [I] said to my dad, "I don't want to cross anymore," and he said "Try again, there is nothing impossible," and I said "No, I don't want to . . ."

C 'Cuz you were so scared, that was the second time.

R And from there I decided to make the decision and I was able to cross. I spent like 4 days in the woods without food.

SOPHIA Do you mind sharing a little bit more about why you came?

R Because, well, my parents told me that here I would have more benefits and the opportunity to know more things and learn more things and be with my family.

C 'Cuz your mom and dad were already here? I bet that was hard for them to leave you.

SOPHIA Did you know about the process to get papers, or how did you learn about it?

R Well now my dad is helping me apply for DACA and is doing my papers.

[Another student, Olivia, joins the conversation.]

C You're from Honduras but your situation, is it the same?

O I don't know.

C How did you get here?

O Um, I also lived with my grandparents and it was good, but I started to have problems with a boy who was a *pandillero* [negative context] and he wanted me to stay with him so I made the decision to come here with my mom.

C So your mom was already over here?

O Yes. I didn't really remember her anymore so I had to come, I tried 4 times. The first time I came, I tried to come, they grabbed me trying to cross [*tratando de pasar por encima*—she is saying "to pass over"] and they returned me, I didn't get to my place or anything, there right at the border I went back. The second time the person my mom paid left me stranded.

C I've heard that happens so many times, the coyote.

SOPHIA Really? They pay them and they just leave them?

C They just kind of left her there, they took the money and left her hanging there. You have to pay up front for a coyote.

O I was lost for a day by myself, it was maybe 6 at night, I didn't know. I walked through some woods and I didn't notice that there was water or anything, and there was like a swamp that I got stuck in and I couldn't get out and I was drowning. Then I felt like someone was [there] and he helped me get out, he was a good man, he helped me he got me out, he gave me food because I had gone the entire day without eating, without drinking water or anything. He got me out and then he turned me in to immigration and they returned me to my country. I tried again and on the next time they also got me, and on the fourth time I got here. I also was in Mexico for like 2 months.

C That's a lot of money, because on average a coyote charges about 3–5,000 dollars to come through.

SOPHIA That's what I've heard.

O Mine was 4,800.

C They want their money first.

O But I was also scared to stay there being a slave to someone I didn't love. Because he didn't just threaten to kill me, but also my family, so even though it wasn't my fault what could I do? It was live or . . .

C So going back was not an option.

O No, it was not an option so I got lots of courage, I alone had to prepare myself psychologically to be able to, I did that alone.

C So that was your driving force to go forward and not look back?

O Exactly, I stayed on the border of Guatemala with Honduras for 6 days until someone came and helped me, they lent me a phone to call my mom and tell her where I was and what I needed, it was hard.

[class talking, moving around]

After these conversations, additional youth shared their stories of migration. Very few had "easy" journeys and had to attempt to cross the border multiple times. As they came *sin papeles*, they recalled not knowing how long they would be held in detention. Many had parents and caregivers here and eventually were released to them. Many also left family members behind or had been separated from parents for several years, like Rafaela and Olivia. The fear associated with crossing the border and the hope of a better life were in conflict.

As they arrived in the United States, many of the youth had to navigate the education system while carrying these hidden traumas and experiences. These experiences enter the classrooms and schools, whether they may or may not be addressed or acknowledged. Continued racialization through schools and communities has a cumulative effect on these young peoples' sense of self and belonging. In chapter 4, I describe the racial dynamics in schools and interactions there, while in chapter 5 I share the lived effects of youths' migration status in the community and how they come to understand their experiences of illegality and perspectives of citizenship through processes of racialization. Recalling my theoretical framework that invokes a multi-level analysis of racialization across state policies, schools as organizations, and community and interactional levels, the chapters explore the journey across such levels; however, these levels of analysis and the accompanying racialization processes are interconnected when viewed through the lived experiences of youth.

I share these vignettes to introduce all that undocumented youth navigate as they come to U.S. schools and systems that are set up to exclude them. The scars that Juan discussed are both physical and emotional. In many cases, educators or school mental health professionals may be unaware of what youth are carrying with them. Making assumptions about their experience or current state occurred due to deficit-based ideologies and a lack of awareness about the spillover effects of migration. While educators like Ms. Ava told me to "listen, hear, and understand" youths' stories, not all educators were as empathetic or exhibited the sociopolitical awareness at Denizen or Citizen. Yet, as the youth navigate border and federal policies, state policies, and the local context, many of their migration stories remain unknown or silenced in the context of the classroom. In this interlude I showed the lived effects of harsh border policies, family separation, and detention practices.

4

"I was born at the border, like the wrong side of it."

●●●●●●●●●●●●●●●●●●●●●

Racialization and
Discrimination at
Denizen West High and
Citizen North High

Denizen West high school—one of the study's focal sites—was located about ten miles from the downtown city center. On my morning drives across the marsh, starting in 2015, I witnessed a growth in housing. In many ways, this was natural given the high interest in living in the Denizen community. The youth referred to the "gentrification" as a "whitetopia," meaning they observed white people moving to the island (described later in the chapter) despite their high school maintaining mostly students of color. The beauty and timelessness of the location made it an iconic place to live for many. The tree-lined, winding road to Denizen made it feel like I had transcended time and space, especially since I was new to living in the South. Most of the students who attended Denizen West lived "on the island," as they referred to it. Youth explained that they did not often leave the island because either their families did not have cars or there was no reason to. There was one grocery store about a mile from the school and a few restaurants, including a McDonald's where a few of the youth worked.

The grounds of the school were covered with oak trees draped with Spanish moss. The beauty of the location overshadowed the fact that the population of Denizen had been steadily dwindling, principal and teacher turnover was a consistent challenge, and limited curricular opportunities and services were available. As I would approach the front door, I would press the button to be let into the school, and immediately be ushered by the security guard to the main office door, where I would wait again to be buzzed in. "Good morning," I'd say to the front office staff, who would print out a sticker with my picture on it, a Visitor Pass, "be sure to wear that everywhere you go." I would head to "Cookie's" office down the hall on the first floor, past the lunchroom, counseling offices, and library. Cookie was the name that the youth gave the school social worker. Cookie's office, the first of three I would visit during the four-year study, was an old storage closet. Cookie described herself as "hippie-like." She would burn incense in her office, and the kids would laugh at her protein shakes. The office held her desk and a small round table; kids sat here and on the floor of the office. Youth filtered through Cookie's office before, during, and in between classes for individual and group sessions, or merely to hang out. I observed all of this and realized immediately how central Cookie was to the youth's belonging at Denizen West.

My time in Cookie's office initially involved my listening and learning from the youth about their experiences and hardships. One youth, Abby, uttered in one of our initial meetings, "I was born at the border, like the wrong side of it. Why couldn't my mom just have me over the border?" She detailed for me her journey as a newborn crossing the border and the hardships that ensued. The youth lived in poverty, and so many were going through evictions and were upset because they would have to switch schools. Mobility and transience often characterized their everyday lives. Others came to Cookie for advice on mental and sexual health, and she drove them to school and to the teen clinic for reproductive health checkups. Cookie also housed kids, often against her better judgment, but she knew that they "just had so much going on in their lives." When I would visit Cookie's house to help pack and deliver care packages for families, often there would be a youth staying at her house for weeks or months, depending on the situation in their home. Over the years, I was able to develop a close friendship with Cookie and she viewed me as a resource in her social work practice. Some nights, around 7 p.m., I would receive texts like, "Miguel got in a fight; he was mixed up with some kids, and now arrested; Will he get deported?" Cookie also asked me to drive kids to a nearby city in North Carolina for immigration hearings. We often navigated legal questions together to advocate for youth. In Cookie's office, I developed and cultivated relationships with the undocumented youth in the study, studying South Carolina state policies with them; writing letters to senators; and learning about their experiences of racism and discrimination, how they engaged with teachers and adults at Denizen West, and how they found solidarity in the storage closet that was Cookie's office. This chapter describes undocumented youths' interactions with teachers and educators in the school, interactions that students or I interpreted as racialized. While Cookie was a critical advocate for undocumented immigrant youth, many educators and teachers in the school contributed to or hindered youths' sense of belonging.

The commute to Citizen North was less dreamy than the drive to Denizen West—just a concrete, two-lane highway lined with car dealerships and fast-food restaurants. The school grounds were nested next to this urban sprawl. Evidence of gentrification was sprinkled along the highway and indicated by increasing housing prices. Entering Citizen North, I was met by security and a friendly office staff. The school was much larger than Denizen West, and a somewhat more modern building. Upon entering the building, I would check in with the front office like at Denizen. After I checked in, I often met with the principal, to say a brief hello, and the coordinator for the language learning classes. The coordinator was a strong advocate for language learners and the newcomers. She explained the types of language learning services available at the school, which had little support, and the informal program was largely driven by her efforts. I would head to the second floor to the corner of the school where all the Spanish and ESL classes were held. Citizen North felt similar to the schools I had studied in the past in Chicago and New York City. It was a large comprehensive high school with approximately 1,000 students, busy during passing periods, and with sterile hallways and a limited sense of community. My observations and interactions were more in classrooms, rather than with support staff like at Denizen, and to some extent were more formal rather than the non-class interactions I had at Denizen. In part this was because I was observing more classroom instructional time.

In both schools, however, I found a wealth of knowledge and experience from critical educators and school-based personnel, which I discuss later in the chapter. These include Cookie, Ms. Ava, and Ms. Constance, as well as educators who expressed troubling deficit-based views rooted in the racial schemas and ideologies they held and that manifested in the racial organization of the schools. Next, I review the central concept of racialization and how it applies to this chapter's discussion of the organizational level of schools through systemic exclusion, lack of access to equitable education, and the reproduction of inequality through the lack of supports for Latinx undocumented immigrant students. Importantly, I also show how institutional agents, who are often reported in the literature to shape immigrant students' trajectories, are key resource brokers and promote opportunities and access. According to Stanton-Salazar (2001), institutional agents hold key positions in institutions that can provide critical forms of social and institutional support. However, I found that the negative racial attitudes of educators and school-based personnel negatively impacted undocumented students' access and sense of belonging. My research indicates the challenge was that teachers and school personnel are not automatically institutional agents that help support youth; while they have the potential to step into this role because of their educational background and job, they may choose not do so, whether consciously or unconsciously, and they may hold values that are not aligned with affirming Latino immigrant youths' backgrounds or cultures.

Racialization

In this chapter I use the concept of racialization as it applies to the meso-organizational level to examine how schools and communities impact immigrant access and mobility. Research often focuses on how racialized minority youth underachieve in school and do not fit in school based on their identities of race and perceived class; this research relegates minoritized youth underachievement to a cultural problem rather than attributing it to structural racism and racialization, which refers to a process of othering and racially categorizing groups (Conchas & Pérez, 2003; Flores-González, 2002). Previous scholarship tends to focus upon barriers to immigrants' academic success without accounting for white-dominant norms in schools (Lareau, 2003; Verma et al., 2017), problematic theories of assimilation and segmented assimilation (Portes & Zhou, 1993; Rumbaut & Portes, 2001; Suárez-Orozco & Suárez-Orozco, 2001), and variation in the racialization processes that impact Latinx immigrant and undocumented immigrant educational achievement. Although previous literature comments on immigrant youth as being voluntary minorities, and thus likely to have a positive outlook for schooling (Fordham & Ogbu, 1986), the Latinx undocumented immigrant youth in this study bear a status of illegality that functions to limit their opportunities and social mobility (Rodriguez, 2020a). The status of illegality—as designated federally—needs to be considered in relation to politics, geopolitical relations, racialization, and the elitism of white nationalism and Americanization (Gerstle, 1997) at the national, state, and local levels, as these frames function to exclude and other Latinx immigrant youth broadly and those with undocumented status particularly (Conchas & Hinga, 2016). Furthermore, these macro frames manifest in communities and schools. As such, schools are important nested contexts and cultural borderlands where the effect of racialization intersect with notions of whiteness and Americanness (Anzaldúa, 1987/2012; Brown & Souto-Manning, 2007; Ong, 1996). In studying these dynamics ethnographically in schools and a local community, I address the process of how Latinx youth make sense of their racial identities and the processes of racialization they encounter at school and in an anti-immigrant state and community.

In this chapter, I examine racialization—an iterative process in which immigrant youth are "placed into the U.S. racial paradigm based upon perceptions and experiences of exclusion, surveillance, and profiling"—to critically show Latinx undocumented youth experiences and promote equity for immigrant youth (Verma et al., 2017, p. 210). Considering "racializing immigration studies" (Sáenz & Manges Douglass, 2015), the ethnographic data revealed how undocumented youth talk about and experience race, racism, and the ascription of identity, and how they negotiate the racialization process to give voice to their own experiences of identity and belonging. The ascription of racial categories to people with perceived common traits is not a politically neutral act. Rather than a fixed aspect of identity, race is a "system of categorization" (Delgado & Stefancic, 2017) designed for the purposes of power and hierarchy (Omi & Winant 2014; Weitz, 2003). As stated in the Introduction, this system of categorization is a historical and ongoing process called *racial formation* (Omi & Winant, 2014). This process includes social and political forces that contribute to generating racial categories and their meanings. Racial formation is embedded in social structures and affects how people understand and frame both themselves and others, and it has material consequences. To explain, Lewis (2003) argues, "Racial categories are not merely sociological abstractions but are potent social categories around which people organize their identities and behavior and that influence people's opportunities and outcomes" (p. 6).

Further, I have argued that racialization occurs at the meso-organizational level, such as in the contexts of schools and communities. In this chapter, I share how processes of racial identification shape youths' life courses and access to resources and affirm or do not affirm a positive sense of self and belonging through the racial messages the youth receive in organizations like schools or in local community interactions they experienced in Denizen. The racial hierarchy in Denizen in particular was determined to some extent by the black-white binary and the invisibility of the Latinx immigrant population. At the two schools and in the community, youth come to understand their racialized identity as Latinx and its intersection with their undocumented immigration status as part of a larger racialized system in the South. Seeing racialized systems helps contextualize the importance of their self-articulated identity expressions because youths' perceptions of themselves are impacted by institutional and structural factors. The youths' dialogue reflects a counternarrative to racialized policies and practices in their schools and local communities.

A key takeaway from my theoretical framework is that racial formation becomes embedded in social structures on a variety of levels and is sustained through implicit practices in organizations such as schools. The youth recognize how their identities are racialized and engage in critical dialogue to educate themselves politically and organize locally in their schools and communities.

Latinos who hold marginalized identities are highly targeted and racialized as criminals. Though Latinos are not a monolithic group, they are stratified by a racialized power structure. Certain sectors of the Latinx community are indeed treated inhumanely, and their rights are not recognized. Other scholars posit the ways in which policy and media discourses produce the category of immigrant not only as a problem, but also as a criminal (Chávez, 1994). Latinx immigrants and undocumented immigrants—problematically assumed to be all Latinos through the production of the criminalizing discourse—have to navigate their illegality (De Genova, 2002, 2004; Rodriguez, 2017b). To contextualize the realities of the students in my study, I next describe the community, the demographics of the school district, and the school itself before moving on to key themes, including deficit-based perspectives, such as "If you want to be American, you need to speak English."

Denizen's District, Community, and School Contexts

In the Denizen community and schools, youth navigated the lack of school district and school-based academic and social resources, highlighting micro-level interactions that contributed to their unbelonging and sense of empowerment. I end with their reflections on identity (re)production in relation to how they are racialized at community and school levels.

The Southern Context and the Denizen Community

In this book I shed light on the racial dynamics and systemic inequities in a Southern community. The racial dynamics are stark, which scholars attribute to the small population of Hispanics in the region (3 percent according to the 2004 census; Smith & Furuseth, 2006, pp. 5, 8). This is common in the South, where states such as Arkansas, Georgia, Mississippi, and Tennessee, which have seen their overall smaller populations steadily increase since the 1900s. Scholars use terms such as the *New Latino/x South, Nuevo South,* and *New Latino Diaspora* to indicate areas in the South where Latino populations are smaller than in urban centers (Guerrero, 2017; Hamann et al., 2015). Additionally, much research on immigration and immigrants occurs in such urban centers, where access to resources tends to exist, even if these resources are limited or problematic. Meanwhile, research shows that in nontraditional receiving contexts, such as rural areas, immigrants face barriers to resources and struggle with identity, community, and belonging. In the Southern contexts state policies and ideologies, including racism and anti-immigrant narratives, are present (Winders & Smith, 2012).

The schools in this study are a part of the larger New Latino South. As outlined in chapter 2 the legacy of Jim Crow and segregation have created a patchwork of racialized policies and practices across Southern states designed to discourage migrants and drive out immigrants already there. This patchwork of state policies is largely based on a racial binary that neglects the Latinx population.

Hamann et al. (2002) argue that Latinx groups face "novel challenges to their senses of identity, status, and community" (p. 1). While research shows that Latinx groups may vary in how they ethnically identify themselves (i.e., Peruvian, Honduran, Guatemalan, etc.), in the South, they are racialized as Hispanic or Latino/x (Rodriguez, 2020b; Sierk, 2019). Browne and Odem (2012) argue that the black-white binary of race is challenged by the influx of Latinx immigrants to the United States, which contributes to ongoing Latinx racialization (Rodriguez, 2020b; Telles et al., 2011). This racial binary of white and nonwhite in the South was present for youth in the current research, who often had to carve out their identities in schools while being racialized as Hispanics and noncitizens. Aligned with this, Browne and Odem (2012), in their study of Guatemalan's and Dominican's experiences of identity, belonging, and exclusion in Atlanta, Georgia, argue: "State laws that racialize Latinos create a two-dimensional category, with a homogenized Latino category as one axis and an illegal/legal distinction as the second axis" (p. 322). For Latinos in Georgia, Latino is not just a racial category, it also implies one's immigrant status. "Legal status thus becomes a second axis in the racialized category of 'Latino'" (Browne & Odem, p. 330). The state and local laws in states across the South (Georgia and South Carolina in particular) racialize Latinos as "illegal" and unwanted, in similar ways to Jim Crow, which leads Browne and Odem to call the racialization of Latinos in the South the *New Juan Crow*. As discussed in the Introduction, it is challenging to think about Latinx experiences in the South without considering the broader racial dynamics and fabric of the racial/ethnic category. This context is critical for understanding the everyday lives of the undocumented youth and their families' experiences.

In South Carolina, Roth and Grace (2015) reported that 54 percent of the 230,000 immigrants in South Carolina were from Latin America—a 19 percent increase between 2008 and 2013. From an analysis of state and local policies, I found that South Carolina has some of the most restrictive laws. For example, in an analysis of 120 state policies from 2000 to 2015 (Rodriguez, 2018a; Rodriguez & Monreal, 2017), I learned that South Carolina's House Bill 4400 (passed in 2008) bans undocumented immigrants from enrolling in public postsecondary education institutions (Roth, 2017), and that South Carolina's Senate Bill 20 (passed in 2011) is a "Show Me Your Papers" law akin to the one in Arizona (Rodriguez & Monreal, 2017).

Denizen's climate toward immigrants was paradoxical. In the city center, it was rare to see nonwhite groups as the richest parts of the city and a local college took up the space downtown and near the tourist areas. Despite the whiteness of Denizen, parts of downtown were historically Black, but at times it felt like gentrification was leading to a pushout of the Black community and an erasure of the Latinx community. However, the Latinx immigrant community near Denizen West was relatively long-standing and provided desirable labor given the agricultural sector and the steady increase in the Latinx population. Many youths reported that Latinos lived in the area, and even the undocumented youth had been there since early childhood. Studying the Denizen community for over three years enabled me to observe shifts in the landscape, both at the rural "island" school Denizen West and the sprawl and at the gentrifying downtown near Citizen North. Youth described their "island community" near Denizen West High as a "whitetopia," saying that the landscape shifted with new subdivisions. I noticed the growth in population on my morning drives across the river onto the island as new housing emerged along the marsh. Meanwhile, youth lived in trailers tucked away from the major thoroughfare. From the urban center of the small Southern city, there is one winding road lined with sweeping oak trees that leads out to the island where Denizen West High School is located. Citizen North High School is located 15 miles north of the urban center, near some of the wealthiest areas in the state. Despite the gentrification, the district maintains a flexible choice policy. These images of the Denizen community were central to my understanding of the physical landscape and led me to notice the wealth of this community and the ways in which inequity was spatial. In other words, this white, affluent city was not the Denizen that the youth in my study experienced. The youth at Denizen West lived secluded from the city center in rural poverty, while youth at Citizen North largely lived in low-income housing near a rapidly gentrifying area north of the city center, which residents worry will push the Black community out of the area due to skyrocketing housing prices.

The Denizen School District

In addition to the social, spatial, and racial inequities in Denizen and the state more broadly, the school district persistently underserved the Latinx (and Black) community. During my time studying Denizen, I witnessed and supported educators in reporting civil rights violations to the district. Language learners were underserved through a low-quality curriculum and a lack of services. Latinx parents were rarely, if ever, provided materials in Spanish or engaged by the school district. In one instance, an educator reported anti-immigrant lesson plans by teachers to me, including when a local teacher had students do an "Immigration Unit," though I would later learn that the lesson plan itself was unclear. The teacher had children draw pictures of immigrants in the state or United States. Many depictions by students were hung in the halls of the school, with stick figures in boats, and maps of the United States, saying "No Immigrants Allowed" and "You're taking jobs." This example shows how curricular debates and activities that claim to present "both sides," such as the immigration debate, in the name of equity reproduce racist structures of oppression.

After these drawings were displayed on the school walls, an educator called me to ask how to report this anti-immigrant hostility to the state office of civil rights. Though she reported it, ultimately no consequences were revealed. When I learned of this incident, I was immediately angry and wanted to support her. Given that teachers in South Carolina do not have many protections as it is a non-union state, the educator was afraid to go public with the anti-immigrant sentiment in schools and at the district level. My research (Rodriguez & McCorkle, 2019, 2020) across the state, including interviews and survey data with teachers, showed a lack of awareness about policies impacting immigrants as well as the tendency for teachers to believe in false narratives about immigrants, such as the ones depicted in the posters that students created. Whether or not this teacher told the students about immigration or not was less relevant for the educator I worked with; what was more concerning was the lack of clarity around the assignment, and the display of false narratives and anti-immigrant sentiments created by the children in the school and unquestioned by any teachers or administrators. Alarmingly, the false narratives about immigrants and negative stereotypes were normalized rather than leveraging the opportunity for critical conversations and breaking down assumptions embedded in these posters. It is likely that the assumptions displayed here were heard by parents or in households through the media. The assignment did not include discussion of the hegemonic discourses that shape narratives about immigrants in the state and nationally.

While the educator noticed some student posters were pro-immigrant, she was concerned with the false and racist narratives about immigrants that were evidenced in the above examples. The teacher did not provide any description of the lesson plan or the discussion and reflection with students. In a 2021 study, Monreal and McCorkle argue that treating sensitive topics as controversies and not reflecting upon them is dangerous in schools, especially when damaging false narratives are plastered on the walls of schools that immigrant students attend, whether they are undocumented or not. In paying heed to both sides, in the name of legitimate or open debate, teachers, along with teaching material, validate, normalize, and (re)produce certain false narratives about immigrants and immigration policy, like the ease of obtaining legal status, the unassimilable nature of certain groups, and an isomorphic Latino Threat (Chavez, 2008). Moreover, Dabach et al. (2018) argue that normalizing immigration as controversy allows anti-immigrant sentiments to prevail and objectifies immigrant populations. Immigrants are thus made objects of discussion and debate, rather than being recognized as agentic subjects with inherent dignity and respect; their humanity, their bodies, their presence in the classroom is legitimately an open controversy (Dabach et al., 2018;

Monreal & McCorkle, 2021). The deficit-based curricular activities and racist sentiments were present in the schools in Denizen and the district failed to address them, often promoting and sustaining colorblindness at best and racial inequity and race-evasiveness at worst.

In addition to these examples of anti-immigrant sentiment in the Denizen schools, the school district woefully underserved immigrant students and their families, as well as Black families. Denizen County School District (DCSD) serves almost 50,000 students. DCSD serves 23,547 white students (47.1 percent of the student population), 19,536 Black students (39.1 percent), 4,692 Hispanic students (9.4 percent), 785 Asian students (1.6 percent), and other (2.8 percent). Additionally, 3,851 students are identified as English language learners, and 4,778 are identified as special education students. Geographically, the district spans 1,000 square miles and incorporates eighty-five schools across urban, suburban, and rural communities. Having studied how minoritized youth and communities struggle for equitable policies and practices by protesting the school board, I learned about the deeply rooted segregation and lack of equity in Title I schools in DCSD and witnessed how community members fought for equity in their schools to no avail. Community members have felt ignored and underserved in these schools for decades, and the lack of resources and investment by the district was evident at Denizen West and Citizen North, such as a lack of services for language learners and a quality curriculum. When I asked an educator who had worked for the district previously, she said:

> I think there is often this deficit mentality on the part of some teachers. Latino students are not necessarily looked at as bilingual or almost bilingual—their less-than-perfect English is seen as an impediment to good test scores. Not all teachers, but definitely some, and I know there are certain schools that keep ESOL students in the ESOL program even after they've tested out so that they don't "pull down" test scores. This is really reflective of how ESEA/NCLB [Elementary and Secondary Education Act (ESEA)/No Child Left Behind Act] has distorted things systematically. (Interview, April 2018)

The district's deficit perspectives toward the language learning population were commonly discussed among teachers at the schools. However, due to the broader racial inequality toward minoritized groups in the district, systemic change was a low priority. It was difficult to parse out perspectives toward Latinx immigrant and language learning students, so when I inquired with district employees about it I was met with ignorance. For example, in an interview with a district representative, he acknowledged these tensions and how limited services were available, noting: "My hands are tied," referring to limited movement on supporting, implementing, and tracking the effectiveness of language learning services. In the face of limited structural supports, teachers and advocates for undocumented students—especially the language learning newcomers—engaged in ad hoc advocacy and coordination, but all commented on the isolation they felt as educators (Rodriguez and McCorkle, 2019. Seeing what was happening in the schools, the lack of ESL classes at Denizen West, and the limited ESL classes at Citizen North, where language learners were often placed in Spanish-as-a-foreign language class, the systemic inequality was apparent. The inequities were structural and hindered the strong efforts by individual teachers and advocates who worked with immigrant and language learning youth. Educators like Ms. Madison tried to make sense of the larger racialized ideologies that perpetuated sustained inequality toward language learning undocumented Latinx immigrants. She explained:

> There is very much an emphasis on assimilation here, rather than embracing different cultures, exploring or learning about other cultures. In the South, the dominant culture/community in power does not make a big effort to reach out to the Latino community (except for money-making purposes), or even really acknowledge it as part of the city's identity. . . . There is fear on both parts concerning lack of knowledge of the other's language, and I think also on the part of Latinos because the large majority here are undocumented—they want to keep off the radar. (Interview, April 2018)

The schools were selected for their rising population of Latinx undocumented students in order to examine how they experience racism. Tables 4.1 and 4.2 provide snapshots of the student demographics at Citizen North and Denizen West, respectively. Citizen North witnessed the number of designated English language learners (ELLs) increase between 2015 and 2017 from approximately 100 to over 300, suggesting a significant number of immigrant youth entered the under-resourced school. There were limited services for them in the district. For instance, at Citizen North there was one beginner ESL teacher, one ESL coordinator, and two Spanish teachers—all of whom were interviewed during the study (Rodriguez et al., 2018). The newly arrived undocumented students were all placed in the beginner ESL classes. I observed that all sections taught by one ESL teacher. At Denizen West, there were no ESL classes. I was told by the youth and the community based organization (CBO) staff that an ESL teacher visited the school weekly, but in my three years at this school I never met her or saw her despite being there several times per week. When I interviewed the director of ESL for the school district in January 2016, a white male, he noted, "I am aware of the limited services, but my hands are tied," referring to the difficulty of broaching this subject with

Table 4.1
Citizen North High School Characteristics (2017)

Description	Urban; neighborhood school; Title I
Enrollment total; number of teachers	1,310; 88
5-year graduation rate	56.5%
Students with disabilities	13.1%
Poverty rate	81%
White	5%
African American	64%
Latinx*	10% (2014–2015), 18% (2015–2016); 30% (2016–2017)
Asian	1%
number of students labeled as English language learners	100 (2015); 140 (2016); 334 (2017)

*All recently arrived undocumented youth
Number of English as a Second Language teachers = 1; number of Spanish teachers that students were placed with after beginner ESL classes = 3 (the number increased slowly over time)

Table 4.2
Denizen West High School Characteristics (2017)

Description	Rural; neighborhood school; Title I
Enrollment total; number of teachers	313; 33
5-year graduation rate	72%
Students with disabilities	12%
Poverty rate	74%
White	10%
African American	66%
Latinx	24%
Asian	0%
Number of students labeled as English language learners	86 (2015); 90 (2016); 104 (2017)

Number of English as a Second Language teachers = 0

the school board. The legal violations that South Carolina counties and districts engage in have remained unpunished or are settled outside of court. These abysmal to nonexistent services for ELLs, except for the work of tireless advocates, were reported as civil rights violations by a female educator who had worked in the district for nearly a decade. There was also one bilingual parent advocate whom I interviewed, who supported nearly 400 Latino families in the school district by herself. By the conclusion of the study, she had been allowed to hire an assistant to help her travel to schools to translate for school staff and Latinx families.

"We should hear their stories and know their rights.": Responses to Racial Ignorance in Schools

Schools as Racialized Organizations

It is important to understand how racialization processes occur in organizations such as schools. Race can be studied as "the background in which organizations operate" (Ray, 2019, p. 29). Organizations are both constitutive of and constituting status quo racial hierarchies; they operate as meso-level racial structures that serve to decrease the agency of people of color and support the unequal distribution of social and material resources. In education, this reproduction of racial inequality has been widely noted (Conchas et al., 2020). Situated at the meso level, organizations affect and are affected by institutional policies at the macro level, (e.g., anti-immigrant state and local policies and laws such as 287[g]), and individual racial prejudice expressed at the micro level (i.e., the teacher-student interactions described below). As such, organizations occupy a central role in reproducing the social order and/or effecting social change. Thinking about schools as racial structures also operationalizes whiteness as a credential that grants access to resources, legitimizes racial hierarchies, and elevates white agency, which often restricts the ability of racially subordinate groups to exercise personal agency, especially when hierarchical relationships, such as those between students and teachers, are involved. Given that the teachers in these schools are mostly white and occupy the top of the racial hierarchy, organizational practices reproduce inequitable conditions. Examples of this were noted above at the level of the Denizen school district, but inequity also manifests at the two high schools through the lack of language learning services, low-quality curriculum, and under-resourced, segregated schools (Capps et al., 2005; Gándara, 2015; Orfield et al., 2014; Suárez-Orozco & Suárez-Orozco, 2001).

A final important component of racialized organizations is that such practices are carried out by actors in the school. Though the school climate certainly shapes Latinx undocumented students' experiences, the climate and organizational practices are informed by prejudices and racial attitudes expressed at the micro level through interactions between educators and students (Rodriguez, 2021). The rest of this chapter details the micro level, which forms a "racial substructure" (p. 33) where subconscious racial schemas composed of implicit biases, racialized emotions, and racial binary-based beliefs manifest.

I detail teacher-student interactions at each school, and then discuss examples of school-based racialization and how youth perceive and respond to it. I begin with teacher perspectives to illustrate how educators' racial attitudes in the form of explicitly racist comments and implicit deficit-based ideologies continued to racialize Latinx youth at these schools, and in their communities.

Educators' Racial Attitudes: Equity or . . .?

The empirical data reveal teachers' racialized and deficit-based ideologies and beliefs about immigrants. Research shows the importance of educators in the lives of immigrant youth as they navigate academics and social belonging in school (Stanton-Salazar, 1997, 2004, 2011; Valenzuela, 1999). Stanton-Salazar (1997, 2011) refers to these individuals as institutional agents. Organizationally, institutional agents are positioned within the school power structure such that they have the influence necessary to direct information and resources to the students who need it. For the undocumented youth in this study, school, and specifically institutional agents such as teachers, is the only potential place to seek support. Many youths in this study would bring immigration papers to school and ask teachers to interpret the meaning of the documents for them. While there were supportive teachers, particularly at Citizen North, many at Denizen West were less inclusive and more biased toward immigrant students. I share examples from Denizen West first, and then supportive examples from Citizen North, before detailing how youth responded.

Racial attitudes at the schools took different forms. I present examples through the narratives of the various teachers, examining teachers' deficit-based perspectives, which ranged from highly deficit-based (Mr. O'Donnell), to advocacy-oriented but holding false beliefs about immigrants (Ms. Madison), to caring and asset-based (Ms. Ava and Ms. Constance). See Table 4.3 for brief descriptions of each of the interview participants. Ms. Madison's comments appear in an earlier section of this chapter titled "The Denizen School District." This continuum of racial attitudes and perspectives offered by teachers reflects

Table 4.3
Participant (Educator) Characteristics

Participant	Race/Ethnicity; Gender	Languages Spoken	Years of Experience	Role	School Site
Ms. Madison	Caucasian; Female	English	10	Adult ESL director; District personnel	District
Ms. Ava	Puerto Rican; Female	Spanish/ English	15 (5 in the United States)	ESL teacher	Citizen North
Ms. Constance	Colombian; Female	Spanish/ English	15	ESL teacher and coordinator	Citizen North
Mr. O'Donnell	Caucasian; Male	English	5	Spanish teacher	Denizen West

the complexity of racialization in an anti-immigrant context, and how systems, structures, and ideologies trickle down into beliefs and (inter)actions.

Racial Attitudes and Processes at Denizen West

Mr. O'Donnell, a Spanish teacher, positions himself as an advocate for undocumented students. However, he displays ignorance regarding the challenges faced by undocumented migrant families in the United States and in the restrictive policy context of South Carolina in particular, attributing these structural constraints to individual failings. In accordance with a deficit-based perspective, this teacher claims that parents and families of undocumented students are "much less likely to try to get involved in [their] child's life as a student." Similarly, he places blame on ESL classes for Spanish speaking students' inability to learn English and reinforcing their tendency to "speak in [their] native language all day." He attributed this tendency to "Mexican students" (despite a diversity of Latinx identities at this school, including students from Honduras, Guatemala, El Salvador, and Ecuador), whose behavior he contrasted with a Brazilian student who, he asserted, does not engage in this particular habit and whom he referred to as a "naturally gifted child" (Interview, March 2018). Based on the example of this child, he advocated for a "sink or swim" approach regarding English language acquisition as opposed to the more gradual scaffolding-based approach used in ESL classes. He also applied this deficit thinking to the immigrant community in South Carolina at large: specifically, he suggested that the lack of access to resources and support systems can be attributed to members of the Latinx immigrant community not wanting to be "recognized" and not "seeking out services." As he put it, "these services just don't exist for them because they don't demand them"; consequently, he underscored, the discrimination they endure "is not intentional at all."

"If you want to be American, you need to speak English.": Assimilationist/Color-Evasiveness Perspectives

Mr. O'Donnell supported the view that immigrant students would have fewer problems at school if they learned English and assimilated better. For instance, when referencing ESL classes again, he made it a point to say that if Spanish speaking students continue to be allowed to speak in their native language, "What incentive do they have to learn English?" Moreover, he claimed that because the United States is a "multicolored society," the one element that binds all Americans together is the English language, concluding that "if you want to be an American, you need to speak English" (Interview, March 2018). He adopted an assimilationist stance, where if one is not completely Americanized and speaks English, then "you're not one of us." In addition to having a deficit-based perspective and promoting an assimilationist stance, this teacher grounded his beliefs in a color-evasive ideology (Annamma et al., 2017). When asked directly whether he saw race as a factor in school-based discrimination toward immigrant students, he insisted that it is "not race based at all," attributing structural discrimination to the unwillingness of the Latinx community to seek resources and assimilate. He also emphasized that students should not be placed in "categories" based on race or ethnic origin or "identified as other," validating the colorblind notion that any mention or connection to race is in itself racist and leading to a complete disregard of race as a contributor to structural inequality and injustice. While Mr. O'Donnell had the least inclusive attitude toward undocumented language learning students, his beliefs were also reflected in the survey data (N = 101) of public-school teachers in the state, reflecting the larger anti-immigrant, deficit-based ideologies that are perpetuated at the macro-policy level that trickle down into schools and interactions.

"We should hear their stories and know their rights.": Racial Attitudes and Processes at Citizen North

Despite the inequitable education and exclusion that language learning undocumented students faced in Denizen, Citizen North educators such as Ms. Ava were aware of legal entitlements and accommodations for English language learners, and they commented on the neglect of the school district and schools. Ms. Ava was one of the first teachers I met at Citizen North. She was the beginning ESL teacher, and received all of the newcomers in her classroom. I observed her morning classes, and often would witness new students arriving each week. The youth referred to her as "madre." She was a bilingual teacher from Puerto Rico. Though new to Citizen North when I began the study, she had been an educator in Puerto Rico about a decade. Immediately, she explained that understanding her students and what challenges they endure is critical to their belonging and her ability to advocate for them despite the limited resources at Citizen North. She explained:

> Some teachers have really negative comments about immigration and how we need to stop letting immigrants in. I don't know what can be done to remove blinders from teachers; school leaders are aware of this; teachers refuse to acknowledge the trauma that some of our recently arrived students have faced. We should hear their stories and know their rights. (Interview, January 2017)

In addition to discussing the discrimination, racism, and ignorance of school-based personnel and teachers, Ms. Ava explained that part of teacher empathy toward their students is "hearing their stories," including the trauma some of her students have faced during their migration journeys to the United States. She described a story of one student who would just start crying because she had been "horrendously raped by multiple people coming through the border." Ms. Ava explained that the girl was cutting herself and missing school. She said, "The way I can describe it is that her soul was broken, so how can she learn?" When describing this story, Ms. Ava's voice cracked. She went on to say, "As a teacher, I think about how to feel informed about these 'taboo' things that the youth experience." She commented on how important it is for her to "hear their stories," noting that "through dialogue there are opportunities for students to feel at ease."

Similarly, Ms. Constance, another ESL teacher who was bilingual in Spanish and English, explained that there was no formal ESOL program for the students. "So, I just made one," she recalled. Given that all of the students at Citizen North were recently arrived newcomers (within the last year, with many arriving by the day and week while I observed), she noticed that students commonly experience the following things: "They feel isolated and alone; they may have had lack of formal school or no schooling; they do not always know their rights once they arrive, which results in deportations of themselves, their friends, or family member[s]." She explained that often when students arrive, "the first thing they need is to receive information related to rights once they are here because ICE is going to job sites of their family or networks, or the apartments where they live" (Interview, February 2016). Ms. Constance took it upon herself to organize Saturday workshops with attorneys to provide youth at the school with assistance and to ensure she had the knowledge and resources to help students, especially given the influx during the years of the study.

In this way, Ava's and Constance's racial attitudes helped students as they understood their positioning in the school as language learners with limited resources. More importantly, they learned of and understood the trauma that many brought with them as migrant students. Because they had a deeper understanding of the systemic racial oppression in the district and schools, and were aware of other teachers' biased attitudes, they were able to provide critical support for students. Though often limited, racialization processes, including understanding one's racial positioning in the school, can promote equity or reproduce inequality. Despite Ms. Ava and Ms. Constance's efforts, the larger meso-organizational racialization, including systemic exclusion and isolation at Citizen North, ensured inequality was reproduced for undocumented language learning youth. The burden to serve these students fell on the shoulders of individual educators who participated in ad hoc advocacy, which I found consistent with other schools in the state serving Latinx undocumented students who were still learning English (Rodriguez & McCorkle, 2019). Although these two educators exhibited care and policy awareness about issues related to immigration and undocumented students, similar to individuals at Denizen West, survey data from 101 public school teachers across the state revealed a common embrace of false narratives about immigrants and a lack of overall awareness of policies impacting undocumented students. The results of the survey regarding teachers' awareness showed a significant lack of policy

Table 4.4

South Carolina Teachers' Awareness of Immigration Restrictions

Question	False (Correct Answer)	True (Incorrect Answer)	I have no idea
Student should receive in-state tuition regardless of immigration status	25.7% (26)	25.7% (26)	48.5% (49)
Students are allowed to enroll in state colleges and universities regardless of immigration status	22.8% (23)	47.5% (48)	29.7% (30)
All students with legal visas can receive in-state tuition	9% (9)	64.4% (65)	26.6% (27)
Immigration status of one's parents affects in-state tuition	9.9% (10)	61.4% (62)	26.7% (28)

* Some totals do not equal 100 due to missing data.

knowledge among public school teachers in the sample. This unawareness was apparent in all of the first section's items, with an overall mean score of 16.85 out of 100 across the four questions (Rodriguez & McCorkle, 2019). This means that teachers selected the wrong answer most of the time. Table 4.4 shows that many respondents selected wrong answers on items related to specific policies that impact college access and eligibility for in-state tuition for undocumented students. There were also two questions about the restrictions for in-state tuition for U.S. citizens with undocumented parents and students on certain legal visas (such as the U visa for victims of domestic violence or other nonimmigrant visas). Both of these groups of students have also been denied in-state tuition in the State of South Carolina. Overall, none of the items in the first section showed an awareness level above 26 percent.

Moreover, the lowest levels of awareness were on the items regarding the eligibility of U.S. citizens with undocumented parents and students with certain legal visas to obtain in-state tuition. Aside from the question on in-state tuition for undocumented students, teachers most frequently selected the wrong choice (as compared to the correct response or the "I have no idea" option). The majority of respondents believed that South Carolina's policies are more inclusive toward immigrant students than they actually are. This lack of awareness is a barrier to teachers' empathy development because if teachers hold inaccurate beliefs about the policies impacting undocumented students, then their advocacy efforts will be distorted or nonexistent. Lack of awareness can also prevent teachers from gaining a sociopolitical consciousness if they already believe they are aware, which is indicated by the fact that they chose the wrong answer more frequently than selecting "I have no idea." This lack of awareness of immigration restrictions in the state as demonstrated in this survey presents significant barriers for undocumented students (Rodriguez & McCorkle, 2019, 2020).

Undocumented Youths' Responses to Racial Ignorance in Schools

Ms. Ava and Ms. Constance, both ESL teachers at Citizen North, were central to the youths' sense of belonging. Belonging research in education and the social sciences shows that young people need to feel validated and respected (Goodenow, 1993). Much attention has linked belonging with positive academic outcomes. Moreover, sociological research about social belonging points to the importance of relationships and critical "institutional agents," or adults in schools that help youth navigate school, access resources, or provide a sense of trust or someone to turn to if they have a social, personal, or academic problem (Rodriguez, 2023; Stanton-Salazar, 2001, 2004). Educators like the ones I observed were critical to providing instructional spaces, but more importantly, they cultivated a sense of home and inclusion in their schools and in this Southern community. Not only did they provide a safe space for youth, but the youth in their class also recognized their caring and sociopolitical awareness of policies impacting them. Juan, an undocumented newcomer from El Salvador and a student in Ms. Ava's class, explained the low quality of his educational experience at Citizen North.

> Everybody assumes we don't know anything or that we can't doing anything. That's ignorance. That is ignorance about Hispanics. I believe education is about awakening the mind. But, the education in this school is easy. They really don't have us do anything. Some teachers help, but in Algebra or Biology [*pauses*], they talk fast and ignore us. In Ms. Ava's class we learn English but we also talk about ideas.

Juan speaks to the broader issues of educational inequity he and his peers face. At best, the teachers talk too fast for them in the school, where there is limited to no English as a second language (ESL) support, and at worst, the students are socially isolated and ignored. Many schools and teachers, particularly in new immigrant destinations, are unprepared to work with their changing student populations (Hamann et al., 2015), and there is a real danger that teachers and administrators will perpetuate inequality either through ignorance or low expectations.

Ignorance, Racial Ascription, and Identity Challenges for Youth

Youth make sense of their identity in relation to how they are perceived or racialized in schools. Many of the youths' shared how their sense of identity is shaped by the school environment and teachers' racialization of them. I found variation across the sites in how youth perceived their identity in relation to how schools and teachers racialized them. Juan felt he had to prove himself in the school because teachers assumed he did not know "anything," since he was Spanish dominant and in language learning classes. He discussed the difference between his school education and family education (*educación*; Valenzuela, 1999). Juan explained family or cultural knowledge as the values you learn to be a kind and good person. Schools do not acknowledge or reward this *educación* that he had learned in his home country of El Salvador, and they did not necessarily see his cultural knowledge as an asset. He and many of the other youth felt valued and intellectually challenged in the ESL classroom, but not often in the broader school. The position of undocumented youth like Juan as racialized and deemed inferior or less than due to white "ignorance" is common in Latinx communities, especially in the South (Villenas, 2001). Villenas's research with undocumented Latina mothers in North Carolina showed how they built *comunidad* among each other and revealed their "educated identities" as part of claiming their dignity and values. Similarly, Juan's noting here of the "ignorance" of many teachers and the school generally is a move toward claiming dignity.

The newly arrived students were more impressionable and subject to internalizing the dominant beliefs in the schools and often associated their Spanish-dominance with a "lack of self-esteem," as one youth named Katarina explained to me during a small group discussion in Ms. Ava's class. It was common at Citizen North to hear the immigrant American dream narrative among teachers. Youth said that teachers would say, "You're here for a better life; it's better in America" and would make assumptions about youths' views of coming to America. Many reported that they came for economic or family reasons, but still had complicated views given their migration experiences and the lack of opportunities for schooling beyond high school in South Carolina. Youth also shared that these "better life" narratives were detrimental because they were figuring out how to fit into school and the larger anti-immigrant context. Promoting the idea that immigrant youth should do well in school to pursue the American dream sustained meritocratic notions on which the American dream is premised, which, in turn, leads to developing deficit perspectives and racializing other racial groups.

As immigrant youth are pushed to do well in school and belong according to the norms of membership to the school through compliance, integration, and assimilation, they in many cases began to question the ideologies underlying these narratives of a better life, given their liminal legal status and limits on their postsecondary opportunities. School settings like Citizen North maintain certain systems of knowledge and preferred norms about doing well in school. Yet the youth in the study perceive that teachers and school personnel are not culturally competent and fail to understand their migration journeys and the lived effects of harmful immigration policies. Youth do not see many teachers and school personnel, with exceptions like Ms. Ava, as effective institutional agents because these educators have deficit views of youths' ability and potential. Instead of the broader school community working to construct a supportive environment for them, the efforts fall on the shoulders of a few advocates like Ms. Ava. Many scholars fail to account for this, instead focusing on how students do not integrate or belong. The undocumented youth here show us how schools ought to respond to them through their critical consciousness. Youth can form bonds with some educators and build trust or *confianza*. These analyses are similar to a body of research that spells out school failure (including dropping out), whether this be in a working-class neighborhood outside of London, or schools in a *favela* outside of Rio de Janeiro. Listening to youth experiences as a starting point for improving school climate is needed. Even with trusted adults like Ms. Ava or Ms. Constance, youth deserve more holistic and systemic supports.

In contrast, for undocumented youth who had lived in the community since childhood, mostly attending Denizen West, identity formation was a more complex process as it involved conflicting and competing views toward immigrants in their school. The dominant deficit perceptions of immigrants promoted in K–12 educational settings and in society at large clash with youths' perspectives of themselves. In this case, dominant, deficit-based perspectives promoted in K–12 educational settings clash with youth perspectives. Youth are entangled in the racial social structure and attitudes in schools but come to understand their immigrant identity as a positive thing in the face of negative racialization. This latter group more regularly expressed awareness of systemic and structural injustice and how they shape immigrant experiences. Both groups of immigrant youth are subjected to processes of racialization by school actors and social institutions, including law enforcement officials and personnel from immigration enforcement agencies. Finally, youth identity formation is shaped by status and early exposure to experiences of illegality, or experiential illegality (Gonzales, 2016; Willen, 2007), drawn from the physical and emotional toll accrued from trying to lead meaningful lives while in the shadows.

Undocumented Latinx Youths' Racial/Ethnic Identification as a Form of Resistance to Racialization

It was important to the youth to carve out their own racial/ethnic identity. As youth named their identities, they exploited racial ignorance, racialization, and educator assumptions about their identity. In some cases, the youth internalized the racialization of their personhood. The effects of this were that some youth felt isolated in school, while others internalized individualistic perspectives about merit and getting ahead in school to survive and access educational resources. For instance, a youth named Alicia was frustrated during a conversation in Cookie's office one day. Her family was undocumented and she had to move several times and often observed the mistreatment of her family members in the community as they were racially profiled and criminalized. She said: "Anybody from a Hispanic background, works as hard as other people, but like they come to America either for family, a better life maybe, not even that some people not everybody is good, so that is why I am saying you can't put everyone in the same category." Alicia points out the underlying processes here of being labeled (racialized as) Hispanic, working as hard as other people (the normative center of hard-working American), and put into a category (a problem—racially categorized as different). She constantly struggled, wanting to do well in school and be understood while observing her family navigate their immigration status and Mexican identity in the community. Of note, Alicia was a strong student but questioned the narratives of merit given that she felt "stuck" and had limited mobility due to her family's immigration status. Her internalization of both the tropes of merit and the pride she had in her family and her immigrant background were ongoing.

Another youth commented on the struggle of identity as an adolescent in general. The challenge of grappling with identity was amplified due to being an immigrant and undocumented. One student shared: "I have been struggling a lot with who I am. . . . The undocumenteds give the Latinos a bad name sometimes. I am undocumented so I don't deny that. It is part of who I am . . . I just never wanted to be *estereotipado* [stereotyped]." Her reflection on her status as a significant marker for her shows how being racialized as Latinx intersects with the "problem" of being undocumented. She went on to describe how policymakers and educators do not always consider the effects on identity development. In many cases youth strongly identified with their Latinx identity but felt that it was undervalued in the school and community space.

Next, I describe how youth self-identified. I provide an overview of participants' responses during interviews to provide a snapshot of youth comments on identity and how they see themselves in relation to how they are racialized in the United States and in school and community contexts. This section directly links with the framework of racialization, specifically showcasing how youth self-identify in relation to the racialized Latinx/Hispanic identities available to them. Central to this self-identification is the background of criminalization, restrictive state policies, and school context. Following this summary table, I delve deeper into youth perspectives by providing a concrete example of how the undocumented youth reject the racialization process. They articulate racial and ethnic identities primarily in relation to immigration status and language use.

Table 4.5 illustrates youth articulations of their racial/ethnic identities, which are complicated and intersect with how Latinx groups are racialized (Cobas et al. 2015; Telles 2018; Vargas et al., 2017). Gabby's comment, for instance, illustrates her awareness of how being born at the border places her on a trajectory that will include barriers to her mobility. She s, "I was born at

Table 4.5

Participant Characteristics and Articulations of Racial/Ethnic Identity Dynamics

Student*	Country of origin/language status	Years in the U.S. (as of 2015)/Age arrived	Site	Racial/ethnic identity dynamics
Gabby	Mexico/Native Spanish and English	14/1	Denizen West	When I learned I wasn't born here, I was like, why didn't you just decide to have me here right like outside the border so I could have an American identity? But my mom crossed several times. I was born like at the border, but on the wrong side.
Emmy	Mexico/Native Spanish and English	6/7	Denizen West	I am Mexican. When I came here I was like freshly Mexican and still had my parents back in Mexico, so I didn't let go of that [part of her identity].
Eileen	Mexico/Native Spanish and English	13/4 or 5	Denizen West	I am always stuck. Kids at school would be like "You're not Mexican, you're white" because I spoke more English. Or, they would be like, "You're white, stop being Mexican." I am Mexican but I also look Asian, so I think I confuse people. Skin color doesn't mean nothing, you know? But with Hispanics, it means all this other stuff.
Pablo	Honduras/Native Spanish and English	13/4	Denizen West	I speak Spanish and like, I get pulled out of class all the time to translate for people in the front office. Like . . . [laughs]. It's not the only thing I am.
Amelia	Mexico/Native Spanish and English	12/5	Denizen West	I'm Mexican. I feel Mexican all the time. I speak with an accent so everyone knows it. The hard part is not all Mexicans and Latinos are undocumented but everybody thinks that. It's so ignorant.
Ana	Mexico/Native Spanish and English	12/5	Denizen West	I'm straight up Mexican. People think I'm Guatemalan 'cuz there are more of them here now, though.
Katerina	Honduras/Spanish dominant	Less than 1/16	Citizen North	I'm Honduran. Here, I am Hispanic or Mexican to people.
Juan	El Salvador/Spanish dominant	Less than 1/16	Citizen North	I'm from El Salvador, but I traveled for many months through Mexico and other places in the United States before coming to here, but I am Latino.
Bevvie	Guatemala/Spanish dominant	Less than 1/15	Citizen North	I am Latina and Guatemalan, but I am more Latina because I speak English.
Manny	Honduras/Spanish dominant	Less than 1/15	Citizen North	I'm from Honduras, but I am Latino, too.

*The students self-reported their racial/ethnic identity.

the border, like the wrong side of it," indicating that being non-American will be a challenge. Youth articulate their identity dynamics in relation to immigration status and broader migration patterns, with comments such as "being Hispanic means all this other stuff," and "people think I look Guatemalan because there's more of them here now." They also connected their identity to language use, for example when Bevvie says "I am more Latina [than Guatemalan] because I speak English." Lastly, how youth look/appear and what that means to the school or community played a role in forming their identities. Amelia explains, "The hard part is not all Mexicans and Latinos are undocumented, but everybody thinks that. It's so ignorant." In these expressions, youth demonstrate awareness of the tenuousness of racial/ethnic identities. This awareness and expression points to the ignorance and assumptions made by those they encounter in the United States (be it in school or society), which exemplifies racialization and how it informs their identity development. To extend this, Emmy's comment illustrates her awareness and expression of a Mexican identity. She elaborates:

> I see myself as Mexican 'cause I am Mexican. I also have to keep in mind where I come from. If they ask me where you from, I'm gonna say I'm from Mexico. I have to interact in English, but I also have to keep in mind where I am from. Trying to speak English makes me feel less Mexican. If I don't say who I am it makes me seem like I want to be something I'm not. But being Mexican is bad or being Latino. Everyone thinks we are job stealers, but we do the work here they don't want to do. (Interview, May 17, 2018)

Emmy self-reports her identity in relation to her racialization based on her non-whiteness and language differences. In doing so, she complicates the broad generalizations about racial identity, and the essentialist ways people perceive and other individuals, whether through looks ("I look Hispanic or Asian, which confuses people"), being Hispanic ("which means other stuff" in the United States, as connected to the racialization process and racial categories of difference), or language use. In the case of Emmy, her preference to identify as Mexican is complicated by what that means in the U.S. South, and she expresses that she has to be "aware" of this, which enables her to provide a counternarrative to the dominant discourses about Mexican-ness, undocumented-ness, and/or Latino-ness in the context of the U.S. South, all of which are conflated as part of Latinx racialization. Counternarratives offer a resistance to racist attributions ascribed to youth.

Table 15 is intended to provide a snapshot of how youth self-identify and make sense of their identity in relation to how their school experiences assign meaning to their racial identities. Aligned with understanding the factors that influence their racialization and how they respond to it, I honor and privilege youth's self-reported identities throughout the study in relation to how they are racialized in school and the Denizen community.

Much like the youth above, additional participants felt marginalized or targeted due to their skin color, which is a component of how groups are racially classified both in society broadly and in school settings more specifically. For example, Alicia expressed her frustration that even when immigrants are "checking all the boxes" and striving to provide for their families and set a good example, they remain targeted by immigration authorities. She concluded that hostility toward immigrants stems from racism, or as she puts it, "other[ing] them because of their skin color." Alicia also noted that immigrant identity often becomes conflated with Latinx identity, and specifically Latinx illegality. "Even if you're from Europe or somewhere . . . you get the assumption that that [immigrant] person only represents the Mexican undocumented community."

The conflation of immigrant identity with illegality, in South Carolina and in other parts of the country in media and political discourse, is significant as it provides the foundation for criminalizing immigrants, or crimmigration (Jones, 2019). Another youth, Adalia, equated her experiences of racialization in school to microaggressions—normalized everyday actions that have negative effects on minoritized groups—which she saw as rooted in systemic racism (Bonilla-Silva, 2019). She said: "There's a lot of like, passive-aggressive, like, institutional racism. Like, it was really hard for me to realize it. Like, even in AP classes, sometimes I felt like you weren't, like, good enough."

By referring to resultant feelings of inadequacy, Adalia pointed to the insidious nature of covert racism premised on individualism and causing racialized subjects to feel that their obstacles to success are self-generated rather than structural. She added that teachers, even those with good intentions early on, "give up after a while." Juan, an El Salvadoran youth, also noted that one of the ESL teachers in his class "helps everyone but she doesn't help me." Students such as Adalia were also implicated in racializing others, specifically, Adalia referred to "white students [who] think they are better." These interactions and perceptions youth have of how they are viewed and/or "helped" in classes reveal the racial dynamics in their schools. Whether intentional or not, these instances are examples of racial microaggressions that communicate "hostile, derogatory, or negative racial slights and insults" to a person or group (Ballinas, 2022; Rodriguez & Conchas, 2022; Sue et al., 2007, p. 273).

Educational settings that promote dominant cultural perspectives, center whiteness, and devalue immigrant youths' racial/ethnic backgrounds can leave some of them with psychological injuries that affect their academic progress in school. For instance, youth can internalize subtle demeaning messages lodged in deficit-based discourses used by teachers and school personnel (Valencia, 2010). Sue and colleagues (2007) explain that racialization and microaggressions can be "microinsults or subtle but insensitive and rude snubs degrading a person's racial identity or heritage microinvalidations or comments that exclude or nullify a person of color's experiences and thoughts" (p. 274). With regard to Latinx undocumented youth, Ballinas (2022) shows that Latinx youth face perceptions of foreignness and are assumed to be less intelligent than whites are. More specifically, Ballinas (2017) found that Mexican students encountered white racial framing and microaggressions in both high school and college, which involved questioning their academic abilities and citizenship status.

In some instances, youth responses to how they were racialized and positioned in their schools led them to internalize individualistic and colorblind meritocratic values. For example, Juan viewed education as a means to combat ignorance even while he was confronting it at Citizen North. He associated ignorance with poverty, stating that "ignorance is because of poverty." He subscribed to a view reflecting the "culture of poverty" perspective, where poverty is framed as the result of individual actions and failures. This phrase has its origins in the work of anthropologist Oscar Lewis (1964). He stated that "people are poor because they want to be," adding: "If someone honestly decides to study . . . they'll come out ahead. Even though they have to walk through any place, they will achieve it."

Juan endured a traumatic experience of multiple attempts crossing the border. He spoke of how his father saved and spent every dollar the family had on getting Juan to the United from El Salvador. He traveled with a coyote, face down in the bed of a truck under a pile of other humans. He described the horrific conditions he endured as a young adolescent. His journey to the United States was built upon the belief that working hard and enduring hardship would lead to a "better life," as he explained. His experience of being ignored in school or thought to be low-skilled motivated him to embrace American meritocratic values—that social mobility was possible as long as you pushed through and worked hard. This bootstraps narrative aligns with a worldview where victims of injustice are blamed for their misfortunes, and ignores the structural components of injustice. Stanton-Salazar (1997) argues that "ideological individualism," such as the beliefs Juan exhibits due to his positioning as an immigrant, thwarts the development of critical consciousness.[1] As Juan further explained, "If one is ignorant in the form of 'I don't believe, I can't do it,' that will never let one to be prosperous." In line with American ideological principles, success is connected to effort and hard work, and is defined in terms of the material wealth one accumulates. These notions are reinforced through the school social structure, where English language learning newcomers like Juan are placed in lower-level courses and receive little academic support or access to quality curriculum unless one merits it by demonstrating exceptional ability.

Adalia's commentary also revealed the importance of proving to be academically and behaviorally exceptional in school, to distinguish herself and get ahead. "I had the goal of going to college ,so I guess in a way I like proved myself to teachers that I was like an exception." To "prove herself" as worthy or deserving of praise, attention, and resources is a key aspect of Latinx immigrant youth racialization. Negrón-Gonzales et al. (2015) explain that deservingness is the rubric by which society determines the worthiness of immigrants to access basic human rights; it is a process with roots in decades past, part of an ongoing effort to further re-entrench borders both literal and figurative (pp. 1–2). The problem with such meritocratic beliefs is that they obscure that academic achievement is also associated with a strong academic support system and caring teachers, both of which are the responsibility of the school. The burden instead falls upon the youth.

Internalizing fictional meritocratic ideals and taking on the ideological individualism of "proving oneself" results in some youth, such as Juan, adopting deficit-based perspectives regarding other racial groups. For instance, Jonathan referred to the "ignorance of Blacks" and noted their affinity for "fighting" and "money," adding that the "majority of them stay poor because they are ignorant." While being a subject of racialization by his white classmates and teachers, Juan engaged in racializing Black students by internalizing not only the ideological premises of the American dream, but also the racial hierarchy of the United States, which relegates Blacks to the bottom tier of the racial order (Omi & Winant, 2014). Juan's racialization of his Black classmates may have been an attempt to resist his own racialization and subconsciously elevate his status. This occurred despite evidence that Black and Latinx individuals generally view race relations between their groups positively, even as they often compete for limited resources (McDermott, 2011; Telles et al., 2011). Juan reveals complex views about his own racial isolation, migration journey, and perceptions of the academic, social, and racial hierarchies at Citizen North. "I am alone here, it's Latinos and others, and we are isolated at school, but what am I going to do? I can't go back. I thought about that many times while crossing the river, praying to God, what am I to do? I can't go back."

"They let you back in the country.": Youths' Perspectives on School-Based Racialization

As youth recalled their perception of their identity in relation to how they were racialized, they reported many instances of the ignorance and racialization above at both schools. In addition, the undocumented youth in this study were subject to racial attitudes, ignorance, and ideologies through the implicit and explicit, racially charged language of teachers in the Denizen schools. As seen above, the variation in teacher perspectives, including knowledge about undocumented experiences, deficit-based thinking, color-evasiveness, and the belief in false narratives about labor opportunity and social mobility, impacts undocumented youth's ability to form trusting relationships with teachers and long-term bonds and social supports that could help youth integrate into school and feel a sense of belonging as well as pursue aspirations. Youth perspectives are provided to show how the above meso- and micro-level structural inequities and racial prejudice and attitudes are detrimental to undocumented youth belonging.

Youth experiences of racialization in teacher-student interactions were rampant in the Denizen community and schools throughout the study. While the anti-immigrant rhetoric and political actions of the Trump administration seemed to heighten these sentiments, in the South, discrimination, racism, and anti-immigrant sentiments pervade state policy discourses and enactments (Rodriguez, 2018a; Rodriguez & Monreal, 2017). Amelia described an encounter between another student and a white teacher at Denizen West:

> The teacher kept telling the student to sit down and stop talking. This was a student who wasn't born here, too. Maria said, "I will do it, just chill." The teacher got upset and said, "That is why they are building a . . ." She didn't finish the sentence, but it was obvious what she was trying to say. The student said, "Finish what you were gonna say."

The youth commented on how these experiences at Denizen West were due to White teachers' "lack of exposure" to "the experiences of non-white races." Such lack of exposure, they believed, resulted in "ignorant" comments about Latinx youth. The "ignorance" of white teachers the youths referred to was a generous characterization—a point I return to later in the chapter. These examples reflect the mechanisms of racialization in the school setting—that is, the actions, speeches, practices, or strategies used by an individual or a group in a position of power and authority (adults/teachers) that are used to mistreat, exclude, marginalize, or disadvantage an individual that is identified as a member of a racialized group in society.

Pablo and Amelia told a story of a Latino student at Denizen West returning to school from Mexico as an example of racialization of Latinx youth and the racial attitudes of the white teacher.

> PABLO A kid returned from visiting Mexico, he's a U.S. citizen by the way, and the teacher said, "They let you back in?" in front of the class. Amelia was like, "What did you say [to the teacher]?" The teacher said, "You know how Muslims are not let back into the country under Trump?"
>
> AMELIA We were like, "Whaaattt!" This is the problem. You will never know what it's like to have to forget WHO YOU ARE or defend WHO YOU ARE because of the COLOR of your SKIN" (emphasis added to indicate raised voices)

In both of these examples, the youth describe encounters with teachers that point to their lack of awareness, showing how racialization operates at school, where assumptions about who they are as Latinx youth are rampant. These assumptions are then conflated with other racialized groups, in this case, Muslims. Considering the concept of racialization provides an important perspective for thinking about racialized organizations and provides the context in which "racialized groups" are created (Hochman, 2019, p. 1245). The example here speaks to the racialization of Muslims post-9/11 in the United States (Rana, 2011; Sriram, 2016). While it is uncommon for Muslims to be referred to as a racial group or to hear the use of the term *Muslim race*, a Muslim identity nevertheless has meaning beyond a religious group in U.S. society and is undergoing racialization. In both examples, regardless of whether the teacher knew the student's immigration status, they assumed things about the students based on their racial attitudes; one teacher associated "building a _____" with the Latinx student and the other referred to "letting you back in" [to the country] when talking with another Latinx student.

Another example of how racialization is enacted in schools occurred when Bevvie, an undocumented youth at Citizen North, described how being Hispanic and a Spanish-dominant language speaker impacted her experiences at school. Specifically, her interactions with non-ESL teachers isolated her. "It's very *preoccupado* or *ansioso* when I am the only non-English speaker. The teacher only explains in English. Tests is English. It's like she doesn't know we're there." These sentiments were common among the Citizen North students because they were Spanish-dominant in a school that had two bilingual Latinx teachers, Ms. Ava and Ms. Constance, and then white Spanish-as-foreign-language teachers. They had limited language services and felt connected with Ms. Ava in the ESL classroom but rarely integrated in the rest of the school context. Manny articulated that he "didn't feel normal because I'm here without papers," referring to his undocumented status and how it weighs on his mind at school. He said, "I break the law everyday driving my cousin to work and we hide when ICE comes to the apartments." While he is referring to his larger racialized positioning in the community and his home, in school, he felt that these were additional things about him that made him abnormal, which was reinforced in school by feeling isolated in most of his classes.

Racial Ignorance in the Everyday Life of Schools

Racialization processes are infused in the core social structures of the schools that purport to serve undocumented and immigrant youth; these processes manifest the schools' power to undermine the development of these youth in multiple ways. Racialization is often the most virulent when it masks the most recognizable and palatable form of racism. The perniciousness of undercover racialization can be identified by the school district's unwillingness to critique and to consider the restructuring of a school environment that immigrant youth find profoundly alienating. The debilitating processes of racialization in the schooling experience occur through the school district's unwillingness to provide the educational services and supports students need, not only to survive the early stages of the settlement process, but also to thrive academically. The institutional culture of the district and school show an unwillingness to confront the cognitively harmful consequences of deficit-based teaching methods as well as forms of school organization that thwart teacher-student bonding and students' sense of safety and belonging. Research has documented how high schools serving students of color from working-class families have been able to radically reorganize the school environment to ensure the academic success and social development of all students (Mehan et al., 1996; Stanton-Salazar et al., 2000). In these schools, the multiplicity of social supports, asset-based pedagogies, and teacher-student relationships come together to make school success inevitable. Schools that produce the opposite effects are equally socially engineered but so as to reproduce class and racial inequality in society.

First, youth are racialized by educators, who position them as others, employing in many instances forms of racial ignorance. Second, youth respond to racialization by self-identification processes that further highlight racial ignorance and attitudes toward them. Yarbrough (2010) argues that "Racialization frameworks focus on the centrality of race in everyday life and demonstrate that individual's experiences are intricately connected to racial structures and their localized manifestations in the U.S." (p. 252). In many instances, these youth experience "differential racialization," which Pulido (2017) uses to describe how different groups are racialized differently based upon history, geography, and capital. This is important in the context of the South where, on the one hand, Latinos do not fit into the historical Jim Crow black-white racial binary. Instead, some teachers create the racial categories in the everyday life of the school to figure out where the Latinx groups fit into racial hierarchies. In addition to the historical and geographical aspects of racialization, we see teachers conflating all Latinx students, even those who are citizens, with being Mexican and undocumented, and as akin to the religious identity of Muslims. This conflation is explained by youth as "ignorance." The point here is to understand that it is racial ignorance, which whites leverage as a way of knowing and non-knowing, and it can be willful or blind (Mueller, 2020).

In the above example, racialization of youth occurs when the Mexican student is assumed to be undocumented ("They let you back in the country?") after a vacation he took with his family. Simultaneously, when youth confront the teacher, racial ignorance is further displayed when the teacher conflates being Mexican and potentially undocumented with being Muslim, which is also not a race. This teacher racializes and then leverages racial ignorance. Mueller (2020) argues that racial ignorance persists because of "white people's militant commitment to an epistemology of ignorance: a way of knowing oriented toward evading, mystifying, and obscuring the reality of racism to produce (mis)understandings useful for domination" (p. 147). This can be observed in the survey data, which showed the lack of awareness about policies impacting undocumented students and teachers' belief that South Carolina had more inclusive laws and policies toward immigrants than in reality. Mueller (2020) argues that "Engaging in a process of knowing designed to resist racial understanding, empathy, and moral responsibility is inevitably more demanding, given 'actual reality' diverges from 'officially sanctioned reality'" (Mills 1997, as cited in Mueller, 2020, p. 18). Additionally, "White ignorance requires real effort and dedication in a world saturated with evidence of racism and the suffering, counterdiscourse, and resistance of people of color" (Mueller, 2020, pp. 146–147). This ignorance was further exemplified when the district's ESL director told me "my hands are tied," referring to his perceived inability to support language learners in the district. At best, educators and district personnel exhibited ignorance about how resources were distributed and conflated racial attitudes and ideologies about racial groups.

White domination was perpetuated when teachers racialized youth as undocumented, Mexican, Hispanic, etc., and this impacted how youth identified racially and ethnically. Latinx racialization is particularly challenging to white domination because of the variation and diversity of Latinx groups. Yarbrough, in a study of Central American immigrants that learned to identify as Hispanic, a term that does not necessarily have meaning in their home country, found that they were commonly misidentified as Mexican, which "was integral to the daily negotiation of an imputed racialized Hispanic identity" (2010, p. 256). Stated differently, the researcher argued that "the recent nature of the demographic transformation coupled with the historical centrality of race in the everyday lives . . . constructs a situation where any Latino-identifying youth is racially marked as Hispanic or Latino in South Carolina and misidentified through other race-making and racial classification" (p. 258). In this way, white ignorance perpetuates racial identification and racialization through uncultured assumptions of social belonging, nationality, and citizenship of Latin American immigrants based primarily on phenotype, skin tone, and/or language/accent" (Yarbrough, 2010, p. 258). Further, Latinx youths' everyday identity experiences shift as they encounter the U.S. racial structure while in the contested spaces of schools. Additionally, Latinx youth identity is entangled with questions of citizenship. In other words, Latinx youth have "their political and cultural membership questioned [and are] positioned outside the boundaries that define who a citizen is and [who] an American [is]" (Flores-González 2017, p. 10). This is evidenced in one teacher's statement: "They [the U.S.] let you [otherized as non-American and non-citizen] back in?" *They* are otherized as noncitizen and non-American.

In this chapter, Latinx youth express their identities to show the ethnic diversity within *Latinidad*. However, there is frequent debate over whether Latino is an ethnic or racial category, as can be seen in discussions over how the term is used in the U.S. Census (Telles, 2018). Latino (or Hispanic), however, functions as a racial category in that race is, in large part, a category that is ascribed to people regardless of how they self-identify (Cobas et al., 2015; Vargas et al., 2016). So, Latino is a racial category because people ascribe to it a certain set of essentialized common traits. In this chapter, such traits are suspected and presumed to be "undocumented" or connected to outsider-ness and illegality. Latino as a racial category is also ascribed to individuals that are assumed to be nonwhite or not clearly African American, and this racial ascription has consequences. Similar to how the teacher referred to Muslim as if it were a racial category, making up racial categories is how white domination persists. Accordingly, Vargas and colleagues (2016) explain, "The notion that others may define one's race regardless of one's own identity is known as 'socially assigned race' or 'ascribed race,' and it has proved to be a very important measure in predicting the level of discrimination an individual will encounter as well as his or her health outcomes" (p. 500). These racial ascriptions enable Latinx groups to think of themselves in racial terms. For instance, "Social science research has found that cognitively, Hispanics consider Hispanic/Latino as both race and ethnicity and, racially, that Hispanic is a group separate and in addition to black, white, Asian, and American Indian" (Telles, 2018, p. 156). Although recent immigrants may identify more with their nationality (as was the case in this study—for example, "I am Mexican. I am Guatemalan."), later generations (e.g., the second and third generation) from Latin American countries identify as Hispanic or Latino (Perez & Hirschman, 2009). The example of Latinx racialization shows not only how racial formation is never absent from power negotiations but also how people are part of the meaning-making of that process.

Racialization processes are negotiated via day-to-day interactions over time. For example, Lewis (2003) argues that "Racial identities do not automatically follow from these early racial assignments. They take shape over time, through multiple interactions. We learn ways to categorize ourselves and others, what the available options and boundaries between categories are" (p. 6). This racial negotiation process can either reinscribe current racial classifications or challenge them. The data reflect this negotiation process for undocumented youth. Although newcomer immigrants arriving from Central and South America may identify, for example, with their nationality, they still navigate a society that racializes them as "Hispanic" in the South, and in schools and communities that assume they are all Mexican. Verma and colleagues (2017) call for examining racialization and immigrant youth and the factors that inform racialization, and the data shows grassroots-level factors that inform and perpetuate racialization, and youth responses. Specifically, this chapter examined youths' interactions with teachers and school-based personnel and the formal and informal school structures that classify youth in particular ways. Youth such as all newly arrived students were placed in ESL classrooms at Citizen North without formal assessments or were provided limited services at the school and district levels. Language learners at Denizen West received no services because the district ESL director claimed his "hands are tied"; that was his explanation for a lack of equitable services. Amidst these structural constraints to their accessing equitable education, youth made sense of their complicated racialized identities; such identities were entangled with race, ethnicity, and countries of origin, and conflated with their immigration status in South Carolina.

This chapter further explored the meso-organizational level of racialization by demonstrating Latinx undocumented youths' racial identification and racialization across two divergent schools and the larger racialization processes and racial attitudes in this school district. Additionally, this conceptual orientation offers an opportunity to examine the ethnographic evidence to understand how the undocumented Latinx youth in this study develop a racial consciousness and enact micro-level forms of resistance that target the organized structural hierarchies of race. From the data, I assert that their responses and self-identification processes are a form of everyday resistance to white domination and dominant deficit-based narratives enabled through white racial ignorance (Mueller, 2020; Scott, 1985); this resistance does not make headlines and is rarely dramatic. Their experiences shed light on the oppressive forces of racialization and racial dominance that impact their sense of belonging, and this has implications for educators and policymakers.

In the next chapter I expand on the racial categorization of undocumented Latinx immigrants, specifically how the concept of race is closely connected to modern conceptions of nation and citizenship, especially what I refer to as *racialized citizenship* (Abrego 2019; Carrillo & Rodriguez, 2016). Once again, I will utilize the micro-level interactions of youth to show how they contest normative categorizations of citizenship and illustrate how racialized citizenship is enacted through policies and laws, and to discuss how youth navigate these categories and lived realities.

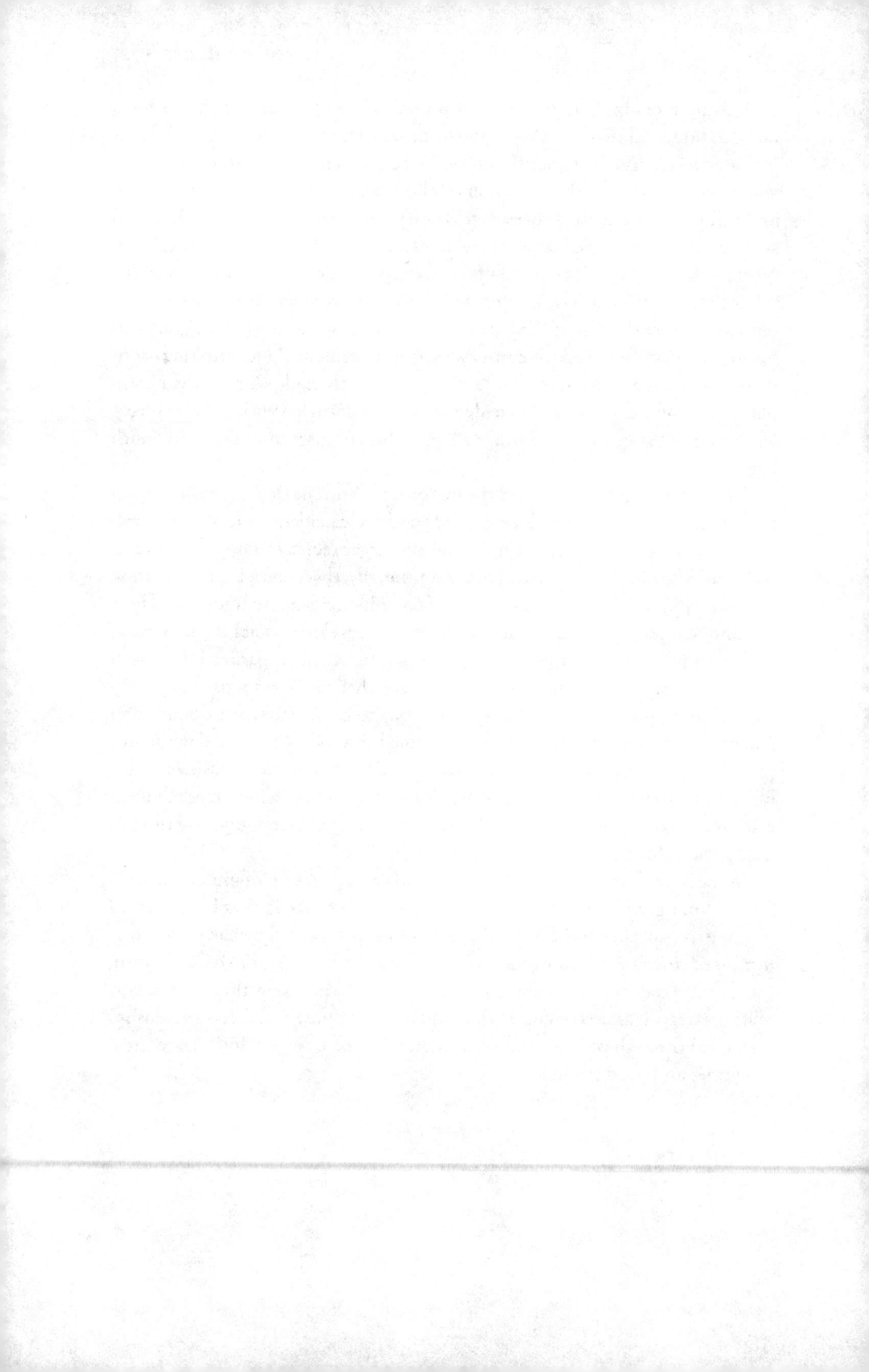

Part 3

Micro-Level Interactional Perspectives

●●●●●●●●●●●●●●●●●●●●●●

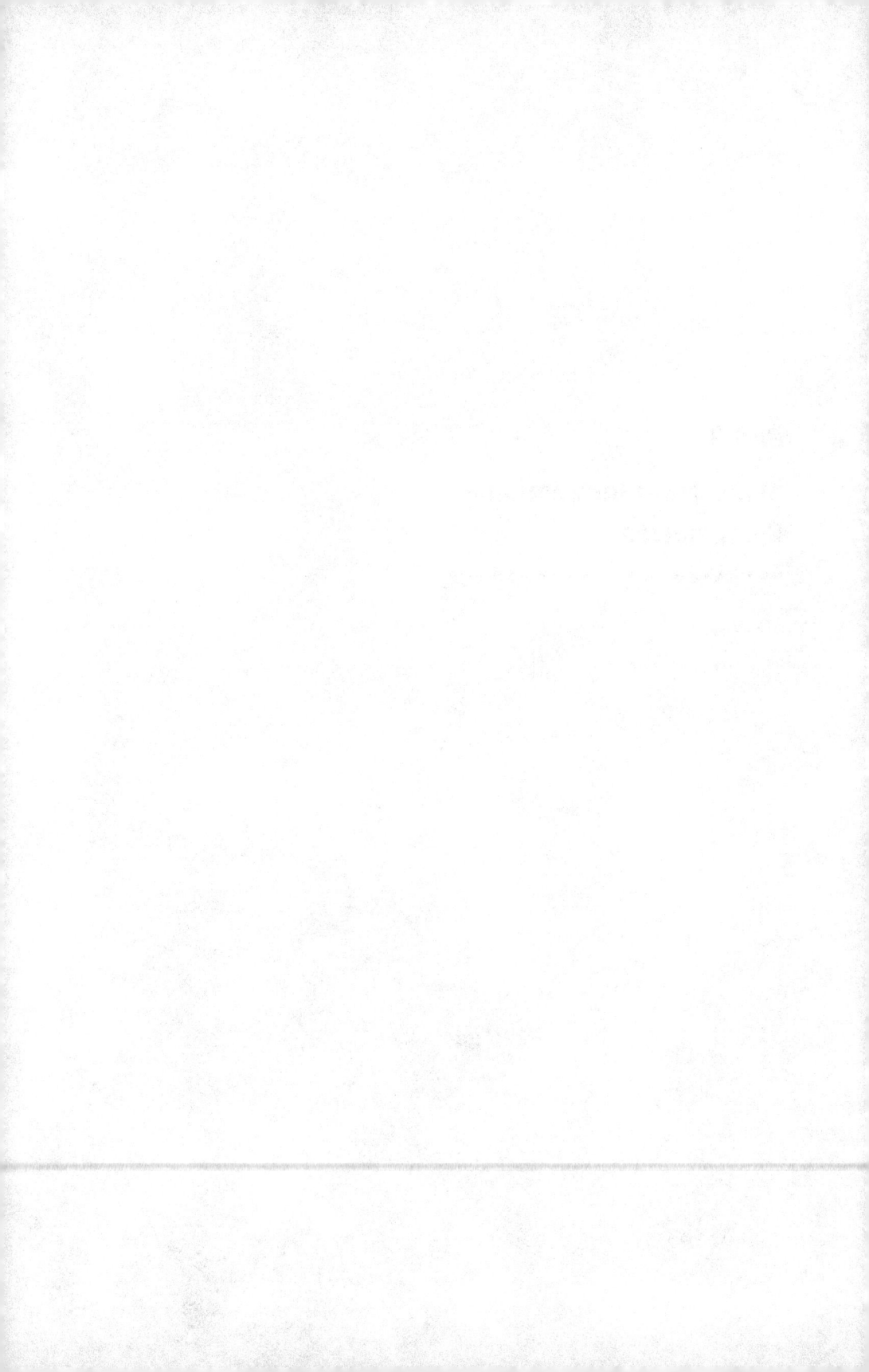

5

"Even being a citizen is not a privilege if you're Hispanic here."

• •

Undocumented Youths'
Perceptions of Racialized
Citizenship

> Citizenship? It's about rights, yeah. But,
> it's also about how hard immigrants
> work. We deserve more than we have.
> —Gabby, undocumented youth,
>   April 2016

I spoke with Gabby in Cookie's (the school social worker's) office, which I visited every day during the initial months of fieldwork. Gabby told me that she wanted to learn about "immigration policies" in order to "help my family with legal struggles" and to try to prevent those all-too-common situations when "immigration knocks at the door." Gabby's story of "trying to understand all the paperwork" and the "lawyers and ICE constantly on us" was common in the undocumented community during my time there. It was in Cookie's office that I learned about the various encounters with local law enforcement, the racialized profiling of ICE in the community, the individual-communal struggles of the Latinx undocumented community, and how youth like Gabby learn to navigate racism, discrimination, and the limits of legal citizenship.

The U.S. political climate entails threats to the livelihood of immigrants, particularly those who are undocumented. During this study, the Trump administration's attempt to include a citizenship question in the 2020 Census presented one of the most recent racialized maneuvers threatening immigrants, particularly Latinx groups, by tying questions of citizenship with other law enforcement regimes, such as ICE. Despite U.S. District Judge George Hazel's comment that "the citizenship question was steeped in discriminatory motive," the Trump administration's attempt to count and classify citizenship was a breach of civil rights (Farias, 2019) that invoked fear across the undocumented community. Political attempts to target Latinx and other foreign-born groups in the 2020 census demonstrate the Trump administration's attempts to juridically encourage exclusionary practices that discriminate against minoritized groups. These forms of symbolic violence have real effects and are at the center of undocumented youths' efforts to belong in the United States. The Latinx youths' perceptions of citizenship and position in school and society are intimately tied to U.S. immigration patterns and histories of Jim Crow segregation in the South (Brown et al., 2018; Guerrero, 2017), and reveal how citizenship has been racialized in the United States (FitzGerald, 2017; Molina, 2014). Additionally, Latinx groups are criminalized and face limited economic and educational opportunities and restricted pathways to citizenship.

This chapter centers youth experiences that disrupt the dominant threatening ideologies and scripts governing U.S. political rhetoric, anti-immigrant policies, and normative conceptions of citizenship. Illustrating my Multilevel Racialization Framework, youth in this study depict the micro-level interactions that expose power and race relations. These dynamics perpetuate a racialized anti-immigrant context and compress immigrants' lives in educational and social spheres. Yet, youth perspectives and activism reveal the relational, institutional, and resistive dimensions of what I refer to as racialized citizenship. Youth contest the boundaries of citizenship, offering alternative, grassroots discourses and practices of citizenship. I show how, on the one hand, undocumented youth are positioned as illegal, meaning outside the normative bounds of citizenship, and are thus made into objects of intervention (e.g., through racial profiling and surveillance from ICE; Arriaga, 2017). On the other hand, they are subject to the racialized logic about Latinx populations in the South, a logic that argues that all Latinx individuals are somehow a threat to the social fabric of society. I provide insight into how youth navigate racialization and perceive citizenship, and how their everyday lives contest traditional, normative views of citizenship as legal/illegal, expanding the boundaries of what citizenship means through thick descriptions of school-based and community-level examples. By centering youth, I expand upon the notion of racialized citizenship, which is grounded in youth experiences and argues that deeper racial meanings and hierarchies undergird categories of citizenship. As part of the larger arc of this book, racialization manifests in conceptions of citizenship and practices that sustain normative (white) institutional views of it.

I assert that citizenship is a racialized category. This critical perspective allows us to exploit how—as a normative, juridical category—citizenship (status) becomes a way to create webs of surveillance over the undocumented Latinx immigrant community and extend the reach of immigration enforcement. The undocumented youths' perceptions of the category of citizenship function as a form of resistance in response to their racialized positioning as other and noncitizen. The context of immigrant criminalization, including racist policies and law enforcement actions, shapes the contexts of reception, impacting migrant mobility. These criminalizing forces leverage normative discourses of citizenship, including the category of legal/illegal, without accounting for the economic contributions of undocumented immigrants and the benefits they bring to the United States.

Citizenship: "It's about rights. But we don't have papers."

Intertwined with undocumented youths' perceptions of citizenship are the mechanisms that reinforce juridical citizenship, such as immigration customs and enforcement. As I tried to make sense of how youth perceived citizenship, youth began interviews and focus groups with their migration stories, first with their encounters with immigration enforcement at the border and then later in the Denizen community. In interviews I asked youth about what came to mind when they heard the word *citizenship*. A few responded:

ALEXA Citizenship, it's about rights. But some Latinos have papers. We don't. My dad has been deported a few times.

MANNY I am *sin papeles*. So, I break the law every day to drive to work.

ALEXA They made the law about an officer being able to walk up and just ask you for ID and don't even have to have a reason. . . . [My dad] could not be doing anything wrong, he could be out in the field working, making a way for us to have what we need, and a cop could be like "Oh where is your ID, don't have one, what is your name?" And that is it, he gets deported. Automatically no if, and or buts.

Alexa's frustration was evident as she described her dad's experience of deportation and their family separation. She refers to the "show me your papers" laws and the cooperation between law enforcement and ICE in the Denizen community (Rodriguez & Monreal, 2017). Research shows that state policies restrict immigrant mobility and criminalize undocumented youth and families. In the South, South Carolina and Alabama are particularly anti-immigrant, akin to

Arizona's "show me your papers" law that racially profiles immigrants based on their perceived "illegality" (Beck & Allexsaht-Snider, 2002; Jones-Correa & de Graauw, 2013). In the above excerpt, Alexa and Manny think of instances involving ICE or the law to make sense of citizenship. In this case, their perceptions of citizenship are of the institutions and mechanisms that sustain its exclusionary juridical forms.

When I asked about his definition of citizenship during a class observation, another youth named Diego began with his encounter with ICE, and the exclusion that ensued from not being a citizen:

DIEGO   They [ICE] grabbed me and asked me so many questions in English that I didn't know and then they returned me. They put me in a car like a van and from there they sent me to a place for underage people, and there they gave us food, there was one bathroom. From there they sent me and they told me, they asked for my papers because they sent me to Mexico and held me there and asked for my papers. Then when I turned 14 my parents told me to come again, and I said okay, so I tried again. On that try they almost grabbed me again because we were crossing and immigration came and there were some *migra* there that I had to cross by. I couldn't run anymore and I said to my uncle—because this time I came with my 2 uncles—so I couldn't run and said "You go, because I know how you'll suffer and I don't want you to suffer," and he said, "No, you can go on." And the car stopped where I think it's like a land obstacle, like a *bache* [hole], and we jumped from there and it was all broken, and I said to my dad, "I don't want to cross anymore," and he said, "Try again, there is nothing impossible," and I said, "No, I don't want to, you are going to be able to."

ATZIN   'Cuz you were so scared, that was the second time . . .

DIEGO   And from there I decided to make the decision and cross. I was able to cross. I spent like 4 days in the woods without food. . . . I was lost for a day by myself, it was maybe 6 at night, I didn't know. I walked through some woods and I didn't notice that there was water or anything and there was like a swamp that I got stuck in and I couldn't get out and I was drowning. Then, I felt like someone was there, and he helped me get out, he was a good man, he helped me—he got me out, he gave me food because I had gone the entire day without eating, without drinking water or anything. He got me out and then he turned me in to immigration and they returned me to my country. I tried again and on the next time they also got me and on the fourth time I got here. I also was in Mexico for like 2 months.

Armenta (2016) argued that in the area of law enforcement, U.S. society has witnessed the emergence of the so-called "crimmigration" system, wherein immigration enforcement is intimately intertwined with the criminal justice system. This means that Latinx groups in particular are highly targeted and racialized as criminals and noncitizens (p. 112). Often Latinx immigrants are problematically assumed to be all undocumented and then have to navigate their status of illegality (De Genova, 2002). These encounters with immigration are racialized and rooted in juridical views of citizenship. I expand on these traditional conceptions next in relation to the research, then return to how youth challenge these normative institutional forms of citizenship.

Categories of Citizenship: Normative (Legal/Illegal), Nation-State, and Cultural Citizenship

Citizenship is a contested notion. Bosniak (2000) finds it important to categorize the debate around citizenship along four main fields: citizenship as legal status; citizenship as rights; citizenship as political activity; and citizenship as collective form of identity and sentiment. Chavez (2013) employs these four fields of citizenship to demonstrate how the rhetoric of us vs. them is experienced by immigrants and becomes a salient aspect of their daily lives. At its root, the notion of citizenship creates a real and symbolic boundary that allows for membership of certain individuals while simultaneously leaving others unrecognized. However, the agency of many people deemed "noncitizens" who are unrecognized by the nation-state influences the way in which this group feels integrated into the social fabric of a given community, or what Bosniak (2000) calls "citizenship as a form of collective identity" (p. 455; see also Flores & Benmayor 1997). Rosaldo (1997) and Ong (1996) have called this process cultural citizenship, which refers to the desire for rights and the inclusion of minoritized groups, including noncitizens, in relation to the state and society. Ong (1996) states that cultural citizenship is "a dual process of self-making and being made within webs of power linked to the nation-state and civil society" (p. 738). In other words, the nation-state creates groups that it ascribes specific ideas of citizenship to. In return, people allow themselves "to be made" as citizens that meet the need of the nation-state in order to acquire membership and recognition by the nation-state.

Of course, there are limitations to cultural, or collective, citizenship as it relates to attaining rights and a sense of recognition from a locality or a nation-state. Scholars have demonstrated Latinos' cultural citizenship is their commitment to cultural as well as political participation and is way to create a space of inclusion for themselves, such as in the "Mega Marches" of the mid-2000s (Chavez, 2013; Gonzales, 2014). Dyrness and Sepúlveda (2020) challenge the singular notion of rights-based citizenship by thinking about citizenship beyond the nation-state, where young people's in-betweenness and transnational connections contribute to the decolonization of citizenship as thought of by political scientists. In his study of Muslim youth, Shirazi (2018) describes how boundaries of citizenship (who has it and who does not; legal/illegal) are drawn across racial lines, where "us" equates to American, understood as whiteness, and "them" equates to other, understood as people of color, regardless of legal citizenship status. Irrespective of legal citizenship status or place of origin, Shirazi (2018) and Abu El-Haj (2007) expose the function of racist discourses in the political and social spheres that attempt to relegate migrants to an inferior status because they are nonwhite. These perspectives demonstrate that juridical, institutional citizenship is not a panacea for belonging and membership in the United States. Furthermore, racialized hierarchies of state membership indicate how and why legal citizenship is not an idealized privilege. Citizenship as an institution produces social inequalities and further stratification based on racial lines, as De Genova and Ramos-Zayas (2003) have rightly suggested.

Racialization and Citizenship

Notably, there are various mechanisms utilized by the institution of citizenship to categorize noncitizens. One of these is a process of racialization, the central concern of this book. The institution of citizenship is then upheld through mechanisms like immigration enforcement, policies and programs like 287(g), which allows for cooperation between ICE and local law enforcement in Denizen, and additional state-policies that allow for racial profiling of immigrants in Denizen. I contend that the racial categorizations created through immigration policies serve as a mechanism that creates a *racialized citizenship* that impacts the undocumented youth who participated in this study (the youth describe this process in earlier chapters. The concept of racialization sheds light on how race operates in society and how conditions of racial inequality are created and sustained, often dehumanizing black and brown bodies through real and symbolic violence influenced by the "white gaze" (Barot & Bird, 2001; Fanon, 1968, p. 612; Gans, 2017; Gonzalez-Sobrino & Goss, 2019; Hochman, 2019).

Advancing Racialized Citizenship and Racial Scripts

This book has leveraged the concept of racialization across macro, meso, and micro contexts. Though citizenship is created through macro-level policies, it is given meaning and enacted through the micro-level, everyday lives of undocumented youth, in how they interact with institutions and the relationships within their families, communities, and schools. I link the evolving racialization process to understandings of citizenship. To deepen and apply the lens of racialization to citizenship from youth perspectives, I draw from Molina's notion of racial scripts. Molina (2014) uses the term to highlight how racialized groups are connected across space and time. For Molina, racial scripts have three main functions: 1) scripts allow for the relational connection between racialized groups; 2) they highlight how racialized groups are treated by institutions and ordinary people; and 3) racialized groups use counterscripts that challenge established racial scripts used to racialize them. I show these functions of racial scripts in connection to how youth make sense of immigration policy and enforcement to expand our understanding of racialized citizenship. For example, undocumented youth comment on how being a citizen in the South does not necessarily confer privilege if one is Hispanic, pointing to the underlying racial hierarchy and potentially multiple citizenships, with white being at the top of the hierarchy (Omi & Winant, 2014). Racialized citizenship helps to draw a racial boundary for Latinx youth based on the valorization of whiteness, which circumvents their sense of belonging and their recognition by the State of South Carolina. Molina's (2014) racial scripts reveal the relational and resistive (counterscript) aspects of the perceptions of citizenship and how they respond to institutional understandings of it. Next, I expand on the concept of racialized citizenship through the experiences youth in the study shared.

Racialized Citizenship, Racial Scripts, and Undocumented Youths' Perceptions of Citizenship

This section discusses three overarching themes utilizing Molina's (2014) racial scripts to advance meanings of racialized citizenship for undocumented youth: social-relational dimensions that youth feel due to being a part of a racialized group ("That's just how it is here"), youths' responses to how institutional forms of citizenship impact their everyday lives ("They make it so confusing! All the shit you have to do"), and the resistive aspects of racialized citizenship through counterscripts: ("I knew we weren't the only ones. Something needs to be done"). These quotes illustrate how youth break boundaries of the normative and empower themselves to network and knowledge-share for their communities' benefit.

"That's just how it is here.": Relational Dimensions of Racialized Citizenship

Gabby discussed her experiences as an undocumented immigrant who is ineligible for DACA, as well as the unique challenges her family has had in the South. Gabby frequently talked about what her citizenship status would mean for her family, noting, "Sure, it would help a little if we were citizens. My dad has already been deported three times." Gabby frequently reflected upon whether she could ever be regarded as a citizen, especially in the current political conjuncture. Because of the intersection of citizenship, ethnicity, and race, "We have gone through a lot here. Trying to figure out our rights. Helping my mom with the lawyers. It's always lawyers and worrying. Where's the money coming from and all that." Hostility toward immigrants has been fueled by the Trump administration and its anti-immigrant and nationalist agenda for most of her time in the United States, and in the Denizen community the fear of deportation and overall criminalization of immigrants is ever-present.

Gabby explained how her dad was pulled over by the police near Denizen West. Her father disputed why he was pulled over in the first place; however, his exchange with the police officer quickly became about his citizenship status rather than the circumstances related to his driving. She recalled her perception of this incident: "[The police officer] takes him out of the car, takes pictures of him on his phone, and is like, 'Be ready for a call, my buddies are going to call you,' which is immigration." Her father's exchange with the police officer reveals how citizenship is constructed via everyday contexts and interactions. It is not only her father's citizenship that comes into question. As she explains, "From that point he was just scared, now if I have a violation, a traffic stop, and if I'm trying to go through the path of getting documentation, will that affect me? With all this new stuff coming in, it's like, now what do we do?" Gabby indicated that there her father wasn't charged with anything and it wasn't clear why the police officer pulled her father over. Gabby said, "That's just how it is here. So now it's like we gotta watch when we go through some intersections at certain times of day."

Gabby highlights the social-relational dimensions of citizenship (Abrego, 2019). This means that she makes sense of citizenship through her relationships and the racialized encounters with law enforcement. Additionally, in South Carolina local law enforcement cooperates with ICE through 287(g) programs (Arriaga, 2017). Such interactions give Gabby the sense that she—and "people who look like her"—will be marked as noncitizens, even if they happen to have citizenship. Gabby's example highlights the relational connection between two racialized groups, which Molina (2014) helps us understand. The socio-relational dimension of citizenship is something that Gabby frequently characterizes as being beyond her reach; there is the sense in her description that she knows the odds are stacked against her. Furthermore, Gabby's experiences show the social and relational meanings of citizenship and her perceptions link to larger questions about her racial/ethnic identity. She reflects on how "the one[s] with the power" will not regard her or others like her as citizens: "They just don't like it, we have to face it. There's no logical reason. It's . . . racism, you just don't give a shit, and they're just going to say no [to institutional, juridical citizenship]." Her father's interaction with police officers became a question of his citizenship because he is marked and racialized as "other," and she believes this will continue to be the case for her and those in the undocumented community. Thus, citizenship isn't only about gaining a legal status (if those "with the power" allow this to happen at all)—importantly, citizenship is bound up with everyday relational processes and interactions.

Another undocumented youth named Elsie told me about her family's experience in relation to her perceptions of citizenship and its limited definition in the United States.

I feel like I am smart. My dad is smart. He knows a lot of U.S. history and stuff like that, he knows the laws, and he knows his rights and things. I feel like that's what really helped him whenever he got deported. ICE was asking all these questions and things like that. We do talk. Recently what we've been talking about is "Should I leave to Mexico and then your sister can get a lawyer and ask for a pardon, and maybe that way I can get in some papers or stuff like that," we've just been going on about that. Just worried about his safety. He works, he has to drive and things like that. We don't know what to do yet. Our family is separated right now, but we will keep talking about it.

Elsie's story showed the ways in which relationships with family factor into understandings of the category of institutional citizenship. She describes her family's life in the United States as "living on the edge," explaining to me that "we risk everything" to come to the United States, and then describes the danger of everyday activities such as driving a car. "That's a risk," she said.

"They make it so confusing. All the shit you have to do.": Youths' Challenges to Institutional Forms of Citizenship

Gabby shared her account of her family's attempt to obtain residency, and it demonstrates how institutional, juridical citizenship constrains immigrants' everyday lives. Her words illustrate youths' responses to the exclusionary institutional dimensions of citizenship. She stated:

It's not just one form or another. It's all this stuff. It's a waste of time. I have to translate everything for my mom. You have to process stuff. That's money. You have to go to the post office or fax things. That's money. You have to get a lawyer. That's money. I had to go to the library for the computer. They make it so confusing.

Gabby's reflections show how the process of gaining legal citizenship is costly and confusing for most families to navigate. Indeed, barriers to it exist, which complicate perceptions of whether it is worth the time to try to obtain it. And something as simple as a traffic ticket, or Gabby's father living with the family while being in the country illegally, could negate the family's chance to obtain legal citizenship.

Gabby concludes that the path to citizenship is complicated, "especially now that anything they have against you. The more people they can get out, the better for them. Like dang, it's screwed up." Even though the dominant racial script about illegal immigrants projects them as deviant or undeserving, for youth, citizenship does not exist apart from these everyday familial and social circumstances. Gabby explains how their process with the lawyer felt like a "waste of time" because the lawyer asked what she perceived as irrelevant questions. Gabby said, "She just wanted to know if we were criminals, and about our past, and how we came here and stuff like that." Embedded in the confusing, contradictory processes for obtaining institutionalized citizenship are also questions about her and her family's personhood, racial/ethnic identities, immigration status, and racialized positioning connected to whether "people who look like her" are "criminals."

Much like Gabby, Alexa explained her process of trying to navigate the threat of immigration and actual deportations of her father, as well as her family's struggle to find pathways toward legal citizenship.

> Back then, once you like lived here for ten years and was working and it was documented you could automatically get your citizenship. . . . I just feel like it just depends. You can have an asshole that deals with your case, or you can have and get away with whatever, or you can have someone really nice who actually cares. . . . sometimes I don't think people step in your shoes and look from, "Oh [what if] that was my family?" They like oh I am illegal, so why does that matter. Immigrants are treated like criminals.

Alexa's story was similar to other youths' stories. They often had several encounters with the mechanisms and forces that reinforce institutional forms of citizenship that maintain the binary of legal and illegal.

Additional participants expressed similar constraints that institutional citizenship presents. One youth stated, "People are still not going to like us even if we are citizens or not." She recounted a story of a man with a Swastika tattoo on his neck coming into her place of work and questioning her about her parents' legal status. She falsely told the man her family members were born in the United States and she only spoke English to him when the man began to speak Spanish to her. Despite her claim to citizenship and language ability, which should have afforded her some cultural citizenship, she was left shaken and scared by the encounter.

While institutional understandings of citizenship legally excluded them from rights and resources, in South Carolina, with its anti-immigrant policies and racial surveillance of Latinx immigrants, youth perceive that even having institutionalized legal citizenship did not confer privilege. During a focus group, youth further connected their racial/ethnic Hispanic identity with broader exclusion. In other words, one has to "deal with being Hispanic," and this racialization as Hispanic, other, did not equate with symbolic privilege.

JUANA When they get here, they don't last the whole year. They look and see. They leave right away. We know why. There's that vibe, like immigration is around. We already know, but then people in the class will be like "Where did they go?" We know. We know they had to go back or they got deported.

AMELIA I wouldn't say it [citizenship] is a privilege. I feel like for society, you're just like, "Who's a different color?" or whatever, and then they're like, "You're Hispanic." And then you get to say, "Oh, you're probably not a citizen," or whatnot. Even if you are, you're still going to be pointed as if you're not, you know?

The "vibe that immigration is around" speaks to the culture of surveillance that Latino youth face. The reality that other youths have disappeared from school impacts these youths' perceptions of citizenship and their racialized positioning in the community. Scholars note that the threat and encroachment of immigration surveillance impacts school attendance and belonging (Dee & Murphy, 2020; Verma et al., 2017). For instance, Juan explained, "It's hard. People here or back home assume that if you're here you're gonna get DACA. Back home, they may say, 'They say life in the United States is great. Let's all go.' They just came. Then, most of them were in the same boat, and then they can't get DACA."

Amelia added, "So, yea, citizenship would help 'cuz then you can have certain things, but then you also have to deal with just being Hispanic here." Lastly, Juana perceived citizenship as complicated by their Hispanic/Latinx immigrant background, "Citizenship, a privilege? I don't think it is. I mean even the Hispanics who are citizens don't speak out. They're scared to talk. Even if they are citizens, they are scared. So, no, I don't think citizenship is a privilege."

From youths' perspective, institutional, juridical citizenship is intertwined with processes of racialization in society, and racial meanings of "just being Hispanic." Amelia said:

That's how I was raised. Don't forget who you really are. Then you go to school and you're put in that situation and it's like, "Oh, you're *this*." I think that's what it comes down to. They see you, like, "Oh, you're Hispanic, you're probably an immigrant." Or, "Oh, you weren't born here." You don't get the same privilege as this person, things like that. It's the same struggle. I think what's been the challenge, the only thing, like, "Oh." Even when you're signing papers and then they're like, "Oh," and they ask you your race or other stuff. It's kind of like you're not really sure what will happen.

Amelia's comments illustrate how being racialized as Hispanic has consequences for belonging regardless of one's citizenship status. Amelia's perceptions show how racialized identities equate with immigration status, and contribute to how "they" (society or institutions) sustain exclusion, or the "struggle" she faces. The category of citizenship, while certainly conferring some rights, does not automatically mean Latinx groups are included or made to feel or a sense of belonging; this further challenges the institutional understandings of citizenship.

"I knew we weren't the only ones. Something needs to be done.":
Resistance as a Counterscript to Racialized Citizenship

While youth expand upon and challenge meanings of citizenship, they also offer forms of resistance to the dominant "script" of institutional citizenship. Amelia explained:

> I knew we were not the only ones. I thought to myself, "How many other people are out here going through the same thing, don't know what's going on?" They're so scared that they just follow without help. They have rights. They can get help. People just didn't know where or didn't know their rights. I feel like that's what drove me. It's like, "Something needs to be done."

Amelia's resistance translated into action in her community—sharing resources and knowledge with other undocumented youth. She said, "I feel like that's just what drove me to be an activist and be the voice for those people that just can't or are scared." These perceptions illustrate how youth relationally connect across racialized identities and positioning as undocumented and offered counterscripts to dominant discourses about citizenship and Latinx immigrants (Molina, 2014).

Emmy shared similar policy thinking and resistive perspectives that counter the limited institutional, juridical forms of citizenship. She explained:

> Policymakers aren't thinking about who they are targeting and who the policies impact. I am here. I am not invisible. These issues need to be brought up and policymakers may not care, but we are here. I am here. I count. Even though policymakers may not want me to count, I am here. I want to tell my story. I crossed the border through a desert. Some people came by planes, some in the desert, and they left their countries for different reasons, and we need to learn about these things.

Thinking about the impact of policy is part of youths' resistive and relational conceptions. Linking racial meaning, relationships, and the limits of institutional systems drives them to action in their communities. For instance, Juana articulated:

> If I were to define it? Hmm, it's more than being born here. The bigger picture is about identity, what you give up to be a citizen. Does it really matter if I am a

citizen but have to give up my other identity or nationality? What does it really mean? I am not eligible for DACA but I have lived a lot of American culture. Am I not American? I would never say that, but my friends don't think I speak Spanish the same or that I am connected with my roots. But I am not trying to be white either. Being a citizen seems to just be that, born here and white.

Youth voices highlight how citizenship (read: juridical and institutional) is not just about being born here or not; rather, it is entangled in broader issues of race, racialization, exclusion, and identity in the United States. Juana's narrative exemplifies counterscripts' objective of claiming dignities that humanize immigrant youths' immigration stories, but also their attempt to become included members of their host communities. Counterscripts highlight their agency in attempting to be seen beyond a racialized and often criminalized perspective, but rather as members of the communities in which they settled.

Alexas's story stuck with me throughout the years of this study because her dad had been deported three times when I met her in 2015 and she had been here less than two years. I asked her how her family's experiences shaped her perspectives toward citizenship and immigration. Unlike some youth, Alexa wanted to resist and take action, but concern for her family weighed on her.

> It would be good [to stand up against immigration policies] but then, you know, because of my dad. . . . it could affect my family a lot. I don't know. A lot of undocumented people could get helped but it could be more of a risk for my family.

The sentiments expressed by Alexa and the other youth illustrate how complex the category of citizenship remains. It is not, to them, just about being legal or illegal. Instead, it connects to their relationships and understandings of their racial identities, including how being "Hispanic" makes them outsiders. But it also connects them and, in many ways, empowers them to resist. Alexa's resistive tendencies challenge institutional, juridical forms of citizenship and the forces that sustain them. She said:

> We misuse our citizenship. Like so many people who have it don't do anything, especially here. Why can't they give their citizenship to someone like my dad, who works so hard for us and who has been through so much for us? I feel like he deserves a lot more than he has.

As part of Alexa's resistance, she connects to citizenship is racialized, and how Latinx immigrants are excluded from institutional, juridical forms of it:

> Anybody from a Hispanic background, works as hard as other people, but like they come to America either for family, a better life. Maybe not, I know not

everybody is good. What I am saying is that you can't put everyone in the same category.

Alexa's expression points to why the category of illegal/noncitizen is problematic and does not humanize the many reasons that undocumented immigrants come to the United States. In addition, her perspective of citizenship in relation to being racialized as Hispanic is important. As I have shown in previous chapters, Latinx racialization functions to exclude these groups from access to resources while also exploiting their labor. Many youths like Alexa have family members who work in the agriculture and poultry industries in Denizen, benefiting local communities while being positioned as criminals and outsiders. These contradictions are revealed through youths' resistance to the dominant "scripts" that criminalize Latinx immigrants. These perspectives offer alternative ways of understanding the relational and resistive aspects of racialized citizenship.

"Even being a citizen is not a privilege here." Reflective Analysis of Youth Sense-Making about Forms of Citizenship

Juana's words, along with the statements of the undocumented youths above, capture the heart of this chapter: youths' relationships and connections across their racialized identities as Latinx and positioning in society as undocumented immigrants, along with their resistance to white, juridical forms of citizenship. To advance the notion of racialized citizenship, or how racialization processes undergird the normative category of citizenship, I outlined youth perceptions of citizenship. To deepen this concept of racialized citizenship, I discuss Molina's (2014) concept of racial scripts as part of the racialization of citizenship experienced by the youth.

This chapter engaged youth perceptions of citizenship. I first explain how racialized citizenship as an alternative to normative, juridical conceptions of the category provides new pathways for understanding its effects on undocumented youths' everyday lives. Youth disrupted categories by connecting relationally across their positioning in a racialized group. Second, I showed how they dismantle institutional understandings of citizenship and its damaging, confusing, and racist undertones, as Alexa's story showed. Third, I show how youth, because of their relational connections, including familial experiences, offered resistive counterscripts to policy thinking and white-dominant discourses.

Moreover, as they foreground racialized citizenship, youth link meanings of citizenship with whiteness, as Juana's comments demonstrate. Youth also connect the broader criminalization and exclusion of being "Hispanic" in their context. A key finding relates to how youth explain their racialized experiences as not only an aspect of being undocumented but also as a larger issue facing Latinx immigrants regardless of citizenship status: the racial meanings ascribed to Latinx immigrants further disrupt any benign institutional or juridical category of citizenship. In other words, Latinx immigrants are deeply and punitively racialized, which leads youth to understand citizenship as "not a privilege," regardless of whether they have citizenship. Flores-González (2017) similarly found that Latinx youth are racialized as other, and thus deemed "citizens but not Americans" because they are outside the white-normative understanding of what "counts" as a citizen.

As youth struggle to belong, they reject belonging to the system because it complicates their lives while providing for them at times. This has significant implications given the current sociopolitical climate and context of schooling. As Abrego (2019) argues, there exist constant reminders of the "idealized privileges of citizenship" (p. 653). Thus, leveraging their relational connections, they challenge the institutionalized version of it. Ybarra (2018) contends that the institution of citizenship as defined in neoliberal discourses depicts undocumented (im)migrants as criminals, regardless of citizenship status, and points to how racist discourses surrounding immigration create the very existence of Latinx immigrants as unlawful and unfit for institutional, juridical citizenship, which youth associate with being white. Ybarra (2018) and others (Abrego, 2019; Flores-González, 2017), call for an expanded view that incorporates Latinx groups' dialogue, resistance, and social group formation as agentic. In this chapter, youths' resistive narratives offer a counterscript that also enables them to gain a sense of solidarity, policy thinking, and in some cases, actions at the local level to support other undocumented community members.

Conceptually, I advance racialized citizenship as an alternative to juridical, institutional citizenship to reflect realities and opportunities for systemic policy change. Ybarra (2018), Pérez Huber (2009), and Ngai (2004) argue that the criminalization of immigrants that results from normative categories such as citizenship is contingent on immigration law. It is also constructed socially through racist nativist discourses that strategically frame immigrants as criminal and thus justify their exclusion in the United States (Pérez Huber, 2009). Thus, the category of citizenship is not just normative; as the data shows, the theoretical category, defined by law, has significant social and material consequences on youths' everyday lives (De Genova, 2002).

The data also have theoretical and practical implications. It entails studying youth actions that counter the restrictive practices of a given society. Attentive to what I highlight as the racialized dimensions of citizenship, Flores (2003) argues that citizenship is not inherently oppositional; though it is sometimes constructed when dominant groups in society restrict membership or cultural rights, in the struggle to belong, groups claim space and enact their cultural practices as resistance. The undocumented youth in this study envisioned and enacted a practice of citizenship that aligned with their racialization as Hispanic and undocumented, resisting dominant, white visions of citizenship in American society. Their experiences and visions allowed them to struggle to gain membership in school-based and local settings and reshape those spaces. The undocumented youth in this study were not seeking to assimilate but to renegotiate what it means to be a citizen as they participated in activities and practices that are allegedly markers of "real" citizens: dialogue, critiques of institutions, and policy thinking. This renegotiation was evident in their everyday activities, particularly as they built knowledge and capital among each other in spaces they carved inside school and undertook visible political acts in the community.

The theoretical framework opens up a critique of institutional citizenship through the lived experiences of undocumented youth. The normative category creates knowledge about these groups and positions them as problems to society. Through this lens of racialized citizenship and racial scripts, there exists an opportunity to intervene in the process of racialization and criminalization of Latinx (un)documented immigrants. As the data show, citizenship is not a benign category but rather one that is perceived by youth as entangled with issues of race, racialization, and exclusion in the United States.

The undocumented youth are entangled in a process of racialized citizenship formation, including personal ties to cultural identity but also engagement with the state and state-like authorities. Ong (1996) demonstrates how "the everyday processes whereby immigrants are made into subjects of a particular nation-state" (p. 737) are especially relevant for newcomers to the United States because "discriminatory modes of perception, reception, and treatment order immigrants" along a racialized continuum (p. 739). Although immigrants are resistant to nation-state-defined citizenship, their interactions with state authorities classify them into racialized categories. Thinking through undocumented youths' perceptions of citizenship provides opportunities to consider relational and material dimensions and effects—specifically, how these young people respond to their context and conditions is resistive.

Citizenship formation is understood as *in process* and thus makes possible interventions into repetitions of the dominant norm. Understanding youth perspectives on the effects of policies and perceptions of citizenship can be informative for educators and researchers, as we engage in the current political climate to advocate for the safety and well-being of immigrant children.

Conclusion

At a time when the basis of citizenship is called into question, we need sustained examinations of the logics that inform citizenship-making. Further, this chapter exploits the detrimental effects of normative, institutional categorizations of citizenship (i.e., legal/illegal) on the lives of undocumented youth. Continued efforts to support undocumented youth are important now more than ever, especially given threats to ending birthright citizenship. Inquiry about the question of citizenship in relation to undocumented students in the South with its anti-immigrant laws and policies acts as the lynchpin for classic and contemporary understandings of freedom and equality. Additionally, the landscape of the South is a site of contestation for competing claims of nationalism and immigrants' rights and provides opportunities for humane dialogue and recognition of the effects of anti-immigrant actions and policies. Undocumented youth typically experience extreme marginalization in society, and yet they remain active participants in and beyond the classroom, showcasing their policy thinking, humanity, and desire for equity. By understanding their experiences, it is hoped that educators and policymakers will call into question pervasive anti-immigrant discourses and practices and act with humanity.

Conclusion

•••••••••••••••••••••••

Implications for Education
Policy and Practice

Collecting data for this study in 2015, on the cusp of Trump's presidential campaign and eventual victory, provided a unique vantage point. As this book now concludes during a period of transition back to a Trump presidency, the initial hope that emerged under Biden has given way to renewed uncertainty. Despite changes in leadership, immigration policies remain uneven, the effects of the pandemic linger, and the legacy of restrictive measures like Title 42 continues to shape migration patterns. My work as an ethnographer in Chicago during the inspirational days when DACA was passed, and the protests and celebrations in the streets of Chicago in 2012, guided my sense of hope as I entered this project in South Carolina. I observed, as an ethnographer in Chicago, thousands of Latinx youth march in the streets and experience the thrill of receiving some protections under DACA, but this was not enough to completely reshape immigrants' lives in many locations.

As I began this book's study in 2015, however, South Carolina's restrictive anti-immigrant policies and legacies of Jim Crow segregation revealed a deeper need to focus on state and local immigration policy and enforcement, and other sectors of social policy and public life that limited immigrants' access to resources and opportunities. I further witnessed the results of these uneven policies, particularly around DACA as a short-term benefit for some in the undocumented community, and then the influx of newcomers who are ineligible and would not be able to attend public institutions in South Carolina even if they were eligible. In many ways, the election of Trump made it seem as if the racist, xenophobic, nativist narratives and policies toward immigrants were novel when in fact they were long-present in the United States, and in the South in particular. While at the national level policies such as the Muslim Ban, threats to DACA and temporary protected status, and more recently the Public Charge rule in 2020 impacted access to resources, undocumented youth and their families also navigated local racialization policies at the community, school, and interactional levels.

Despite initial hope at the start of the Biden administration—when he, like many presidents before him, vowed to pass immigration reform—it is important not to overlook the overlapping meso- and micro-level policies that shape immigrant youths' daily experiences. This is especially true now that an increasing number of states—often led by "Make America Great Again" (MAGA) Republican governors—have decided to seize the powers of the federal government to further militarize their borders and criminalize migrants, as is the case with Texas, where Governor Greg Abbott announced a multibillion-dollar initiative in 2021 that has resulted in further weaponization of local law enforcement to detain migrants, mobilization of the National Guard and state troopers to the border, and the installation of razor wire and floating barriers along the Rio Grande (Sandoval, 2023). These tactics have already resulted in two rumored deaths and several severe injuries. The number of migrants entering the United States continues to climb, influencing the rhetoric of traditionally blue sanctuary states and cities like New York, whose "right to shelter" mandate makes it an appealing destination for new migrants (Cineas, 2023). New York City Mayor Eric Adams stated in a town hall, "All of us are going to be impacted by this. I said it last year when we had 15,000, and I'm telling you now at 110,000. The city we knew, we're about to lose," echoing sentiments expressed by a youth in this study that immigrants are "blamed for everything" (Cineas, 2023). As these new migrants enter the public school system, the Multilevel Racialization Framework can serve to help scholars and practitioners better understand immigrant youth experiences, especially as Trump has again been elected president. The framework was intended to be an entry point into a multilevel analysis of racialization processes across policy, community, school, and interactional contexts and dynamics. My hope is it can be adapted to account for forms of racialization processes impacting immigrant youth as deportation threats and racist, discriminatory policies and organizational practices continue.

At the heart of *Undocumented in the U.S. South* are the stories of undocumented youth, and how racialization processes of othering them manifest at the policy and institutional levels and impact their everyday lives and realities. This last chapter engages undocumented youths' voices once again to revisit the core argument in this book: racialization occurs at the macro, meso, and micro levels, and limits access to social and educational resources. While Wacquant

(2002) and Lewis (2003) extend the argument that schools are "race-making" institutions, this book shows that policies, institutions, and practices at multiple levels engage in race-making. Importantly, the book demonstrates how undocumented youth are racialized in connection with their immigration status. Not only are they made into racial subjects and problems in society, communities, and schools, racial disparities in outcomes and access to resources are also produced at multiple levels. The ways that undocumented youth are racialized as Latinx and undocumented, and are assumed to all be Mexican, are but a few examples of these processes at work. Additionally, establishing the impact of racialization processes is not just to show that race should be centered in my analysis but to begin to understand how racialization operates in the everyday activities of institutions such as schools, through discourses and policy effects, assumptions, attitudes, ideologies, and values in schools and communities.

The narratives presented in this book depict the positioning of Latinx immigrant youth of the New Latino South, framing their experiences in relation to the political and social history of South Carolina. In this book I have outlined the contours of citizenship, racialization, identity, and belonging through scholarship and ethnographic accounts from youth. Using a Multilevel Racialization Framework, I challenge binary thinking about immigrant youth as deserving/undeserving and position them as policy thinkers and actors, or authors of their experiences and ones that we ought to learn from at policy, community, and school levels.

Viewing racialization as a multilevel process helps explain the structural opportunities and barriers to immigrant youth mobility. As I demonstrated in my analysis of the macro (historical and policy) level chapter 2, the U.S. immigration law has used racialization and citizenship to both include certain groups when interests converge and exclude certain groups when it was most convenient for the United States; these U.S. practices mark Latinx immigrants as a perpetual "other" regardless of their citizenship status. This gets reflected and compounded in state policies, particularly in the South, where racialized immigrants are excluded from public spaces including schools. Other state policies do not explicitly exclude but do enshrine a trope of "deservingness" that also is applied to Latinx immigrants, especially privileging "high achievers" (Flores, 2021; Marquez et al., 2022).

I explored the meso-institutional level, the role of the school, in chapter 4. Through the voices of immigrant youth, I traced how they are constructed as deviant problems in two Title I high schools in the New Latino South and how they critique their positioning through activism and participation in school and community activities. Schools structure themselves in line with American meritocratic values, promoting the idea that social mobility is possible as long as you work hard. The bootstraps narrative results in placing the blame on the individual for any misfortunes and ignores the structural components. This leads to youth like Adalia, who often work twice as hard for the same opportunities as other students just to "prove" to teachers "that I was like an exception," reinforcing "deservingness" narratives that are often applied to immigrant groups (Jimenez, 2022). In chapter 5, I further explored the concept of citizenship through the undocumented youths' perspectives, specifically how youth come to interpret citizenship in theory and practice through the microinteractional level, in their relationships with family members and teachers.

The schools and the larger South Carolina context reveal processes of racialization, racial ascription, and racial meanings assigned to the undocumented youth in the study. Constantly under surveillance in the state and local Denizen community, undocumented youth try to make sense of the policy, organizational, and interactional levels they encounter. Conceptually, few studies have treated these multilevel racialization processes as central to youth experiences. Methodologically, the ethnographic project allowed me to explore and center youth experiences. Next, I connect this multilevel analysis to racialization processes and demonstrate how the latter shape youths' sense of self, belonging, and thinking through impacts across the macro-policy level, meso-organizational level (which includes racial practices and attitudes), and micro-interactional level and revisit some key moments from youth.

Policy

Thinking of racialization as a multilevel phenomenon is useful for understanding the root of opportunities and barriers to immigrant youth mobility. Through almost four years of fieldwork, I spent time with undocumented youth as they came to school with stories of how policies affected their everyday lives. One youth shared how the lack of immigration policies to support pathways to citizenship shaped her experience and how short-term policies like DACA fell short of assisting her in realizing her aspirations and completely demoralized other undocumented youth:

> I feel like I would always have to work harder, two times, three times harder than anyone else sitting next to me because of the whole college thing . . . because I do want to go to college, and it's really hard for me because I can't take out loans, and the FAFSA doesn't apply to me. There are some students, or friends, that simply just have given up and don't try and don't do anything because they know somehow that because of their status they just won't get anywhere . . . even if they try . . . but that's not me.

Limited access to financial resources for college forces many undocumented students to confront similar barriers. While this challenge is well-documented in research, my study highlights how K–12 educational settings contribute to the miseducation of Latinx immigrant students. As discussed in earlier chapters, lack of services and institutional supports contribute to the miseducation of Latinx youth, and the organization of schooling furthers racialization. Even when students receive school support in applying to college, they still face significant barriers in securing financial aid. As youth noted, many students give up because of the limitations of their immigration status.

Though each chapter laid out the macro, meso, and micro levels where racialization occurs, it is difficult in reality to separate processes from the everyday lives and interactions that undocumented youth talked about. Even the youth above explains that the challenges of gaining financial aid and resources are due to an unequal distribution of resources that originates from decades of racialized federal- and state-level policies toward immigrants. In addition to the macro-policy level, what sociologist Victor Ray (2019)refers to as the "racial state," ideologies are also enshrined in the state policy proposal and enactment process; this was evident in the explicit and implicit forms of exclusion in South Carolina policies. At some points, immigrants have been referred to as terrorists and jihadists and explicitly excluded from higher education (Rodriguez, 2018a; Rodriguez & Monreal, 2017; Roth, 2017). On the other hand, tropes of deservingness and uplift are applied to white European immigrants in state policy (Rodriguez, 2018a). And while policy is often thought of in the abstract, the critical perspective that I take in this book shows how policy is lived and experienced, and how processes of racialization are embedded in policy and lived. For instance, Gwen said, while explaining the impact of policy on her life choices and aspirations, "These policymakers aren't thinking about who they are targeting and who the policies will have an impact [on]."

Another way that the macro-level policies and forces impacted students through racialization processes occurred through immigration enforcement and the mechanisms and technologies of surveillance (Foucault, 1982) at the meso (community and school) level. Youth feel the macro-policy, meso-institutional (ICE), and micro-interactional impact of enforcement. Gwen explained:

> All these negative thoughts and comments about undocumented immigration, but no one really hears or sees a different point of view because people hide . . . or people don't take the time to tell someone, and things still stay the same, so if no one else does, I should.

The lived experience of "illegality" is personal and risky (De Genova, 2002). When youth feel "the vibe of immigration" (chapter 5) they refer to the surveillance apparatus of immigration enforcement. This extends beyond just pointing out how exclusionary laws seek to criminalize immigrants and inherently carry the threat of deportation (Menjívar, 2014b), often carried out in local spaces such as schools. Gwen also refers to other undocumented members of the community who hide. In many instances, youth observed classmates disappearing (Dee & Murphy, 2020) as was noted in chapter 5 when a youth said, "We know what happened, and where they go." When someone is removed from a community by ICE, it shapes "the consciousness, lives, and, potentially, the politics of those who remain" (Maldonado, 2014, p. 1933). Patler and Gonzalez (2020) assert that "the ever-present fear of enforcement makes its way through entire families regardless of citizenship status" (p. 24). The fear of immigration enforcement causes many immigrants to try to avoid going out in public as much as possible because of "policeability," which Maldonado (2014) defines as the "state of constant surveillance and regulation of the daily activities of immigrants and their families" (p. 1935). Not surprisingly, then, local immigration enforcement activities impact academic outcomes for immigrant students (Ee & Gándara, 2019) and access to food and secure housing (Amuedo-Dorantes et al., 2018; Potochnick et al., 2017). Amuedo-Dorantes and Lopez (2015) found that among children from mixed-status households, an increase in immigration enforcement was associated with a higher risk of repeating a grade and dropping out of school. Bellows (2019) examined the effects of the staggered rollout of the Secure Communities policy on student achievement measures using the Stanford Education Data Archive (SEDA) and found that the implementation of Secure Communities and its associated removals had a negative impact on Latinx students' scores in English language arts (ELA). Dee and Murphy (2020) found that local ICE partnerships reduced the number of Latinx students by almost 10 percent over a two-year period, with nearly 300,000 Latino students moving districts between 2000 and 2010. The effects on the social and academic outcomes for undocumented youth are significant, as they are both racialized as immigrants and made into subjects of intervention and surveillance.

Racialization and Ignorance

The reach of the racialization process is evident in this project at the meso-organizational level, in the school and community. Youth often attributed racialization to a great "ignorance" in society, community, and school spaces. Gwen explained: "The community is kind of ignorant too, because you meet someone and you assume everyone is Mexican . . . or even if you don't know about their status, you assume they're Mexican because of the, I guess, the population that immigrates here. . . . It's kinda rude, even for us to point out." Meanwhile, Alexa exclaimed in one interview: "Society thinks we've ruined everything," referring to the persistent negative perceptions of Latinx immigrants. In the community, youth referred to assumptions about Latinos, such as when a youth was working the drive-thru at McDonald's and a white male with a Confederate flag on his truck ordered food from her and asked her if she was Hispanic. He also asked if she and her parents were born here. As a teenager working her afterschool job, she said, "I was like yeah and yeah, even though we weren't born here. She explained he was like "those typical white supremacist looking guys. With the swastika, the shaved head, he . . . so I guess he was looking for something so that he could say something to me, but I didn't give it to him. That's what he wanted." In addition to having to navigate the macro-policy level and lived effects of policies, youth must navigate ignorant and racist interactions in the community. This youth explained: "People are still not going to like us even if we are citizens or not. They feel like we take everything they have." Like Alexa's reflection that it is believed that Latinos have "ruined" everything in society and in the local Denizen community, youth dealt with racism, discrimination, and ignorance. In many cases, youth experienced overt racism, but in other interactions they were attuned to the values and beliefs of local community members and educators in their schools. Mueller (2020) offers a Theory of Racial Ignorance (TRI) to "study how (and why) people produce and abide by ignorance" (p. 163). She argues that to maintain racism, "white actors *need* to 'not-know' in a certain way in order to 'not-do' (i.e., not make different choices)" (p. 159). An epistemology of ignorance is "a way of knowing oriented toward evading, mystifying, and obscuring the reality of racism to produce (mis)understandings useful for domination" (p. 147). This was common in school-based racialization as educators would confuse religious or cultural identities with immigration status (e.g., "They let you back in the country?"). Mueller (2020) argues that this is how racial ignorance is reproduced on both a micro and meso level (p. 148). Other scholars have explained that ignorance can persist through institutions, interactions, and policies, which I describe using my Multilevel Racialization Framework. In the context of Denizen, there were more instances of overt racism, and racial ignorance, than there were converging interests, perhaps due to the anti-immigrant climate of South Carolina.

Using the Multilevel Racialization Framework, I show the deeply problematic ways in which racial othering occurs in the everyday lives, structures, and interactions of undocumented youth. The impact on youth identity and sense of belonging was shown when youth carved out spaces to self-identify. One youth noted, "I have been struggling a lot with who I am. . . . The undocumenteds give the Latinos a bad name sometimes. I am undocumented, so I don't deny that. It is part of who I am." Many youths proudly shared their Latinx identities, or more specific ethnic identities, and unraveled the myth that a monolithic Latinx identity exists.

In school, youth grappled with the identity they have and the ones that schools and policies ascribe to them. The intersection of identity, immigration status, and belonging were important for youth as they considered their educational futures and aspirations. Many had low-quality curriculum and classes while others felt that educators held low expectations of them. Several youths noted the limited support they had from educators or counselors. When thinking about educational opportunities, one commented, "There was nobody there to help me" and that she had to "find out on my own" about scholarships and potential ways to pay for college. Given their immigration status, many youths shared that educators were unaware of the restrictions they faced in state policy and more broadly. This was corroborated in a state-level survey I completed with South Carolina teachers as well as a larger sample of 5,200 teachers in the United States, where we found a lack of awareness about DACA and educational restrictions for undocumented students (Rodriguez & McCorkle, 2019, 2020).

The low expectations, akin to the "poor dear" syndrome referred to by Ladson-Billings (2007), impact their sense of identity, efficacy, and belonging. One youth explained that Latinos work in low-wage jobs often because people assume they do not have any assets. One youth explained an instance where she was working at McDonald's, and "They automatically sent me to the kitchen and I was like, 'I am bilingual, shouldn't I be up front?' Y'all call me every other time when y'all need help, why don't you just, like, let me work up front?' and they never quite gave me a response." Similarly, youth recalled how the counselor and front office staff at Denizen West would pull them out of class to translate for parents; yet they were persistently kept in the "lower-track" classes. One youth explained how he was in ESL classes his whole high school career even though he passed the tests. "They just kept me in there." He explained how he was always curious to take other classes and get more help at Denizen. In many instances, youth do not know they can advocate for themselves or have a caregiver do so. Yet many youths associated educational aspirations in the United States with "going to college." They do not have support or awareness of the pathways they might take to get there. One youth explained the need for someone in the school to actually "sit there and dedicate time to us," because many undocumented and Latinx youth drop out of high school if they need to work to support themselves or family.

The Multilevel Racialization Framework depicts the experiences of these youth to comprehensively demonstrate how the racialization of immigrant studies occurs at the macro-policy level through current and past federal immigration law and enforcement, as well as through popular media discourses; the meso-organizational level through schools, institutional agents, and community ideologies and practices; and at the micro-interactional level through racialized individual interactions. Taken together, these layers influence access and mobility in ways youth describe throughout this study. The above reflects the theoretical, empirical, and policy contributions of the book. Next, practice contributions are discussed.

Practice

As a result of this ethnographic study and the stories youth shared with me, I have come to a set of policy and practice implications as well as a set of recommendations for educator and school administrators to help mitigate the impacts of racialization on immigrant youths' opportunities and resources: Offer districtwide "know your rights" training; hire and support educators of color; use teacher training to increase strategic, sociopolitical empathy; engage immigrant-serving community organizations to provide wraparound services and support for youth, and advocate for pathways to college and the workforce. These practices range from structural, to occur through district-level decision-making (i.e., hiring, professional development, and training, to individual, where educators need to engage in self-reflection about their identities and power dynamics in relation to the populations they serve.

Offer Districtwide "Know Your Rights" Training

First, districts and schools can engage in structural transformation to combat macro-level policies that are harmful to undocumented immigrant youth, such as "know your rights" trainings and further professional development about immigration and its impact on youth and families. Youth in this study described fear and trepidation for themselves and their family members as local law enforcement continues to strengthen their partnerships with ICE. Youth described being racially profiled and stopped by police on the road and ICE knocking on their doors. After the Trump election, many youths also temporarily stopped attending school for fear they might be deported. With a second Trump presidency that is once again making immigration and "securing the border" a central issue, it is imperative that schools and school districts provide their immigrant students and families with peace of mind and reassurance. Every school district should provide basic "know your rights" trainings to their students and families as a baseline, and support educators in developing safety plans and protocols, as well as updating communication trees for youth and families in the event of family separation. These trainings should specify the constitutional and basic rights of immigrant students and their families. This information already exists in "know your rights" materials provided by organizations such as the American Civil Liberties Union (ACLU).

Hire and Support Educators of Color

Second, schools should improve their hiring practices. In contrast to Mr. O'Donnell, an educator at Denizen West, who held deficit-based views of immigrant youth who failed to learn English quickly and of families for not advocating for services, educators and school-based personnel like Ms. Ava, Ms. Constance, and Cookie retained an asset-based framework that allowed them to connect with students. These educators shared racial/ethnic or immigrant identities with the community they serve, had a "border-crossing/ *nepantla*" orientation (Rodriguez et al., 2020), or simply were aware of their students' challenges and advocated for them. They held a wealth of knowledge and demonstrated a high level of cultural competency. Part of their role as *nepantleras*, which Anzaldúa (1987) describes as individuals who navigate in-between spaces to mediate, bridge, and transform oppressive structures, Rodriguez et al. (2020) argue, is to understand the macro, meso, and micro contexts of immigration law and policy, migration journeys, family conditions, and their own identities in relation to the immigrant youth in order to build strong, trusting relationships and advocate for this population. Educators like the ones mentioned above often must navigate barriers themselves to broker resources and provide access to opportunities. They cannot always bear the burden of such an important institutional agent. In South Carolina and other anti-immigrant states, doing advocacy work and brokering resources for immigrant youth and families also poses professional risks (Rodriguez et al., 2020, 2021). Instead, schools and districts need to think structurally about how to improve access for immigrant youth.

Schools must strive to employ high-quality teachers that reflect the community they serve. Teachers who speak the same language as their students and who have similar backgrounds and sometimes similar immigration statuses, can use these similarities to foster relationships with their students and between the school and community. It is important for students to see themselves reflected in their teachers so that they can begin to imagine themselves as professionals and watch as their teachers navigate U.S. and home culture (García & Bartlett, 2007). Whether or not teachers share similar racial/ethnic or cultural backgrounds with their students, they should approach their work with an asset-based mentality and authentic caring where students' needs are at the center. Hiring more teachers of color might be one pathway for this, as barriers to educational access and resources are not just a problem affecting immigrant youth.

Teacher Training to Increase Strategic, Sociopolitical Empathy

Third, alongside specific trainings on immigration issues, broader teacher training beyond instructional practices such as culturally relevant or multicultural pedagogies is needed. By this, I mean engaging in conversations about the population and understanding the sociopolitical contexts. Similar to the immigration-related trainings, this would involve deeper understanding of immigration policy as it invades schools through the lived experiences of youth (Lowenhaupt et al., 2021; Verma et al, 2017). Throughout my study teachers demonstrated a lack of awareness of basic policies impacting immigrants and tended to believe in false narratives about immigrants. There was even a tendency to believe that South Carolina policies are more inclusive than they are in reality. Worse still, the lowest levels of awareness were regarding the eligibility of U.S. citizens with undocumented parents and students with certain legal visas to obtain in-state tuition for postsecondary education. As educators, they should be aware of these kinds of policies to appropriately guide their students, and this lack of awareness is a consistent barrier to teacher empathy and trust-based relationships with students. If teachers hold inaccurate beliefs about the policies impacting undocumented students, then their efforts to advise and advocate for them will be distorted or nonexistent. To counter this, teachers need two types of training: teacher-focused "know your rights" trainings and trauma-informed practices. Teacher-focused "know your rights" training will help educators understand the overlapping policies that impact their immigrant students' everyday lives and actions. It will also help educators know what options are available for their immigrant students post–high school. Additionally, it is important for educators to recognize the trauma that comes from being an unaccompanied minor, refugee, asylee, and/or student with interrupted formal education. A trauma-informed approach to teaching is essential to building successful relationships with students. Schools should focus on professional development that will add to teachers'—and school-based personnel such as school social workers'— knowledge of student's cultures and communities but also the ways in which trauma affects learning and the brain (Bajaj & Suresh, 2018, Rodriguez et al., 2020, 2021). Scholars such as Lowenhaupt and colleagues (2021) have offered "domains of practice" that ought to guide such professional development, including schoolwide affirmation and welcoming of immigrant students; building shared knowledge and capacity across staff and educators (so that the burden does not fall on one educator or social worker, as was the case at both Denizen West and Citizen North); mobilizing resources within and outside of the school; and creating space for conversations.

Engage Immigrant-Serving Community Organizations to Provide Wraparound Services and Support for Youth

Fourth, schools need to engage and develop partnerships with individuals and organizations to support immigrant students and families. It is clear from youth stories that immigrant students need more than academic support in their daily lives. Educators like Ms. Ava, Ms. Constance, and Cookie provided emotional and mental support and housing, and at times they attempted to provide legal support. While the work of these educators is necessary and greatly contributes to the immigrant youths' sense of belonging in their schools, it places an undue burden on individual educators, who are not receiving the proper support, training, and compensation to engage in this work. Additionally, not every school will have an Ava, Constance, or Cookie. To systematize these much-needed services and off-load some responsibility from individual educators, schools should partner with already existing immigrant-serving community organizations to provide wraparound services for youth. Community partnerships have been demonstrated to help schools provide holistic wraparound services (Martin & Suárez-Orozco, 2018). Through community partnerships, schools can provide legal information sessions, housing support, mental and physical health services, and recreational activities. Schools can engage families through food drives and even community gardens (Bajaj & Suresh, 2018). With a more holistic community model, the school can become a welcoming environment for all and the bedrock of the community, not an institution to be distrusted and suspicious of. Often community-based organizational spaces offer affirming curriculum and relationships that Latino immigrant youth can develop among other Latino and/or immigrant peers, organizers and adult staff (Rodriguez, Roth, and Murillo, 2024). Youth can build social relationships and a sense of belonging that can be counterspace to negative racial climates in schools (Rodriguez & Wy, 2024). In many cases, youth in community-based spaces also leverage these relationships and networks of support to inform future aspirations and decision-making about postsecondary opportunities.

Advocate for Pathways to College and the Workforce

Lastly, schools must support the aspirations of young people, both immigrant youth and racially/ethnically minoritized students more broadly, by leveraging asset-based approaches. A common sentiment expressed by immigrant youth was a sense of frustration and hopelessness about life post–high school. One youth shared that most of his friends had stopped trying to enroll in college, while others expressed working even harder to be the exception. While there is broad support for DACA, and a 2020 Pew Research Center poll showed that 74 percent of Americans were in favor of the program, it is insufficient (Krogstad, 2020). Recently arrived students are ineligible for DACA. More advocacy needs to be done by educators in partnership with advocacy organizations to implement both federal and state policies that provide pathways to higher education. Without such pathways we cannot uphold the promise of *Plyler v. Doe* of an equitable education for immigrants or the children of immigrants; instead, we are limiting their opportunities to "contribute in even the smallest way to the progress of our Nation" (*Plyler v. Doe*, 1982, p. 223). In our contemporary moment, *Plyler* is and will continue to face threats from a second Trump administration, and increasing racism and discrimination at federal and state levels. It is imperative that advocates, policy-makers, and researchers continue to be equity-centered and show the contributions of immigrant youth, and sustain the educational rights that they are entitled to. As a researcher, I invite our scholarly community to leverage research that is useful and policy-relevant in what feels like insurmountably dark times for our country.

Final Thoughts

Since the completion of this study, I have engaged with migrant youth across the Mid-Atlantic and Northeast. While I began with an understanding of undocumented youth who were eligible for DACA while I researched in Chicago, moving to the Southeast gave me the opportunity to explore how contexts of reception varied a great deal by region. In learning more about the impact of state policy on the everyday lives of youth, I also encountered variation across school districts and schools themselves both within and across sanctuary and non-sanctuary community, school, and policy contexts. Most students in the Denizen community were ineligible for DACA, or the state did not acknowledge DACA as a valid way to access postsecondary opportunities. While the excitement regarding the creation of DACA in 2012 was cautiously palpable in Chicago, the youth I studied across the United States have never seen DACA as the be all and end all to improving outcomes and mobility. Yet scholars and policymakers alike have continued to perpetuate deservingness and meritocracy as ways to improve life chances for many immigrants and are quick to point to economic advantages and disadvantages to educating immigrant children and youth. Continued diligence toward federal policy changes are part of the movement, but local communities and schools are also spaces that can mitigate and exacerbate social inequalities and economic costs to states and local communities.

The youth at Citizen North were newly arrived in the country. Youth like Juan shared deep aspirations for education beyond high school and yet pathways were limited. During my writing of this book, additional research has come out about the impact of policies on undocumented youth. Yet less attention has been paid to those youth who are separated from their families for long periods, have interrupted schooling, endure trauma and violence pre- and post-migration, and who remain unaccompanied in the United States. In the many conversations I have had in hundreds of districts with school-based leaders and personnel since this study's conclusion, it is common to hear the about "newness" of the crisis of immigrant youth. In South Carolina, I heard this "newness" discourse, and about the "influx" of immigrants posing a "crisis" for many school personnel. I continue to hear this in anti-immigrant contexts as well as in more inclusive states and communities. While the study and its focus on racialization was heightened in the Southeast, many communities in rural and suburban localities face similar increases in their population of Latinx immigrant and newcomer students, and similar forms of racism, discrimination, and exclusion. I continue to hear about the "crisis" of "new arrivals," and the "what do we do" comments. Often these statements are made with the best intentions of supporting young people. My observations over the years have led me to also view this positioning of "new" immigrant youth or "newcomers" as a potential strategy to delay structural transformation and the creation of positive supports and systems. Without structural change, the amazing work of educators like Cookie, Ms. Ava, and Ms. Constance remains limited, despite the significant ways that individual educators support immigrant youth every day in many locations beyond the South. Being undocumented in the U.S. South meant that youth needed these agents, and relied on them for emotional, financial, academic, and relational support. My hope in sharing these stories and the courageous work of educators is that one day personnel like Cookie will not have to text me in fear that her youth are going to be deported for getting into a fight at school, or that families will not need frantic legal advice as immigration officers raid local apartments where they are trying to survive.

While questioning their identity and belonging due to macro policies and meso school and community dynamics and practices, youth also question larger political and media discourses about what it means to be American and to belong. Not only do the youth know more about immigration policy and its effects than many researchers and educators, their voice is also central to policy thinking and policymaking. Youth noted that they are not invisible even though "policymakers are not thinking about who they are impacting." I end as I started, knowing that youth voices matter and that youth are the experts of their experience. As we move into new election cycles, questions of the border remain at the top of partisan politics. My hope is that *Undocumented in the U.S. South* prevents these questions from overshadowing the lived realities and existence of undocumented young people in the South and beyond. It is also my hope that exposing the racialization process across policy and school contexts can be a learning opportunity to policy-makers and leaders and educators as they attempt to transform educational and social systems to support immigrant youth and children from immigrant backgrounds as they navigate school and society. Focusing on racialization in this book revealed troubling policies, practices, and interactions; yet, listening to the voices and experiences of youth also provides an opportunity to transform educational and social systems in race-conscious, caring ways.

Acknowledgments

Over the years, many people contributed to this book. I am deeply grateful to the educators and youth that talked with me during the project. While I cannot name all of the amazing educators here, I continue to be in awe of the advocacy work that they do for immigrant youth and their families in an anti-immigrant policy context. In addition, the brilliant and strong young people that I encountered over the years made the story of this project possible and filled with unexpected learning, labor, and love.

I began this project in 2014, when anti-immigrant sentiment was pervasive in the political rhetoric and national policy discourse. I was truly out of my element as I moved to South Carolina for my first job as a professor after graduate school in Chicago. I had mainly lived and taught in large urban cities. Upon moving, I experienced my own culture shock, and many friends along the way supported me and my research. I am also indebted to many individuals who helped during the research and writing stages. To help me understand the policy landscape in South Carolina, Timothy Monreal sifted through countless policy documents and assisted by writing several articles with me based on this project. As a thought partner and friend, Tim, I am grateful and so proud to witness your scholarly journey.

I also wish to thank several individuals for talking with me about South Carolina politics and immigration policy, including Alessandra Bazo Vienrich, Felicia Arriaga, Ben Roth, Jon Hale, Joy Howard, Will McCorkle, and Ben Roth. I especially thank Will McCorkle for working with me as he was completing his dissertation about teachers in South Carolina through survey research. We were able to develop an amazing collaboration and think through how teachers and other school-based personnel were understanding immigration policies and their impact on immigrant youth and families. To Felicia Arriaga and Alessandra Bazo Vienrich, I am so grateful for our friendship and to have the opportunity to learn from you on all things related to immigration and criminal justice. Thank you, Felicia, for North Carolina check-ins and writing retreats, and Alessandra, for ongoing advice and podcasts about life, immigration policy, and how to improve the lives of immigrant youth in schools. To Ben Roth, one of my first scholarly friends in the South, and who I met through Roberto Gonzales, thank you for our collaboration and thinking across disciplinary boundaries to consider how we could bridge conversations in education and social work. Our work together was a form of *nepantla* in many ways, and I learned a great deal from our reflections, struggles, and achievements. To Jon Hale and Quinn Burke, you two were and are like brothers to me, and you helped me navigate the landscape of being a new professor living in the South. Jon, thank you for always answering any question and confirming things related to the history of the South. Quinn, thank you for being such a dear friend and supporter, from our Charleston days to the present. I also thank Brian Lanahan for many conversations about research and wanting to write a book during my time in the South.

The mentorship I received during the process of writing the book was profoundly helpful. I thank Ricardo Stanton-Salazar for his incisive critique and feedback on the chapters as well as on the theoretical endeavor I was attempting. Ricardo, thank you for giving me the confidence to stand by what I observed about race and racism and its intersections with policy and educational practice. I would also like to thank Kathy Hytten and Christine Finnan for talking with me about ethnographic data and dilemmas and helping me to clarify what the story is really about.

I also wish to thank several friends and colleagues for later conversations about the work, including Eric Macias, Ted Hamann, Aaron Kuntz, Becca Lowenhaupt, Theresa Ambo, and Cam Scribner. Cam, thank you for always listening and being willing to do a (not so) quick read when I ambush you for help. To Ted, thank you for being a scholarly guardian angel and mentor as this work took shape and grew. I also want to express gratitude to Dr. Gilberto Conchas for taking me under his wing and inviting me to contribute a chapter for a book from my research in the South on racial and social inequality in educational systems. This led to our co-editing a book together titled *Race Frames in Education: Structuring Inequality and Opportunity in a Changing Society*, which was my first edited book. I learned a great deal from working with you, Gil, and carried so much new knowledge into writing my own book. I thank Dustyn Martincich for over twenty years of friendship, including our early years as professors and our writing retreats as I tried to get this book over the finish line.

There were also many people not in academia that supported my many moves, research, struggles, and achievements. I am so grateful for the countless friends such as Amanda Skrzypchak, Jason Bissonnette, Shanna Mann, and Kristina Jelinek (Bronx forever!). Thanks also to Pamela Konkol, Ali

Torrence-Hale, Jordan Kardasz, Tim Specht, Alicia Haller, and Deb Baron for all the support over the years about life and research and everything in between; and many thanks for listening in recent years to conversations about academic things and taking trips for reprieve, Scott Davis, Ziggy Pop Star Dust (RIP, July 11, 2023), and Ralphie the bull terrier.

There were many interruptions over the years, including a global pandemic, so having friends and colleagues who encouraged this work meant the world to me. I am also deeply grateful to Betty Malen, my dear friend and mentor at the University of Maryland, for her thoughts on chapters in this book and other publications. Betty passed away before this book was finished, but her kindness and generosity with very honest feedback is evident throughout the book. Betty, you continue to be in my thoughts with everything I write, every class I teach, and every student I mentor.

I also have much appreciation for my students at the University of Maryland, University of North Carolina Greensboro (UNCG), and College of Charleston, who allowed me the privilege of teaching courses on immigration and race in education, topics I am passionate about. I am particularly grateful to former students at UNCG and Maryland for being thought partners and helping to analyze the mountains of data for this project, including research assistants Katya Murillo, Manny Zapata, Staci-Pippin Kottkamp, and Gisell Ramirez. Thank you to Lisa Lopez-Escobar, who will defend her dissertation in 2025 after working with me for four years on multiple projects about immigrant youth and belonging, and whose amazing talents and ideas pushed this work in many ways.

I also wish to thank the editors, associate editors, journal leaders, and reviewers from *Educational Policy, Anthropology & Education Quarterly, Teachers College Record,* and *Sociology of Race & Ethnicity,* whose feedback over the years on iterations of this project greatly improved and challenged my thinking. Additionally, I thank friends from American Educational Studies Association, which was one of my first academic conferences and forever home, for sharing work and support. I also thank the Spencer and William T. Grant foundations for support of my research on immigrant youth and for learning how school-based personnel and educators can better advocate for immigrant youth and families.

This book is freely available in an open access edition thanks to TOME (Toward an Open Monograph Ecosystem)—a collaboration of the Association of American Universities, the Association of University Presses, and the Association of Research Libraries—and the generous support of the University of Maryland. Learn more at the TOME website: openmonographs.org.

Notes

Introduction

1 "Immigrant-background" refers to children and youth who were not born in the United States, or children who were born in the United States but may have one or more parents who are foreign-born.

2 States are also responsible for helping EL and immigrant-background students to achieve English proficiency and meet academic standards using data and evidence-based practices. Schools should, to the extent they can, communicate with parents in a language the parents understand, make outreach efforts toward them, and hold regular meetings with them to partner in support of students (Sugarman, 2017).

3 I recognize the larger academic debates about this term. I chose to use Latino (unless referring to scholarly literature) to acknowledge the communities we serve and the term they use. I recognize Latinx is used in academic spaces as a term that acknowledges gender-neutral, inclusive and, in some cases, Indigenous languages (Salinas, 2020) to describe people from Latin American countries (Rodriguez et al, 2024). I further acknowledge the diversity of Latinidad.

4 As noted earlier, in most of the literature the term *Latino* is used. I use *Latinx* to reflect the current attempts at inclusivity in academic and public discourse.

5 Rios's (2017) use of cultural framing is useful to describe this negotiating process. He argues that "a cultural frame is a system of meaning-making, identity formation, and presentation of self based on material and symbolic resources that influence peoples' perceptions of the world and their choice of actions and behaviors" (p. 24). Rios also explains that the culture, policies, and practices of educational institutions affect the cultural frames in which young people engage. For undocumented Latinx youth, the cultural framing they engage with regarding their identities is racialized and informed by school and local community contexts. The point here is that in the context of the South, youth are limited in the way they can express resistance explicitly.

6 Critical to the relationship between power and knowledge creation about subjects is how Foucault defines the process of subjectification. Like mechanisms of power, individual subjects are, for Foucault (1982), always produced by a pre-existing

system of power relations that makes their existence possible. Heller (1996) argues that "Foucault's insistence that a subject's ability to speak is ontologically bounded by the discourses through which his or her subjectivity is constructed—a process that is always determined by the subject's location within the specific institutional topography of a particular social formation—is particularly relevant to the question of intentionality: if subjectivity is essentially discursive, then subjects can only choose tactics they are able to discursively formulate" (p. 91). This is significant in the context of the Southeast and the broader context of Latinx immigration in the United States as youth navigate the boundaries of exclusion.

Chapter 2   "This state is racist with its policies toward Hispanics. We work, but don't have rights."

1   "Second-generation immigrants" refers to young people that were born in the United States but who have at least one parent who is born outside of the United States.

2   Section 287(g) of the Immigration and Naturalization Act allows the Department of Homeland Security to enter into formal agreements with local and state police so that local law enforcement officers can perform some functions of federal immigration agents (American Immigration Council, 2016).

3   As Rodriguez (2018a) argues, other policy documents produce migrants as illegal threats to the social and economic fabric of the state. Along this line of argument, De Genova (2013) argues: "Discursive formations that uphold and propagate the notion of migrant 'illegality' more than mere 'consequences' of a more elementary (prior) violation persistently serve as veritable conditions of possibility for the larger sociopolitical procedures that generate and sustain this 'illegality'" (p. 1181). In other words, the state's policy produces notions of "good" and deserving immigrants while positioning others as "bad immigrants." Worse yet is that policy production of migrant illegality fails to acknowledge how such "bad immigrants" enter into a racialized social structure that produces and reproduces their illegality by making it illegal and difficult to do anything right in their daily lives. Positioning Latinx undocumented immigrants in this way is an intended consequence of the construction of good immigrants; it also sustains a belief in the "naturalness" and "putative necessity of exclusion" that must be "verified" and "legitimated" through this larger policy process, which appears empathetic and protective of the state and its good immigrants while reifying notions of migrant illegality through a "grandiose gesture of exclusion" in a different form (De Genova, 2013, p. 1181).

Chapter 4   "I was born at the border, like the wrong side of it."

1   There are additional terms that scholars have used to explain the individualism that obscures structural oppression and racialized social systems. These individualism perspectives obscure the structures that ensure educational and economic success for some and obstruct it for others. There are critiques of the meritocracy views. Different terms have been used, including fictional meritocratic ideals, meritocratic mythologies, and ideological individualism (Stanton-Salazar, 1997, pp. 28–29).

References

Abbott, G. (1917). *The immigrant and the community*. Century Company.

Abrego, L. (2008). Legitimacy, social identity, and the mobilization of the law: The effects of Assembly Bill 540 on undocumented students in California. *Law & Social Inquiry, 33*(3), 709–734.

Abrego, L. J. (2006). "I can't go to college because I don't have papers": Incorporation patterns of Latino undocumented youth. *Latino Studies, 4*(3), 212–231.

Abrego, L. J. (2019). Relational legal consciousness of US citizenship: Privilege, responsibility, guilt, and love in Latino mixed-status families. *Law & Society Review, 53*(3), 641–670.

Abrego, L. J., & Gonzales, R. G. (2010). Blocked paths, uncertain futures: The postsecondary education and labor market prospects of undocumented Latino youth. *Journal of Education for Students Placed at Risk, 15*(1–2), 144–157.

Abu El-Haj, T. R. (2007). "I was born here, but my home, it's not here": Educating for democratic citizenship in an era of transnational migration and global conflict. *Harvard Educational Review, 77*(3), 285–316.

Abu El-Haj, T. R. (2010). "The beauty of America": Nationalism, education, and the war on terror. *Harvard Educational Review, 80*(2), 242–275.

Abu El-Haj, T. R. (2015). Belonging in troubling times: Considerations from the vantage point of Arab American immigrant youth. In J. Wyn & H. Cahill (Eds.), *Handbook of children and youth studies* (pp. 433–445). Springer.

ACF Press Office. (2021). Unaccompanied Children (UC) Program [Fact Sheet]. US Department of Health and Human Services. https://www.hhs.gov/sites/default/files/uac-program-fact-sheet.pdf.

Agamben, G. (2005). *State of exception* (K. Atteil, Trans.). University of Chicago Press.

Alba, R., Sloan, J., & Sperling, J. (2011). The integration imperative: The children of low-status immigrants in the schools of wealthy societies. *Annual Review of Sociology, 37*, 395–415.

Aleaziz, H. (2019). *US border officials pressured asylum officers to deny entry to immigrants seeking protection, a report finds*. BuzzFeed News. https://www.buzzfeednews.com/article/hamedaleaziz/dhs-asylum-report-mpp-immigration-remain-mexico

Alvarez, P., Sands, G., & Brown, R. (2019, August 28). U.S citizenship will no longer be automatic for children. *Pittsburg Post Gazette.*

American Immigration Council. (2016, October 24). *Public education for immigrant students: Understanding* Plyler v. Doe. https://www.americanimmigrationcouncil .org/research/plyler-v-doe-public-education-immigrant-students

Amuedo-Dorantes, C., Arenas-Arroyo, E., & Sevilla, A. (2018). Immigration enforcement and economic resources of children with likely unauthorized parents. *Journal of Public Economics, 158,* 63–78.

Amuedo-Dorantes, C., & Lopez, M. J. (2015). Falling through the cracks? Grade retention and school dropout among children of likely unauthorized immigrants. *American Economic Review, 105*(5), 598–603.

Annamma, S. A., Jackson, D. D., & Morrison, D. (2017). Conceptualizing color-evasiveness: Using dis/ability critical race theory to expand a color-blind racial ideology in education and society. *Race ethnicity and education, 20*(2), 147–162.

Anzaldúa, G. (2012). *Borderlands/La frontera: The new mestiza* (4th ed.). Aunt Lute Books. (Original work published 1987)

Armenta, A. (2016). Between public service and social control: Policing dilemmas in the era of immigration enforcement. *Social Problems, 63*(1), 111–126.

Arriaga, F. (2017). Relationships between the public and crimmigration entities in North Carolina: A 287(g) Program focus. *Sociology of Race and Ethnicity, 3*(3), 417–431.

Atkinson, P., Delamont, S., Coffee, A., Lofland, J., & Lofland, L. (2007). *Handbook of ethnography.* Sage.

Bajaj, M., & Suresh, S. (2018). The "warm embrace" of a newcomer school for immigrant & refugee youth. *Theory Into Practice, 57*(2), 91–98.

Ballinas, J. (2017). Where are you from and why are you here? Microaggressions, racialization, and Mexican college students in a new destination. *Sociological Inquiry, 87*(2), 385–410.

Ballinas, J. (2022). No margin for error: Racialization along the transition to higher education. In S. Rodriguez & G. Q. Conchas (Eds.), *Race frames in education: Structuring inequality in a changing society* (pp. 216–235). Teachers College Press.

Banton, M. (1977). The adjective "black": A discussion note. *New Community, 5*(4), 480–482.

Barot, R., & Bird, J. (2001). Racialization: The genealogy and critique of a concept. *Ethnic and Racial Studies, 24*(4), 601–618.

Batalova, J. (2024, March 13). Frequently requested statistics on immigrants and immigration in the United States. *Migration Information Source.* https://www .migrationpolicy.org/sites/default/files/publications/FRS-PRINT-2024-FINAL.pdf

Beck, S. A., & Allexsaht-Snider, M. (2002). Recent language minority education policy in Georgia: Appropriation, assimilation, and Americanization. In S. Wortham, E. G. Murillo Jr., & E. T. Hamann (Eds.), *Education in the new Latino diaspora: Policy and the politics of identity* (pp. 37–66). Ablex Publishing.

Bellows, L. (2019). Immigration enforcement and student achievement in the wake of secure communities. *AERA Open, 5*(4), 2332858419884891.

Bennett, M. T. (1966). The Immigration and Nationality (McCarran-Walter) Act of 1952, as amended to 1965. *The Annals of the American Academy of Political and Social Science, 367*(1), 127–136.

Bettie, J. (2003). *Women without class: Girls, race, and identity.* University of California Press.

Bickham Mendez, J., & Nelson, L. (2016). Producing "quality of life" in the "Nuevo South": The spatial dynamics of Latinos' social reproduction in Southern amenity destinations. *City & Society, 28*(2), 129–151.

Bjorklund Jr., P. (2018). Undocumented students in higher education: A review of the literature, 2001 to 2016. *Review of Educational Research, 88*(5), 631–670.

Bloemraad, I. (2004). Who claims dual citizenship? The limits of postnationalism, the possibilities of transnationalism, and the persistence of traditional citizenship. *International Migration Review, 38*(2), 389–426.

Blumer, H. (1958). Race prejudice as a sense of group position. *Pacific Sociological Review, 1*(1), 3–7.

Bohon, S. A., Macpherson, H., & Atiles, J. H. (2005). Educational barriers for new Latinos in Georgia. *Journal of Latinos and Education, 4*(1), 43–58.

Bonilla-Silva, E. (2019). Feeling race: Theorizing the racial economy of emotions. *American Sociological Review, 84*(1), 1–25.

Bosniak, L. S. (2000). Citizenship denationalized. *Indiana Journal of Global Legal Studies, 7,* 447.

Brint, S. and Teele, S. (2006). Professionalism under siege: Teachers' views of the No Child Left Behind Act. In A. R. Sadnovik, G. Bohrnstedi, K. Borman, and J. O'Day (Eds.), *Federal legislation, No Child Left Behind, and the reduction of the achievement gap: Sociological perspectives on federal education policy.* Routledge.

Brown, H. E., Jones, J. A., & Becker, A. (2018). The racialization of Latino immigrants in new destinations: Criminality, ascription, and countermobilization. *RSF: The Russell Sage Foundation Journal of the Social Sciences, 4*(5), 118–140.

Brown, S., & Souto-Manning, M. (2007). "Culture is the way they live here": Young Latin@s and parents navigate linguistic and cultural borderlands in US schools. *Journal of Latinos and Education, 7*(1), 25–42.

Brown, S. K., & Bean, F. D. (2006, October 1). Assimilation models, old and new: Explaining a long-term process. *Migration Information Source.* http://www.migrationpolicy.org/article/assimilation-models-old-and-new-explaining-long-term-process/

Browne, I., & Odem, M. (2012). "Juan Crow" in the Nuevo South: Racialization of Guatemalan and Dominican immigrants in the Atlanta Metro Area. *Du Bois Review: Social Science Research on Race, 9*(2), 321–337.

Canaday, M. (2009). *The straight state: Sexuality and citizenship in twentieth-century America.* Princeton University Press.

Canizales, S. L. (2021). Work primacy and the social incorporation of unaccompanied, undocumented Latinx youth in the United States. *Social Forces, 101*(2), 725–748.

Capps, R., Fix, M., Murray, J., Ost, J., Passel, J. S., & Herwantoro, S. (2005). *The new demography of America's schools: Immigration and the No Child Left Behind Act.* Urban Institute (Report No. NJ1).

Carlton, J., Ramey, C., & Lazo, A. (2019, July 14). Large-scale immigration raids fail to materialize. *The Wall Street Journal.*

Carrillo, J. F., & Rodriguez, E. (2016). She doesn't even act Mexican: Smartness trespassing in the New South. *Race, Ethnicity and Education, 19*(6), 1236–1246.

CBP (2024). Southwest land border encounters. U.S. Customs and Border Protection. https://www.cbp.gov/newsroom/stats/southwest-land-border-encounters

Chang, R. S. (2003). Teaching Asian Americans and the law: Struggling with history, identity, and politics. 10 *Asian L.J.* 59.

Chávez, E. (1994). *Creating Aztlán: The Chicano Movement in Los Angeles, 1966–1978*. Doctoral dissertation, University of California, Los Angeles.

Chavez, J. M., & Provine, D. M. (2009). Race and the response of state legislatures to unauthorized immigrants. *The Annals of the American Academy of Political and Social Science, 623*(1), 78–92.

Chavez, L. (2008). *The Latino threat: Constructing immigrants, citizens, and the nation*. Stanford University Press.

Chavez, L. (2013). *The Latino threat: Constructing immigrants, citizens, and the nation* (2nd ed.). Stanford University Press.

Chavez, L. (2020). *The Latino threat: Constructing immigrants, citizens, and the nation* (3rd ed.). Stanford University Press.

Chishti, M., & Bush-Joseph, K. (2023, May 25) U.S. border asylum policy enters new territory post-Title 42. *Migration Information Source*. https://www.migrationpolicy.org/article/border-after-title-42

Chung, S. F. (2018). Chinese exclusion, the first Bureau of Immigration, and the 1905 special Chinese census: Registered, counted, arrested, deported—1892–1906. *Chinese America: History and Perspectives*, 21–36. Gale Academic.

Cineas, F. (2023, September 26). New York City's not-so-sudden migrant surge, explained. *Vox*. https://www.vox.com/policy/2023/9/26/23875580/new-york-city-migrant-crisis-influx-eric-adams

Cobas, J., Duany, J., & Feagin, B. (2015). *How the United States racializes Latinos: White hegemony and its consequences*. Routledge.

Colomer, S. E. (2010). Dual role interpreters: Spanish teachers in new Latino communities. *Hispania, 93*(3), 490–503.

Conchas, G. Q., & Hinga, B. (2016). *Cracks in the schoolyard—Confronting Latino educational inequality*. Teachers College Press.

Conchas, G. Q., & Pérez, C. C. (2003). Surfing the "model minority" wave of success: How the school context shapes distinct experiences among Vietnamese youth. *New Directions for Youth Development, 100*, 41–56.

Coutin, S. B., (2005). Contesting criminality: Illegal immigration and the spatialization of legality. *Theoretical Criminology, 9*(1), 5–33.

Crawford, E. R. (2017). The ethic of community and incorporating undocumented immigrant concerns into ethical school leadership. *Educational Administration Quarterly, 53*(2), 147–179.

Crawford, E. R. (2018). When boundaries around the "secret" are tested: A school community response to the policing of undocumented immigrants. *Education and Urban Society, 50*(2), 155–182.

da Silva, D. F. (2011). Note for a critique of the "metaphysics of race." *Theory, Culture & Society, 28*, 138–148.

Dabach, D. B. (2015). "My student was apprehended by immigration": A civics teacher's breach of silence in a mixed-citizenship classroom. *Harvard Educational Review, 85*(3), 383–412.

Dabach, D. B., Merchant, N. H., & Fones, A. K. (2018). Rethinking immigration as a controversy. *Social Education, 82*(6), 307–314.

Darolia, R., & Potochnick, S. (2015). Educational "when," "where," and "how" implications of in-state resident tuition policies for Latino undocumented immigrants. *The Review of Higher Education, 38*(4), 507–535.

De Genova, N. (2002). Migrant "illegality" and deportability in everyday live. *Annual Review of Anthropology, 31*(1), 419–447.

De Genova, N. (2004). The legal production of Mexican/Migrant "illegality." *Latino Studies, 2*(2), 160–185.

De Genova, N. (2013). Spectacles of migrant "illegality": The scene of exclusion, the obscene of inclusion. *Ethnic and Racial Studies, 36*(7), 1180–1198.

De Genova, N., & Ramos-Zayas, A. Y. (2003). *Latino crossings: Mexicans, Puerto Ricans, and the politics of race and citizenship.* Routledge.

Deaux, K. (2006). *To be an immigrant.* Russell Sage Foundation.

Dee, T., & Murphy, M. (2020). Vanished classmates: The effects of local immigration enforcement on school enrollment. *American Educational Research Journal, 57*(2), 694–727.

Delgado, R., & Stefanic, J. (2017). *Critical race theory: An introduction* (3rd ed.). NYU Press.

Dreby, J. (2012). The burden of deportation on children in Mexican immigrant families. *Journal of Marriage and Family, 74*(4), 829–845.

Dwyer, C. (2018). ICE carries out its largest immigration raid in recent history, arresting 146. *NPR.* https://www.npr.org/2018/06/20/621810030/ice-carries-out -its-largest-immigration-raid-in-recent-history-arresting-146

Dyrness, A., & Sepúlveda, E. (2020). *Border thinking: Latinx youth decolonizing citizenship.* University of Minnesota Press.

Ee, J., & Gándara, P. (2019). The impact of immigration enforcement on the nation's schools. *American Educational Research Journal, 57*(2), 840–871.

Embrick, D. G., & Henricks, K. (2013). Discursive colorlines at work: How epithets and stereotypes are racially unequal. *Symbolic Interaction, 36*(2), 197–215.

Erickson, F. (1984). What makes school ethnography "ethnographic"? *Anthropology & Education Quarterly, 15*(1), 51–66.

Faier, L., & Rofel, L. (2014). Ethnographies of encounter. *Annual Review of Anthropology, 43,* 363–377.

Fanon, F. (1968). *The wretched of the earth.* Grove Press.

Farias, C. (2019). Is there racist intent behind the census citizenship question?" *The New Yorker.* https://www.newyorker.com/news/news-desk/is-there-racist-intent -behind-the-census-citizenship-question-wilbur-ross

Fassin, D. (2011a). *Humanitarian reason: A moral history of the present.* University of California Press.

Fassin, D. (2011b). Racialization: How to do races with bodies. In F. E. Mascia-Lees (Ed.), *A companion to the anthropology of the body and embodiment* (pp. 419–434). Wiley.

Filindra, A., Blanding, D., & Coll, C. G. (2011). The power of context: State-level policies and politics and the educational performance of the children of immigrants in the United States. *Harvard Educational Review, 81*(3), 407–438.

FitzGerald, D. S. (2017). The history of racialized citizenship. In A. Shachar, R. Bauböck, I. Bloemraad, & M. Vink (Eds.), *The Oxford handbook of citizenship* (pp. 128–152). Oxford University Press.

Flores, A. (2021). *The succeeders: how immigrant youth are transforming what it means to belong in America.* University of California Press.

Flores, R. D., & Schachter, A. (2018). Who are the "illegals"? The social construction of illegality in the United States. *American Sociological Review, 83*(5), 839–868.

Flores, W. V. (2003). New citizens, new rights: Undocumented immigrants and Latino cultural citizenship. *Latin American Perspectives, 30*(2), 87–100.

Flores, W. V., & Benmayor, R. (1997). Constructing cultural citizenship. In W. V. Flores & R. Benmayor (Eds.), *Latino cultural citizenship: Claiming identity, space, and rights* (pp. 1–23). Beacon Press.

Flores-González, N. (2002). *School kids/street kids: Identity development in Latino students*. Teachers College Press.

Flores-González, N. (2017). *Citizens but not Americans: Race and belonging among Latino millennials*. NYU Press.

Fong Yue Ting v. United States 149 US 693. (1893). https://supreme.justia.com/cases/federal/us/149/698/

Fordham, S., & Ogbu, J. U. (1986). Black students' school success: Coping with the "burden of acting white." *The Urban Review, 18*(3), 176–206.

Foucault, M. (1982). The subject and power. *Critical Inquiry, 8*(4), 777–795.

Foucault, M. (1989). *Foucault Live: Interviews, 1961–1984* (S. Lotringer, Ed.) Semiotext(e).

Foucault, M. (1994). Subjectivity and truth. *Ethics: Subjectivity and truth* (P. Rabinow, Ed.). The New Press.

Foucault, M., (2008). *The Birth of Biopolitics: Lectures at the Collège de France, 1978–1979* (M. Senellart, Ed.). Palgrave Macmillan UK.

Galindo, R. (2012). Undocumented and unafraid: The DREAM Act 5 and the public disclosure of undocumented status as a political act. *Urban Review, 44*(5), 589–611.

Gallo, S., & Link, H. (2016). Exploring the borderlands: Elementary school teachers' navigation of immigration practices in a new Latino diaspora community. *Journal of Latinos and Education, 15*(3), 180–196.

Gamez, R., & Monreal, T. (2021). "We have that opportunity now": Black and Latinx geographies, (Latinx) racialization, and "New Latinx South." *Journal of Leadership, Equity, and Research, 7*(2), 1–24.

Gándara, P. (2015). With the future on the line: Why studying Latino education is so urgent. *American Journal of Education, 121*(3), 451–463.

Gándara, P. (2017). The potential and promise of Latino students. *American Educator, 41*(1), 4–11, 42.

Gans, H. J. (2017). Racialization and racialization research. *Ethnic and Racial Studies, 40*(3), 341–352.

García, O., & Bartlett, L. (2007). A speech community model of bilingual education: Educating Latino newcomers in the USA. *International Journal of Bilingual Education and Bilingualism, 10*(1), 1–25.

Gelatt, J., & Zong, J. (2018). Settling in: A profile of the unauthorized immigrant population in the United States. Migration Policy Institute Fact Sheet. https://www.migrationpolicy.org/research/profile-unauthorized-immigrant-population-united-states

Gerstle, G. (1997). Liberty, coercion, and the making of Americans. *The Journal of American History, 84*(2), 524–558.

Gildersleeve, R. E., & Hernandez, S. (2012). Producing (im)possible peoples: Policy discourse analysis, in-state resident tuition, and undocumented students in American higher education. *International Journal of Multicultural Education, 14*(2). https://doi.org/10.18251/ijme.v14i2.517

Golash-Boza, T. & Valdez, Z. (2018). Nested contexts of reception: Undocumented students at the University of California, Central. *Sociological Perspectives, 61*(4): 535–552.

Gonzales, A. (2014). *Reform without justice: Latino migrant politics and the Homeland Security state*. Oxford University Press.

Gonzales, R. G. (2016). *Lives in limbo: Undocumented and coming of age in America*. University of California Press.

Gonzales, R. G., Heredia, L. L., & Negrón-Gonzales, G. (2015). Untangling *Plyler's* legacy: Undocumented students, schools, and citizenship. *Harvard Educational Review, 85*(3), 318–341.

Gonzales, R. G., & Ruiz, A. G. (2014). Dreaming beyond the fields: Undocumented youth, rural realities and a constellation of disadvantage. *Latino Studies, 12*, 194–216.

Gonzalez-Sobrino, B., & Goss, D. R. (2019). Exploring the mechanisms of racialization beyond the black–white binary. *Ethnic and Racial Studies, 42*(4), 505–510.

Goodenow, C. (1993). Classroom belonging among early adolescent students: Relationships to motivation and achievement. *The Journal of Early Adolescence, 13*(1), 21–43.

Goodman, A. (2015). Nation of migrants, historians of migration. *Journal of American Ethnic History, 34*(4), 7–16.

Gratton, B., & Gutmann, M. P. (2000). Hispanics in the United States, 1850–1990: Estimates of population size and national origin. *Historical Methods, 33*(3), 137–153.

Guerrero, P. M. (2017). *Nuevo South: Latinas/os, Asians, and the remaking of place*. University of Texas Press.

Gulson, K. N., & Webb, P. T. (2013). "A raw, emotional thing": School choice, commodification and the racialized branding on Afrocentricity in Toronto, Canada. *Education Inquiry, 4*, 167–187.

Hamann, E. T. (2004). The local framing of Latino educational policy. *Harvard Journal of Hispanic Policy, 16*, 37–50.

Hamann, E. T., & Harklau, L. (2010). Education in the new Latino diaspora. In E. G. Murillo Jr., S. A. Villenas, R. Trinidad Galván, J. Sánchez Muñoz, C. Martínez, & M. Machado-Casas (Eds.). *Handbook of Latinos and education: Theory, research and practice* (pp. 157–169). Routledge.

Hamann, E. T., & Rosen, L. (2011). What makes the anthropology of educational policy implementation "anthropological"? In B.A.U. Levinson & M. Pollock (Eds.), *A companion to the anthropology of education*, (pp. 461–477). Wiley.

Hamann, E. T., & Vandeyar, T. (2018). What does an anthropologist of educational policy do? Methodological considerations. In A. E. Castagno & T. L. McCarty (Eds.), *The anthropology of education policy: Ethnographic inquiries into policy as sociocultural process* (pp. 42–60). Routledge.

Hamann, E. T., Wortham, S., & Murillo, E. G. (2002). Education and policy in the new Latino diaspora. In S. Wortham, E. G. Murillo, & E. T. Hamann (Eds.), *Education in the new Latino diaspora* (pp. 1–16). Ablex Publishing.

Hamann, E. T., Wortham, S., & Murillo Jr., E. G. (Eds.). (2015). *Revisiting education in the new Latino diaspora*. Information Age Publishing.

Hamilton, E. R., Patler, C. C., & Hale, J. M. (2019). Growing up without status: The integration of children in mixed-status families. *Sociology Compass, 13*(6), Article e12695. https://doi.org/10.1111/soc4.12695

Harklau, L., & Colomer, S. (2015). Defined by language: The role of foreign language departments in Latino education in Southeastern new diaspora communities. In E. T. Hamann, S. E. F. Wortham, & E. G. Murillo (Eds.), *Revisiting education in the new Latino fiaspora* (pp. 153–170). Information Age Publishing.

Heidbrink, L. (2020). *Migranthood: Youth in a new era of deportation*. Stanford University Press.

Heller, K. J. (1996). Power, subjectification and resistance in Foucault. *SubStance, 25*(79), 78–110.

Hennessey-Fiske, M., Del Rio, Carcamo, C., Castillo, A., Sahagun, L., & Nieto del Rio, M. (2019). Threatened ICE raids create more political noise than police action. *The San Diego Union-Tribune*. https://www.sandiegouniontribune.com/news /california/la-me-ln-ice-raids-trump-immigration-20190715-story.html

Hernandez, D. J., Denton, N. A., & Macartney, S. (2009). School-age children in immigrant families: Challenges and opportunities for America's schools. *Teachers College Record, 111*(3), 616–658.

Hochman, A. (2019). Racialization: A defense of the concept. *Ethnic and Racial Studies, 42*(8), 1245–1262.

Huber, L. P. (2009). Challenging racist nativist framing: Acknowledging the community cultural wealth of undocumented Chicana college students to reframe the immigration debate. *Harvard Educational Review, 79*(4), 704–730.

Irwin, K. (2006). Into the dark heart of ethnography: The lived ethics and inequality of intimate field relationships. *Qualitative Sociology, 29*(2), 155–175.

Jackson, J. L., Jr. (2010). On ethnographic sincerity. *Current Anthropology, 51*(S2), S279–S287.

Jaffe-Walter, R., & Lee, S. J. (2018). Engaging the transnational lives of immigrant youth in public schooling: Toward a culturally sustaining pedagogy for newcomer immigrant youth. *American Journal of Education, 124*(3), 257–283.

Jimenez, A. M. (2022). "All are deserving": Racialized conditions of immigrant deservingness in a Catholic Worker Movement-inspired non-governmental organization. *American Behavioral Scientist, 66*(13), 1758–1776.

Jones, J. A. (2019). *The browning of the New South*. University of Chicago Press.

Jones-Correa, M., & de Graauw, E. (2013). The illegality trap: The politics of immigration & the lens of illegality. *Daedalus, 142*(3), 185–198.

Katz, V. S. (2014). *Kids in the middle: How children of immigrants negotiate community interactions for their families*. Rutgers University Press.

Kerwin, D. (2018). From IIRIRA to Trump: Connecting the dots to the current US immigration policy crisis. *Journal on Migration and Human Security, 6*(3), 192–204.

Kingdon, J. W. (1984). *Agendas, alternatives, and public policies*. Little, Brown.

Kochhar, R., Suro, R., & Tafoya, S. (2005). *The New Latino South: The context and consequences of rapid Population growth*. Pew Hispanic Center.

Kovacs, K. (2018). *"We've failed them": How South Carolina education policy hurts "Dreamers"—and costs taxpayers*. The Hechinger Report. https://hechingerreport .org/weve-failed-them-how-south-carolina-education-policy-hurts-dreamers-and -costs-taxpayers/

Krogstad, J. M. (2020). Americans broadly support legal status for immigrants brought to the U.S. illegally as children. Pew Research Center, June 17. https:// www.pewresearch.org/short-reads/2020/06/17/americans-broadly-support-legal -status-for-immigrants-brought-to-the-u-s-illegally-as-children/

Lacy, E., & Odem, M. E. (2009). Popular attitudes and public policies: Southern responses to Latino immigration. In M. E. Odem & E. Lacy (Eds.), *Latino immigrants and the transformation of the U.S. South* (pp. 143–163). University of Georgia Press.

Ladson-Billings, G. (2007). Pushing past the achievement gap: An essay on the language of deficit. *The Journal of Negro Education, 76*(3), 316–323.

Lamont, M., Welburn, J. S., & Fleming, C. M. (2012). Introduction. Varieties of responses to stigmatization: Macro, meso, and micro dimensions. *Du Bois Review, 9*(1), 43–49.

Lareau, A. (2003). *Unequal childhoods: Class, race, and family life.* University of California Press.

Lau v. Nichols 414 U.S. 563 (1974). https://supreme.justia.com/cases/federal/us/414/563

Lee, E. (2002). The Chinese exclusion example: Race, immigration, and American gatekeeping, 1882–1924. *Journal of American Ethnic History, 21*(3), 36–62.

Leiden, W. R., & Neal, D. L. (1990). Highlights of the U.S. Immigration Act of 1990. *Fordham International Law Journal, 14*(1), 328–340.

Lewis, A. E. (2003). *Race in the schoolyard: Negotiating the color line in classrooms and communities.* Rutgers University Press.

Lewis, G. (2005). Welcome to the margins: Diversity, tolerance, and policies of exclusion. *Ethnic and Racial Studies, 28*(3), 536–558.

Lewis, O. (1964). The culture of poverty. In J. J. TePaske & S. N. Fisher (Eds.), *Explosive forces in Latin America* (pp. 149–173). Ohio State University Press.

Lindblad, S., Pettersson, D., & Popkewitz, T. S. (Eds.). (2018). *Education by the numbers and the making of society.* Routledge.

Longazel, J. G. (2013). Moral panic as racial degradation ceremony: Racial stratification and the local-level backlash against Latino/a immigrants. *Punishment & Society, 15*(1), 96–119.

López, R. M. (2021). *The (mis)treatment and (non)education of unaccompanied immigrant children in the United States.* National Education Policy Center. http://nepc.colorado.edu/publication/immigrant-children

López, R. M., & Giraldo-Santiago, N. (2023). A critical examination of policies and practices impacting the education of unaccompanied immigrant children in the United States. *Education Policy Analysis Archives, 31.* https://doi.org/10.14507/epaa.31.7386

Lowenhaupt, R., Dabach, D. B., & Mangual Figueroa, A. (2021). Safety and belonging in immigrant-serving districts: Domains of educator practice in a charged political landscape. *AERA Open, 7,* 23328584211040084.

Ludden, J. (2006). 1965 immigration law changed face of America. *NPR.* https://www.npr.org/templates/story/story.php?storyId=5391395

Maldonado, M. M. (2014). Latino incorporation and racialized border politics in the heartland: Interior enforcement and policeability in an English-only state. *American Behavioral Scientist, 58*(14), 1927–1945.

Marrow, H. (2011). *New destination dreaming: Immigration, race, and legal status in the rural American South.* Stanford University Press.

Martin, P., & Midgley, E. (1994). Immigration to the United States: Journey to an uncertain destination. *Population Bulletin, 49*(2), 2–45.

Martin, M., & Suárez-Orozco, C. (2018). What it takes: Promising practices for immigrant origin adolescent newcomers. *Theory Into Practice, 57*(2), 82–90.

Marquez, B. A., Williams, A. A., Plankey-Videla, N., & Diaz, S. I. (2022). The discourse of deservingness: Racialized framing during rumored ICE raids. *Ethnicities, 22*(2), 318–342.

McDermott, M. (2011). Black attitudes and Hispanic immigrants in South Carolina. In E. Telles, G. Rivera-Salgado, & M. Sawyer (Eds.), *Just neighbors? Research on*

African American and Latino relations in the United States (pp. 242–266). Russell Sage Foundation.

Mehan, H., Villanueva, I., Hubbard, L., & Lintz, A. (1996). *Constructing school success: The consequences of untracking low-achieving students*. Cambridge University Press.

Mellon, P. J. Straubhaar, R., Balderas, C., Ariail, M., & Portes, P. R. (2018). "They come with nothing": How professional development in a culturally responsive pedagogy shapes teacher attitudes towards Latino/a English language learners. *Teaching and Teacher Education, 71*, 98–107.

Menjívar, C. (2014a). Immigration law beyond borders: Externalizing and internalizing border controls in an era of securitization. *Annual Review of Law and Social Science, 10*, 353–369.

Menjívar, C. (2014b). The "poli-migra": Multilayered legislation, enforcement practices, and what we can learn about and from today's approaches. *American Behavioral Scientist, 58*(13), 1805–1819.

Menjívar, C. (2021). The racialization of "illegality." *Daedalus, 150*(2), 91–105.

Menjívar, C., & Kanstroom, D. (Eds.). (2013). *Constructing immigrant "illegality": Critiques, experiences, and responses*. Cambridge University Press.

Migration Policy Institute. (2023a). *Profile of unauthorized population in the United States*. https://www.migrationpolicy.org/programs/us-immigration-policy-program-data-hub/unauthorized-immigrant-population-profiles

Migration Policy Institute. (2023b). *State immigration data profiles. South Carolina*. https://www.migrationpolicy.org/data/state-profiles/state/demographics/SC

Miles, R. (1982). *Racism and migrant labour*. Routledge.

Miroff, N. (2021). At border, record number of migrant youths wait in adult detention cells for longer than legally allowed. *The Washington Post*. https://www.washingtonpost.com/national/unaccompanied-minors-detention-cells/2021/03/10/a0d39390-81c6-11eb-bb5a-ad9a91faa4ef_story.html

Molina, N. (2014). *How race is made in America: Immigration, citizenship, and the historical power of racial scripts*. University of California Press.

Monreal, T., & McCorkle, W. (2021). Social studies teachers' attitudes and beliefs about immigration and the formal curriculum in the United States South: A multi-methods study. *The Urban Review, 53*(1), 1–42.

Mueller, J. C. (2020). Racial ideology or racial ignorance? An alternative theory of racial cognition. *Sociological Theory, 38*(2), 142–169.

Murillo Jr., E. G. (2002). How does it feel to be a problem?: "Disciplining" the transnational subject in the American South. In S. Wortham, E. G. Murillo Jr., & E. T. Hamann (Eds.), *Education in the new Latino diaspora: Policy and the politics of identity* (pp. 215–240). Ablex Publishing.

National Conference of State Legislatures. (n.d.). Resources and tools for legislative staff. Retrieved March, 2025. https://www.ncsl.org/

National Park Service. (2017). *Closing the door on immigration*. https://www.nps.gov/articles/closing-the-door-on-immigration.htm

Negrón-Gonzales, G. (2014). Undocumented, unafraid and unapologetic: Re-articulatory practices and migrant youth "illegality." *Latino Studies, 12*(2), 259–278.

Ngai, M. (2004). *Impossible subjects: Illegal aliens and the making of modern America*. Princeton University Press.

Ngai, M. M. (2017). The architecture of race in American immigration law: A reexamination of the Immigration Act of 1924. In I. H. Lopez (Ed.), *Race, law and society* (pp. 351–376). Routledge.

Nostrand, R. L. (1980). The Hispano homeland in 1900. *Annals of the Association of American Geographers, 70*(3), 382–396.

Oboler, S. (2010). On race, racial profiling and states of mind(lessness). *Latino Studies, 8*, 149–155.

Odem, M. E., & Lacy, E. (Eds.). (2009). *Latino immigrants and the transformation of the U.S. South.* University of Georgia Press.

Office of Refugee Resettlement (ORR). (2021). *ORR guide: Children entering the United States unaccompanied.* Administration for Children and Families. https://www.acf.hhs.gov/orr/policy-guidance/children-entering-united-states-unaccompanied

Ogbu, J. U. (1978): *Minority education and caste: The American system in cross-cultural perspective.* Academic Press.

Ogbu, J. U. (1987). Variability in minority school performance: A problem in search of an explanation. *Anthropology & Education Quarterly, 18*(4), 312–334.

Olneck, M. R. (1989). Americanization and the education of immigrants, 1900–1925: An analysis of symbolic action. *American Journal of Education, 97*(4), 398–423.

Omi, M., & Winant, H. (1994). *Racial formation in the United States* (rev ed.). Routledge.

Omi, M., & Winant, H. (2014). *Racial formation in the United States* (3rd ed.). Routledge.

Ong, A. (1996). Cultural citizenship as subject-making: Immigrants negotiating racial and cultural boundaries in the United States. *Current Anthropology, 37*(5), 737–762.

Orellana, M. F. (2016). *Immigrant children in transcultural spaces: Language, learning, and love.* Routledge.

Orfield, G., Frankenberg, E., Ee, J., & Kuscera, J. (2014, May 15). Brown *at 60: Great progress, a long retreat and an uncertain future.* The Civil Rights Project (*Proyecto Derechos Civiles*). https://www.civilrightsproject.ucla.edu/research/k-12-education/integration-and-diversity/brown-at-60-great-progress-a-long-retreat-and-an-uncertain-future

Patel, L. (2013). *Youth held at the border: Immigration, education, and the politics of inclusion.* Teachers College Press.

Patel, L. (2015). Deservingness: Challenging coloniality in education and migration scholarship. *Association of Mexican American Educators Journal, 9*(3), 11–21.

Patton, M. C. (2017). Teacher tells student: "Go back to where you speak Spanish." *KSAT-TV News.* https://www.ksat.com/news/teacher-tells-student-go-back-to-where-you-speak-spanish

Peffer, G. A. (1986). Forbidden families: Emigration experiences of Chinese women under the Page Law, 1875–1882. *Journal of American Ethnic History, 28*–46.

Perez, A. D., & Hirschman, C. (2009). The changing racial and ethnic composition of the US population: Emerging American identities. *Population and Development Review, 35*(1), 1–51.

Perez, N. (2021). Nested contexts of reception: Latinx identity development across a new immigrant community. *Ethnic and Racial Studies, 44*(11), 1995–2015.

Pérez Huber, L. (2009). Challenging racist nativist framing: Acknowledging the community cultural wealth of undocumented Chicana college students to reframe the immigration debate. *Harvard Educational Review, 79*(4), 704–730.

Plyler v. Doe, 457 U.S. 202 (1982). https://supreme.justia.com/cases/federal/us/457/202/

Portes, A., Fernandez-Kelly., P & Haller, W. (2009). The adaptation of the immigrant second generation in America: Theoretical overview and recent evidence. *Journal of Ethnic and Migration Studies, 35*(7), 1077–1104.

Portes, A., & Rumbaut, R. G. (2001). *Legacies: The story of the immigrant second generation*. University of California Press.

Portes, A., & Rumbaut, R. G. (2006). *Immigrant America: A portrait*. University of California Press.

Portes, A., & Zhou, M. (1993). The new second generation: Segmented assimilation and its variants. *Annals of the American Academy of Political and Social Science, 530*, 74–96.

Portes, P. R., & Salas, S. (2010). In the shadow of Stone Mountain: Identity development, structured inequality, and the education of Spanish-speaking children. *Bilingual Research Journal, 33*(2), 241–248.

Potochnick, S., Chen, J. H., & Perreira, K. (2017). Local-level immigration enforcement and food insecurity risk among Hispanic immigrant families with children: National-level evidence. *Journal of Immigrant and Minority Health, 19*(5), 1042–1049.

Powell, J. (2009). *Encyclopedia of North American immigration*. Infobase Publishing.

Pulido, L. (2017). Geographies of race and ethnicity III: Settler colonialism and nonnative people of color. *Progress in Human Geography, 42*(2), 309–318.

Rana, J. (2011). *Terrifying Muslims: Race and labor in the South Asian diaspora*. Duke University Press.

Ray, V. (2019). A theory of racialized organizations. *American Sociological Review, 84*(1), 26–53.

Reese, E. (2005). Policy threats and social movement coalitions: California's campaign to restore legal immigrants' rights to welfare. In D. S. Meyer, V. Jenness, & H. Ingram (Eds.) *Routing the opposition: Social movements, public policy, and democracy* (pp. 259–287). University of Minnesota Press.

Reynolds, W. M. (Ed.). (2014). *Critical studies of southern place: A reader*. Peter Lang.

Ribas, V. (2016). *On the line: Slaughterhouse lives and the making of the new South*. University of California Press.

Rios, V. M. (2017). *Human targets: Schools, police, and the criminalization of Latino youth*. University of Chicago Press.

Robles, J. (2023, May 13). Title 42 migration restrictions have ended, but Biden's new policy is tougher. *The Guardian.* https://www.theguardian.com/us-news/2023/may/13/title-42-migration-biden-new-policy-tougher

Rodriguez, S. (2015). The dangers of compassion: The cultural positioning of refugee students in policy and education research and the impact on teacher education. *Knowledge Cultures, 3*(2), 112–126.

Rodriguez, S. (2017a). "My eyes were opened to the lack of diversity in our best schools": Re-conceptualizing competitive school choice policy as a racial formation. *The Urban Review, 49*, 529–550.

Rodriguez, S. (2017b). "People hide, but I'm here. I count": Examining undocumented youth identity formation in an urban community-school. *Educational Studies, 53*(5), 468–491.

Rodriguez, S. (2018a). "Good, deserving immigrants" join the Tea Party: How South Carolina policy excludes Latinx and undocumented immigrants from educational opportunity and social mobility. *Education Policy Analysis Archives, 26*, 103. https://doi.org/10.14507/epaa.26.3636

Rodriguez, S. (2018b). "Risky" subjects: Theorizing migration as risk and implications for newcomers in schools and societies. *European Education, 50*(1), 6–26.

Rodriguez, S. (2019). "We're building the community; it's a hub for democracy.": Lessons learned from a library-based, school-district partnership and program to increase belonging for newcomer immigrant and refugee youth. *Children and Youth Services Review, 102*, 135–144.

Rodriguez, S. (2020a). "I was born at the border, like the 'wrong' side of it": Undocumented Latinx youth experiences of identity, belonging, and racialized discrimination in the U.S. South. *Anthropology & Education Quarterly, 51*(4), 496–526.

Rodriguez, S. (2020b). "You're a sociologist, I am too": Theorizing disruption in fieldwork with undocumented youth. *Journal of Contemporary Ethnography, 49*(2), 257–285.

Rodriguez, S. (2021a). "They let you back in the country?": Racialized inequity and the miseducation of Latinx undocumented students in the New Latino South. *The Urban Review, 53*(4), 565–590.

Rodriguez, S. (2021b, November 30). "The system makes it hard for them:" Exploring the challenges and strategies for schools in supporting newcomer unaccompanied immigrant youth. [Policy Brief]. William T. Grant Foundation. http://wtgrantfoundation.org/the-system-makes-it-hard-for-them-exploring-the-challenges-and-strategies-for-schools-in-supporting-newcomer-unaccompanied-immigrant-youth

Rodriguez, S. (2022). "Immigration knocks on the door. We are stuck.": A multi-level analysis of undocumented youths' experiences of racism, system failure, and resistance in policy and school contexts. *Teachers College Record, 124*(6), 3–37.

Rodriguez, S. (2023). *Latino youth struggle with sense of belonging in schools.* The Conversation. https://theconversation.com/latino-youth-struggle-with-sense-of-belonging-in-school-203385

Rodriguez, S., Bonezzi, D., & Koehler, K. (2019). "How long do we have to wait?": Examining school choice, selective enrollment schools, and the reproduction of racial inequality in a Southern community. In G. Conchas, B. Hinga, M. N. Abad, & K. Gutierrez (Eds.), *The complex web of inequality in North American schools* (pp. 23–45). Routledge.

Rodriguez, S., & Conchas, G. (2022). *Race frames: Structuring inequality and opportunity in a changing educational landscape.* Teachers College Press.

Rodriguez, S., & Crawford, E. R. (2023). School-based personnel advocacy for undocumented students through collective leadership in urban schools: A comparative case study. *Journal of Research on Leadership Education, 18*(3), 347–377.

Rodriguez. S., Escobar, L.L., & Murillo, K. (2024). The bureaucratic paradox: Newcomer unaccompanied children, educational access, and strategies for increasing flourishing through an ecosystem of care. In E. Hamann, S. Herrera, E.G. Murillo, Jr. & S. Wortham (Eds.), *Imagineering education in the new Latinx diaspora: Anti-nativist visions of promising and inclusive practices* (pp. 169–190). Teachers College Press.

Rodriguez, S., & Kuntz, A. M. (2021). Avowing as healing in qualitative inquiry: Exceeding constructions of normative inquiry and confession in research with undocumented youth. *International Journal of Qualitative Studies in Education, 34*(8), 746–762.

Rodriguez, S., & Macias, E. (2022). "Even being a citizen is not a privilege here": Undocumented Latinx immigrant youth and perceptions of racialized citizenship. *Sociology of Race & Ethnicity, 9*(1), 21–36.

Rodriguez, S., & McCorkle, W. (2019). Examining teachers' awareness of immigration policy and its impact on attitudes toward undocumented students in a Southern state. *Harvard Journal of Hispanic Policy, 31*(1), 21–44.

Rodriguez, S., & McCorkle, W. (2020). On the educational rights of undocumented students: A call to expand teachers' awareness of policies impacting undocumented students and strategic empathy. *Teachers College Record, 122*(12), 1–34.

Rodriguez, S., McCorkle, W., & Ma, C. (2021). School-based personnel advocacy for undocumented students: Examining the role of context in shaping educators' sense of agency. *Journal of Education for Students Placed at Risk (JESPAR), 26*(2), 168–187.

Rodriguez, S., & Monreal, T. (2017). "This state is racist.": Policy problematization and undocumented youth experiences in the New Latino South. *Educational Policy, 31*(6), 764–800.

Rodriguez, S., Monreal, T., & Howard, K. J. (2018). "It's about hearing and understanding their stories": Teacher empathy and socio-political awareness toward newcomer undocumented students in the New Latino South. *Journal of Latinos and Education, 19*(2), 181–198.

Rodriguez, S., Murillo, K., & Roth, B. (2024). "Like they're my same people. They've probably been in my shoes . . .": Community-based organizations' role in fostering social and organizational ties for Latino/x immigrant youth. *Journal of Adolescent Research.* https://doi.org/10.1177/07435584241280265

Rodriguez, S., Roth, B., & Sosa, L. V. (2020). School social workers as nepantleras in equity work for immigrant students: A conceptual exploration. *Social Service Review, 94*(4), 748–780.

Rosaldo, R. (1997). Cultural citizenship, inequality, and multiculturalism. In W. V. Flores & R. Benmayor (Eds.), *Latino cultural citizenship: Claiming identity, space, and rights* (pp. 27–38). Beacon Press.

Roth, B. J. (2017). When college is illegal: Undocumented Latino/a youth and mobilizing social support for educational attainment in South Carolina. *Journal of the Society for Social Work and Research, 8*(4), 539–561.

Roth, B. J., & Grace, B. L. (2015). Falling through the cracks: The paradox of post-release services for unaccompanied child migrants. *Children and Youth Services Review, 58*, 244–252.

Roth, W. (2016) The multiple dimensions of race. *Ethnic and Racial Studies, 39*(8), 1310–1338.

Ruiz, R. (1984). Orientations in language planning. *NABE Journal, 8*(2), 15–34.

Ruiz-de-Velasco, J., & Fix, M. E. (with Clewell, B. C.). (2000). *Overlooked & underserved: Immigrant students in U.S. secondary schools.* The Urban Institute. https://www.urban.org/research/publication/overlooked-and-underserved-immigrant-students-us-secondary-schools

Rumbaut, R. G., & Portes, A. (2001). Ethnogenesis: Coming of age in immigrant America. In R. G. Rumbaut & A. Portes (Eds.), *Ethnicities: Children of immigrants in America* (pp. 1–19). University of California Press.

Sáenz, R., & Manges Douglas, K. (2015). A call for the racialization of immigration studies: On the transition of ethnic immigrants to racialized immigrants. *Sociology of Race and Ethnicity, 1*(1), 166–180.

Sandoval, E. (2023, August 22). Texas Governor's multibillion-dollar border operation drags on despite criticism. *The New York Times.*

Scott, J. C. (1985). *Weapons of the weak: Everyday forms of peasant resistance.* Yale University Press.

Shachar, A. (2009). *The birthright lottery: Citizenship and global inequality*. Harvard University Press.

Shirazi, R. (2018). Decentering Americanness: Transnational youth experiences of recognition and belonging in two U.S. high schools. *Anthropology & Education Quarterly, 49*(2), 111–128.

Sierk, J. (2019). White girls and the "other" in the new Latino diaspora: The conflation of deviance and immigration and the role of language. *Theory in Action, 12*(2), 46–70.

Silva, K. (2016). *Brown threat: Identification in the security state*. University of Minnesota Press.

Smith, H. A., & Furuseth, O. J. (Eds.). (2006). *Latinos in the New South: Transformations of place*. Ashgate Publishing.

Smith, S., & Vasudevan, P. (2017). Race, biopolitics, and the future: Introduction to the special section. *Environment and Planning D: Society and Space, 35*(2), 210–221.

Sriram, S. K. (2016). A Foucauldian theory of American Islamophobia. *International Journal of Islamic Thought, 10*, 47–54.

Stanton-Salazar, R. D. (1997). A social capital framework for understanding the socialization of racial minority children and youths. *Harvard Educational Review, 67*(1), 1–41.

Stanton-Salazar, R. D. (2001). *Manufacturing hope and despair: The school and kin support networks of U.S.-Mexican youth*. Teachers College Press.

Stanton-Salazar, R. D. (2004). Social capital among working-class minority students. In M. A. Gibson, P. Gándara, & J. P. Koyama (Eds.), *School connections: US Mexican youth, peers, and school achievement* (pp. 18–38). Teachers College Press.

Stanton-Salazar, R. D. (2011). A social capital framework for the study of institutional agents and their role in the empowerment of low-status students and youth. *Youth & Society, 43*(3), 1066–1109.

Stanton-Salazar, R. D., & Spina, S. U. (2003). Informal mentors and role models in the lives of urban Mexican-origin adolescents. *Anthropology & Education Quarterly, 34*(3), 231–254.

Stanton-Salazar, R. D., Vásquez O. A., & Mehan H. (2000). Engineering success through institutional support. In S. T. Gregory (Ed.), *The academic achievement of minority students: Comparative perspectives, practices, and prescriptions* (pp. 213–247). University Press of America.

Stuesse, A. (2016). *Scratching out a living: Latinos, race, and work in the Deep South*. University of California Press.

Stuesse, A., Staats, C., & Grant-Thomas, A. (2017). As others pluck fruit off the tree of opportunity: Immigration, racial hierarchies, and intergroup relations efforts in the United States. *Du Bois Review, 14*(1), 245–271.

Suárez-Orozco, C., & Suárez-Orozco, M. M. (2001). Immigrant children and the American project. *Education Week, 20*(7), 40–56.

Suárez-Orozco, C., & Suárez-Orozco, M. (2009). Educating Latino immigrant students in the twenty-first century: Principles for the Obama administration. *Harvard Educational Review, 79*(2), 327–340.

Suárez-Orozco, C., Yoshikawa, H., Teranishi, R., & Suárez-Orozco, M. (2011). Growing up in the shadows: The developmental implications of unauthorized status. *Harvard Educational Review, 81*(3), 438–473.

Sue, D. W., Capodilupo, C. M., Torino, G. C., Bucceri, J. M., Holder, A., Nadal, K. L., & Esquilin, M. (2007). Racial microaggressions in everyday life: Implications for clinical practice. *American Psychologist, 62*(4), 271.

Sugarman, J. (2017). *Beyond teaching English: Supporting high school completion by immigrant and refugee students.* Migration Policy Institute. https://www.migrationpolicy.org/research/beyond-teaching-english-supporting-high-school-completion-immigrant-and-refugee-students

Szathmary, Z. (2016, June 4). North Carolina high school "Trump wall" prank upsets Latino students. *Daily Mail.* http://www.dailymail.co.uk/news/article-3625535/North-Carolina-high-school-prank-upsets-Latino-students.html

Taparata, E. (2016). The U.S. has come a long way since its first, highly restrictive naturalization law. *Public Radio International.* https://theworld.org/stories/2016-07-04/us-has-come-long-way-its-first-highly-restrictive-naturalization-law

Tarasawa, B. (2013). Fight or flight? Immigration, competition, and language assistance resources in Metropolitan Atlanta. *Journal of Latinos and Education, 12*(3), 186–201.

Telles, E. (2018). Latinos, race, and the US Census. *ANNALS of the American Academy of Political and Social Science, 677*(1), 153–164.

Telles, E. E., Ortiz, V., Edward, E., & Telles, V. (2011). Generations of exclusion: Mexican Americans, assimilation, and race. *Du Bois Review, 8*(2), 506.

USCIS. (n.d.). Immigration and Nationality Act. https://www.uscis.gov/laws-and-policy/legislation/immigration-and-nationality-act

Valencia, R. R. (2010). *Dismantling contemporary deficit thinking: Educational thought and practice.* Routledge.

Valencia, R. R. (2019). *International deficit thinking: Educational thought and practice.* Taylor & Francis.

Valenzuela, A. (1999). "Checkin' up on my guy": Chicanas, social capital, and the culture of romance. *Frontiers: A Journal of Women Studies, 20*(1), 60–79.

Vargas, E., Sanchez, G., and Valdez, J. (2017). Immigration policies and group identity: How immigrant laws affect linked fate among U.S. Latino populations. *The Journal of Race, Ethnicity, and Politics, 2*(1), 35–62.

Vargas, E. D., Winston, N. C., Garcia, J. A., & Sanchez, G. R. (2016). Latina/o or Mexicana/o? The relationship between socially assigned race and experiences with discrimination. *Sociology of Race and Ethnicity, 2*(4), 498–515.

Verma, S., Maloney, P., & Austin, D. (2017). The school to deportation pipeline: The perspectives of immigrant students and their teachers on profiling and surveillance within the school system. *ANNALS of the American Academy of Political and Social Science, 673*(1), 209–229.

Villenas, S. (2001). Latina mothers and small-town racisms: Creating narratives of dignity and moral education in North Carolina. *Anthropology & Education Quarterly, 32*(1), 3–28.

Villenas, S. (2002). Reinventing educación in new Latino communities: Pedagogies of change and continuity in North Carolina. In S. Wortham, E. G. Murillo Jr., & E. T. Hamann (Eds.), *Education in the new Latino diaspora: Policy and the politics of identity* (pp. 17–35). Ablex Publishing.

Wacquant, L. (2002). *From slavery to mass incarceration: Rethinking the "race question" in the US. New Left Review, 13*(1), 41–60.

Warikoo, N., & Carter, P. (2009). Cultural explanations for racial and ethnic stratification in academic achievement: A call for a new and improved theory. *Review of Educational Research, 79*(1), 366–394.

Weise, J. M. (2015). *Corazón de Dixie: Mexicanos in the U.S. South since 1910.* The University of North Carolina Press.

Weitz, E. D. (2003). *A century of genocide: Utopias of race and nation*. Princeton University Press.

White, S. (2012). Property-owning democracy and republican citizenship. In M. O'Neill & T. Williamson (Eds.), *Property-owning democracy: Rawls and beyond* (pp. 129–146). Wiley

Willen, S. S. (2007). Toward a critical phenomenology of "illegality": State power, criminalization, and abjectivity among undocumented migrant workers in Tel Aviv, Israel. *International Migration, 45*(3), 8–38.

Winders, J., & Smith, B. E. (2012). Excepting/accepting the South: New geographies of Latino migration, new directions in Latino studies. *Latino Studies, 10*(1–2), 220–245.

Wortham, S., Murillo, E. G., & Hamann, E. T. (Eds.). (2002). *Education in the new Latino diaspora: Policy and the politics of identity*. Ablex Publishing.

Yarbrough, R. A. (2010). Becoming "Hispanic" in the "New South": Central American immigrants' racialization experiences in Atlanta, GA, USA. *GeoJournal, 75*, 249–260.

Ybarra, M. G. (2018). "Since when have people been illegal?": Latinx youth reflections in Nepantla. *Latino Studies, 16*(4), 503–523.

Ybarra, V. D., Sanchez, L. M., & Sanchez, G. R. (2016). Anti-immigrant anxieties in state policy: The Great Recession and punitive immigration policy in the American states, 2005–2012. *State Politics & Policy Quarterly, 16*(3), 313–339.

Zak, D. (2020, November 2). *Fact sheet: Unaccompanied migrant children (UACs)*. National Immigration Forum. https://immigrationforum.org/article/fact-sheet -unaccompanied-migrant-children-uacs/

Index

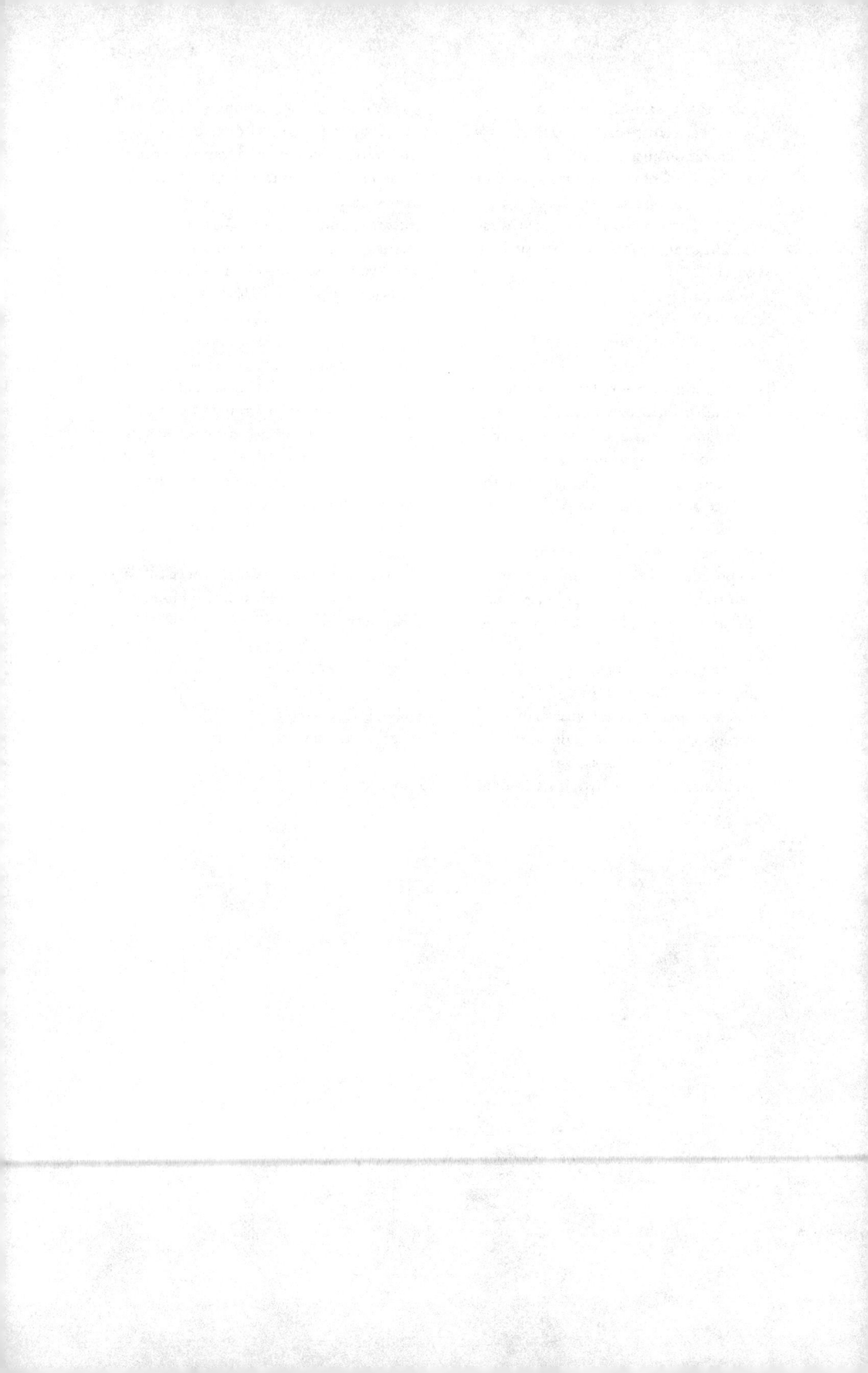

About the Author

SOPHIA RODRIGUEZ is an associate professor of educational policy studies and sociology at New York University's Steinhardt School of Culture, Education, and Human Development in New York City. She is the coeditor of *Race Frames in Education: Structuring Inequality and Opportunity in a Changing Society.*

About the Artist

YEHIMI CAMBRÓN ÁLVAREZ is an interdisciplinary artist, activist, and public speaker born in Michoacán, Mexico. She immigrated to Georgia at seven, grew up undocumented in Atlanta, and has been a DACA recipient since 2013.

Cambrón's work explores the nuances of undocumentedness and its thread in the movement toward collective liberation. Through public art, she has served as a monument-maker asserting the humanity of immigrants in Atlanta, claiming barren walls to paint landmarks that belong to undocumented people. Her work institutes a space for immigrants within the South's dominant racial binary. From her first mural on Buford Highway to her mural at the Mercedes-Benz Stadium, she confronts the idea of who is worthy of public celebration in the home of the largest Confederate monument in the nation. She has worked to complicate the immigrant narrative beyond murals through portraits and site-responsive installations. Cambrón has had solo exhibitions at the University of South Carolina's Upstate Art Gallery and Oglethorpe University Museum of Art, and has exhibited at Agnes Scott College's Dalton Gallery, Atlanta Contemporary Art Center, Museum of Contemporary Art of Georgia, and the High Museum of Art.

Cambrón received a BA in studio art from Agnes Scott College. Her degree was fully funded by the Goizueta Foundation. In 2015, she became an educator and one of the first Teach for America DACAmented Corps Members placed in Georgia. She returned to Cross Keys High School, her alma mater, two years later to teach art. In 2019, Cambrón left the classroom to pursue art full time. Cambrón was named a 2023 Fellow of the Paul & Daisy Soros Fellowship for New Americans to support her MFA at the School of the Art Institute of Chicago. She has expanded her practice into matriarchal, intergenerational fiber modes of making to reclaim discarded materials from her family's commercial furniture-making practice.